Tracking Anthropological Engagements

Histories of Anthropology Annual

EDITORS

Regna Darnell
Frederic W. Gleach

EDITORIAL BOARD

Lee D. Baker, *Duke University*
Sally Cole, *Concordia University*
Alexei Elfimov, *Russian Academy of Sciences*
Geoffrey Gray, *University of Queensland*
Robert L. A. Hancock, *University of Victoria*
Richard Handler, *University of Virginia*
Erik Harms, *Yale University*
Curtis M. Hinsley, *Northern Arizona University*
Christer Lindberg, *Lund University*
Jonathan Marks, *University of North Carolina, Charlotte*
Marie Mauzé, *l'Ecole de Hautes Etudes en Sciences Sociales*
Stephen O. Murray, *El Instituto Obregón*
Robert Oppenheim, *University of Texas*
Vilma Santiago-Irizarry, *Cornell University*
Joshua Smith, *University of North Carolina, Chapel Hill*
Susan R. Trencher, *George Mason University*

Tracking Anthropological Engagements

Histories of Anthropology Annual, Volume 12

EDITED BY REGNA DARNELL AND
FREDERIC W. GLEACH

University of Nebraska Press | Lincoln and London

© 2018 by the Board of Regents of the University of Nebraska. All rights reserved. Manufactured in the United States of America. ♾

Library of Congress Cataloging-in-Publication Data

Names: Darnell, Regna, editor. | Gleach, Frederic W. (Frederic Wright), 1960–, editor.
Title: Tracking anthropological engagements / edited by Regna Darnell and Frederic W. Gleach.
Description: Lincoln: University of Nebraska Press, 2018. | Series: Histories of anthropology annual; volume 12 | Includes bibliographical references.
Identifiers: LCCN 2018027844
ISBN 9781496208934 (paperback)
ISBN 9781496213020 (epub)
ISBN 9781496213037 (mobi)
ISBN 978-1-4962-1304-4 (pdf)
Subjects: LCSH: Anthropology—Philosophy—History. | Anthropology—Methodology—History. | BISAC: SOCIAL SCIENCE / Anthropology / Cultural.
Classification: LCC GN33 .T69 2018 | DDC 301.01—dc23 LC record available at https://lccn.loc.gov/2018027844.

Set in Arno Pro by Mikala R. Kolander.

CONTENTS

	List of Illustrations	vii
	Editors' Introduction	ix
1.	Topography and Cosmography in the Sixteenth Century: A Window into Early Ethnography DRITON NUSHAJ	1
2.	Faded Tracks of Austrian Anthropology: Hans Sidonius (von) Becker (1895–1948) and Some of His Contemporaries CHRISTIAN FEEST	45
3.	Is It Anthropology?: Exhibiting Latin American Cultures at the 1892 Madrid International Expositions NANCY J. PAREZO AND CATHERINE A. NICHOLS	133
4.	Worcester, Massachusetts, 1909: Language, Culture, and the Boas-Freud Intersection JOHN LEAVITT	175
5.	Karl Popper's Enheartening of Derek Freeman's Attacks on Margaret Mead's *Coming of Age in Samoa* STEPHEN O. MURRAY	199
6.	Anthropology's Camelot Myth—And What We Can Learn from It HERBERT S. LEWIS	213

7. A Model for Open Community Engagement: Six Nations, the GWCA, and the Production of Wartime Narratives   229
   EVAN HABKIRK

8. Guns and Ivy: An Anthropologist's Memoir   249
   ANTHONY F. C. WALLACE

   Contributors   267

ILLUSTRATIONS

Figures

1.	Two Indians with a parrot and monkey	30
2.	Psychology Conference group photo, 1909	180
3.	The hand-embroidered battalion flag of the 114th battalion	230
4.	Somerville's banjo containing the signature of W. E. Davis	242
5.	W. E. Davis's signature on Somerville's banjo	242

Tables

1.	Brinton's assessments of national exhibit's anthropological value	149
2.	Important or especially interesting objects in exhibits	158

EDITORS' INTRODUCTION

The array of papers included in this volume attests to anthropology's attunement to the contemporary interdisciplinary climate of the social sciences and humanities. What might once have been seen as poaching on the boundaries of others is increasingly interpreted as innovative exploration of issues that are of interest to readers from a broad range of backgrounds. Long-established ethical, social, and political entanglements engage audiences across the social sciences, cultural studies, and the history of science as well as in the no longer exclusively isolated communities where anthropologists do their research. Anthropologists are less likely to offer firm answers intended to stand for all time and more likely to pose questions in open-ended and continuing dialogue.

From the onset of *HoAA*'s experiment in the potential plurality of the discipline's understanding of its own past, contributors have not necessarily been anthropologists by training or present employment. An "anthropological lens"—a commonly used formulation, evoking a range of theoretical and methodological perspectives as well as the notion of "seeing" as filtered through but still based on an external reality—can be deployed by others. And throughout their history, anthropologists have been bricoleurs, borrowing conceptual tools and research methods at hand wherever they find them and integrating them into a perspective on the study of humankind that carves out an evolving identity that we believe is a particular characteristic and strength of anthropology. Is this conundrum about anthropology or about its history? Perhaps it is both. How we got there is an integral part of where we are now and what comes next.

This diversity of anthropology's contemporary engagements has led us as editors and, by extension, our readers, far afield from a traditional "classical" definition of the discipline. Yet there is a startling conservatism in how narrowly many colleagues continue to define the history of anthropology in a postwar positivist mode. While acknowledging that trends in the discipline as a whole come and go, and that our elders have lived through multiple paradigm shifts, disciplinary history too often diminishes itself by self-imposed confinement to older boundaries; it becomes a specialization somehow insulated from the burning issues of present-day scholarship and its public relevance rather than an active participant in current discourse.

The University of Nebraska Press has supported our efforts to broaden these assumptions, to revisit the interpretations of anthropology's history that reflect ideas otherwise outdated in the theoretical apparatus of the discipline. With a dozen volumes in print (volumes 1–7 in the journal series and volumes 8–11 as stand-alone titled volumes within the *HoAA* umbrella), the range of contents and genres render visible the viability of our claim that a new vision of the history of anthropology is overdue. Sometimes we cannot distinguish anthropologist as author from historian as author; at other times, historians and science studies scholars call for a standard of purported objectivity that seems on the surface to contradict the reflexivity of recent anthropological thinking, and not just about disciplinary history. By juxtaposing different genres of writing, different approaches, different visions, their equally valid but discretely grounded premises emerge in contrast. In this issue, for example, Canadian military historian Evan Habkirk employs a documentary descriptive voice to contextualize a collaborative interactive website merging both Indigenous and non-Indigenous memories; the late Anthony F. C. Wallace returns to his World War I military experience and makes sense of the role of war in human history and civilization by reflecting on the contrast to his experience of the Iroquois tradition of warfare as he came to understand it over six decades "in the field"; Herbert Lewis provides a commentary on the internal workings of the American Anthropological Association, yet another distinct genre, in which it is very clear what Lewis thinks about matters of activism, counterinsurgency and war—matters in which Wallace was a key participant. When these chapters are examined together, questions are posed that transcend the explicit intentions and expertise of any one contributor. Such serendipities were not planned in advance. Our editorial policy is to see what comes in and how the papers play off of one another. We are consistently gratified to find such links and draw them to readers' attention. This is what history of anthropology looks like.

The days are long gone when the required History of Anthropology course was automatically taught by the oldest member of each department, who would take a role somewhere between witness and dinosaur. Both Lewis and Wallace are senior figures who have already contributed broadly to the discipline as well as to the writing of its history; their reflections are of interest to anthropologists but also provide grist for historians and public interlocutors. As president of the AAA amid the tumult of the 1960s, Wallace sought rapprochement where everyone seemed compelled to choose one side and demonize the other. One of us (Darnell) clearly recalls the dissension of Project Camelot that fractured the discipline in those years; the papers evoke parallel reflections and reassessment half a century plus later. These are issues that contemporary students want to discuss as they sort out the political struggles of their times. Past, present, and future intersect. The histories of anthropology are plural.

We have occasionally been able to include major essays that are too long for most journals but not long enough to stand alone as books. Christian Feest's essay traces the engagements of Hans Sidonius (von) Becker, a German anthropologist little known in North America and almost not known at all for his work beyond the scope of anthropology in the narrow sense, with the intellectual groundings of national socialism. The documentary value of this detailed biography poses useful contrasts to the anglophone sphere of the same period. The history of anthropology properly includes instances where anthropologists engage larger public contexts and when their work has direct public consequences.

Our contributors have included indigenous scholars and community members as well as academics of various stripes. Habkirk's engagement with Indigenous and non-Indigenous collaborations in documenting shared wartime experience in the area around Brantford ON provides one model for cross-cultural appreciation of mutual memories and commemorations. The Great War Centenary Association is an institutional site that inherently requires cross-cultural communication. Although Hapkirk doesn't call what he does "anthropology," public history and collaborative anthropology share many of the impulses that motivate and disseminate scholarship. One form of collaboration in producing histories of anthropology is to amplify the voices of all parties to events described.

Some of the essays that follow are more conventional in their scope within the history of anthropology, but they are still not much like one another. Driton Nushaj's comparison of two sixteenth-century missionary reports from the Amazon reveals systematic underlying differences between the cosmography on the Catholic Andre Thevet and the topographic approach of the Calvinist Jean de Léry. At the time, the two were in direct competition for authority to speak for Indigenous peoples deemed incapable of speaking for themselves. Read together, their juxtaposed accounts enrich contemporary understanding of "the same" people despite the blinders of racism and chauvinism characteristic of the age of European expansion and Christian missionization.

Nancy Parezo and Catherine Nichols focus on a single event much later in the cross-cultural mélange of anthropology's emergence: the International Exposition held in Madrid in 1892, almost simultaneously with Chicago's World's Columbian Exposition of 1893–94. Spanish hosts emphasized the homogeneity of the Latin American cultures showcased in the various pavilions. Regardless of the intensions of exhibit organizers, or the sources of their collections, viewers were strongly encouraged to embrace a national heritage of Spanish triumphal exploration and capitalist innovation. Expositions constituted a major force in public understanding of cultural diversity as Americans in Chicago were in their turn encouraged to celebrate technology and progress. The diversity of American positions in Madrid emerges from the contrastive evaluation of the scientific value of the collections, with Walter Hough representing the emergent professionalism of the Bureau of American Ethnology and the aging amateur Americanist Daniel Garrison Brinton, who saw the academy as the future of anthropology. National traditions coalesced outside of directly academic contexts in expositions and world's fairs, but their effects fed back into the self-presentation and self-confidence of the nascent anthropological discipline (especially in the context of museums, where science and pedagogy vied for priority, funding, and public support). Neither the

Spanish nor the Americans presented unitary interpretations of exploration and discovery, even though both aspired to hone a visible and easily consumed national imaginary.

Still within the naissance of the disciplines we know today, John Leavitt turns to an event well known in outline but not previously analyzed in the context of its failures. Psychologist G. Stanley Hall, president of Clark University, where Franz Boas taught until 1892, attracted a stellar cast for a conference aimed at cross-fertilization between European psychoanalysts and their American counterparts of their understandings of the unconscious. Freud indeed met Jung, but there was no meeting of minds. Leavitt argues persuasively that the ethnographic bent of Boasian thinking about language, culture, and personal identity, with its explicit rejection of evolutionary hierarchies, was alien to the intents of Freud's more biologically based theorizing. Scientific evidence from ethnography, for Boas, could falsify generalizations about human nature, but for Freud the evolutionary framework was already given, and his science did not seek to falsify it.

Stephen O. Murray explores the alliance of strange bedfellows when anthropologist Derek Freeman and philosopher of science Karl Popper teamed up to undermine the reputation of Margaret Mead, whose anthropology was of a very different type than Freeman's. Murray uses archival traces of mutual academic opportunism to demonstrate the systematic ideological selectivity with which Freeman drew authority from Popper's "scientific" approach to validation and disconfirmation, but quietly ignored Popper's political agendas. Popper in turn was not convinced that Freeman's science allowed the possibility of falsification.

The cross-overs of chapter topics, time periods, and methodological approaches are multiple and we have been able to explore only a few here. Readers are encouraged to wend their own paths through these offerings.

REGNA DARNELL
FREDERIC W. GLEACH

DRITON NUSHAJ

1

Topography and Cosmography in the Sixteenth Century
A Window into Early Ethnography

The history of anthropology rarely extends beyond the turn of the nineteenth century. But before anthropologists took up the study of culture, historians, missionaries, ambassadors, and other travelers with an interest in the language and customs of the people they visited produced their own written accounts. Where do these pre-ethnographic accounts fit in relation to a contemporary understanding of "ethnography"? Ancient writers such as Herodotus, Strabo, Ptolemy, and Tacitus did not differentiate ethnographic interests from their broader historical and geographical inquiries (Vermeulen 2015, 2–3). Nevertheless, the questions, methods, and paradigms that travel writers have employed since antiquity to describe otherness provide a glimpse into the epistemological evolution of "ethnography."

Margaret Hodgen (1964), in her historical comparison of pre-ethnographic genres, has shown that early ethnography should not be dismissed simply because it does not conform to secular and rationalist social science originating with Enlightenment thought. Moreover, the sentiments expressed by sixteenth-century writers like Michel de Montaigne and Bartolome de las Casas show an appreciation for a premodern conception of cultural relativism (Martin 2007, 134–35). The history of ethnography is partly a question of legitimacy: Are its origins in Enlightenment science or did it begin as a colonial enterprise in the Age of Discovery (Vermeulen 2015, 24)? While it can be argued that the first usage of the terms "ethnography" and "ethnology" corresponds to the inception of the epistemological foundation of the two concepts (Vermeulen 2015, 269–71), it is equally valid to claim that methods and perspectives that formed a "discipline" may predate its foundation. Moreover, a dialogue about the genealogy of ethnography avant la lettre—the exploration of the tangled roots of the well-defined contemporary discipline—need not lead to the "projecting [of] later epistemological views on the past" (Vermuelen 2015, 270).

This paper will compare the ethnographic and literary techniques used by two mid-sixteenth-century French missionaries—the Catholic Andre Thevet and the Calvinist Jean de Léry—who came into contact with the Tupinambas around Guanabara Bay in Brazil. The approaches that Thevet and de Léry used to write about the indigenous populations amounted to two divergent methods: "cosmography" and "topography," respectively. "Cosmography" reflected Thevet's desire to order the world according to schema used by Renaissance science, combining classical—especially Aristotelian—paradigms within a Catholic worldview (Nushaj 2016). By contrast, the topographic narrative of de Léry is a personal history embedded in the greater struggle of Protestant Huguenots against the Catholic French majority. De Léry's account is therefore structured by a confessional mode of retelling an adventure that tests the fortitude and righteousness of the author as he lands in a remote settlement in Brazil (Lestringant 1990). The clash of methods leads each author to affirm the veracity of his account based on a claim of direct experience. This claim to direct experience was noticeably lauded by Montaigne as a prerequisite for a reliable account about faraway "savages" (de Certeau 1986).

THE CLAIM TO TRUTH

The requirement of firsthand knowledge reflects a new spirit of skepticism expressed by Montaigne in the sixteenth century. The Protestant Reformation and the discovery of the "New World" brought about fundamental changes in the European view of the world (Neto et al. 2009). The formulation of an empirical, (pre)scientific *autopsy* (Lestringant 1994, 13) was taking hold, pitting the experience of the New World against the received knowledge of Renaissance civilization with its basis in classical thought (Neto et al. 2009). Montaigne, in his essay "Of Cannibals," even proposes that the ideal witnesses should be "simple [and] crude" and thus not so clever as to twist information to their own ends (2003, 184). Moreover, when it comes to writing reports,

> we ought to have topographers who would give us an exact account of the places where they have been. But because they have over us the advantage of having seen Palestine, they want to enjoy the privilege of telling us news about all the rest of the world. I like everyone to write what he knows, and as much as he knows, not only in this, but in all other subjects; for a man may have some special knowledge and experience of the nature of a river or a fountain, who in other matters knows only what everybody knows. However, to circulate this little scrap of knowledge, he will undertake to write the whole of physics. From this vice spring many great abuses. (2003, 184–85)

Montaigne comes down firmly on the side of reports that limit themselves to the author's direct observation and no more. Topography moved toward describing what was seen and experienced in a single place (*topos*) with attention to minor details guided by an inquisitive and close enquiry. The importance of observation is fundamental to de Léry's *Histoire d'un voyage faict en la terre du Brésil*; the author is more emphatic than Thevet in the importance of sensory experience (Lestringant 1990, 129). "Mon intention et mon sujet sera en ceste histoire, de seulement declarer ce que j'ay pratiqué, veu, ouy et observé" (de Léry 1994, 105). (My intention and my subject in this history will be to declare only what I have experienced, seen, heard and observed [trans. mine]). The avowed commitment to empirical observation for de Léry is a matter of personal circumstances as opposed to a demand made by a preexisting topographic *method*. Nevertheless, by writing in a mode that emphasizes sensory experience, de Léry was moving away from the conventions of earlier travel writers and cosmographers. By limiting the scope of his account, de Léry avoids some of the "abuses" that are committed by the unbounded epistemological breadth of cosmography.

Jean de Léry and Andre Thevet write in a "poetics of extreme witness" that highlights the adventures and risks undertaken by the voyager (Williams et al. 2006, 34). The claim of personal endangerment gives each writer his authority and the prerogative to contradict the other. Within the text, the appearance of danger simultaneously appeals to a sense of pathos and the credibility of the narrator, who was in the midst of tumultuous events. Yet, for de Léry, the witness claim is not just a rhetorical trope (as it often is for Thevet) but a consistent narrative theme that portrays his *Histoire d'un voyage* as a testament to a personal mission sanctioned by God as well as an attempt to correct the lies of Thevet (de Léry 1990, xlvi). Around 350 years before Bronislaw Malinowski set foot on the Trobriand Islands, de Léry claimed that his work was conducted through direct observation and living among the natives of Guanabara Bay:

> When I speak of savage customs, I often use this kind of expression—"I saw," "I found," "this happened to me," and so on (as if I wanted to show myself off)—I reply that not only are these things within my own subject but also that I am speaking out of my own knowledge, that is, from my own seeing and experience; indeed, I will speak of things that very likely no one before me has ever seen, much less written about. I mean this however, not about all of America in general, but only about the place where I lived for about a year: that is, under the tropic of Capricorn among the savages called the *Tupinamba*. (1990, lxi)

Attempting to safeguard his reputation after de Léry's assault on *Les singularités*, Thevet writes in his subsequent publication ("La cosmographie universelle"):

> It is true that the ancients have written about this place, but for the most part their words were based on their own imaginations, or mere reports; whereas I call on only the evidence of what I have myself ocularly seen [*ce qu'oculairement i'ay veu*], or heard from those who are in the place itself. (Thevet, cited in Williams 2006, 30)

Thevet noticeably fortifies his assertion of firsthand knowledge as a way of defending the authority of his text. By the late sixteenth century, Thevet's writings were "outmoded" (2011, 12); however, the preference for topography may not have lasted long—for instance, in the year of his death, de Léry's account was summarized and integrated into a multiauthor cosmography entitled "The manners, lawes, and customes of all nations" (Boemus et al. 1611). The seventeenth and eighteenth centuries saw a return to a cosmographic, encyclopedic urge to chart the world (Hodgen 1964).

ENTERING THE WORLD OF THE TUPIS: ORIENTATIONS TOWARD SAMENESS AND DIFFERENCE

Thevet begins his description of the Tupis (chapter 28) by assuming an almost ironic tone that appears to mock their beliefs: "Les uns ont reconnu le Soleil commme souverain, les autres la Lune, et quelques autres les etoiles; les autres autrement ainsi que nous recitent les histoires" (1983, 39–40). (Some recognized the Sun as their lord, others the Moon, yet others the stars; the others worshiped differently, as the histories tell us [trans. mine]). The statement conveys a lack of surprise that plays with the audience's expectations. It confirms that the Tupis are polytheistic and immediately superimposes on them the typologies of the "savage" developed by earlier writers. Thevet suggests that his readers already know what to expect of the "savages"; as soon as the cosmographer enters into the region inhabited by the Tupis, he already sees that they are "like" others he has already encountered. The friar adopts a dismissive, distant tone to make his cosmographic perspective appear earnest—readers realize later on that Thevet is hardly an impartial witness. The cosmographer attenuates the novel customs of the "savages" by a direct analogy to other pantheistic peoples that removes the need to consider this particular polytheism as something new. The cosmographer is therefore prepared to observe new beliefs and customs only as they illustrate existing forms seen elsewhere. The application of the cosmographic paradigm creates the impression that new things are quite like the old. Frank Lestringant calls this a "montage" of new observations onto existing knowledge (Thevet 2011, 6). Typological and analogical connections bridge current and past knowledge in order to illustrate a topic. This manner of comparison was also frequently used by other cosmographers. For example, Sebastian Muenster's *Cosmographia* notes that the Turks abstain from wine just like Roman women (Hodgen 1954, 520). Thevet uses the same strategy to append his observations to similar cases cited in cosmographic works. For instance, he tells readers that, like the

Romans, Tupi men incite their young to be belligerent (1983, 97–98). Thus, analogy is the act of an a priori principle that seizes two distinct things, rejects their differences, and declares them to be alike according to some common perceived quality. Michel Foucault, however, is highly skeptical of the epistemological validity of cosmography and other contemporary disciplines.

> By positing resemblance as the link between signs and what they indicate (thus making resemblance both a third force and a sole power, since it resides in both the mark and the content in identical fashion), sixteenth-century knowledge condemned itself to never knowing anything but the same thing, and to knowing that thing only at the unattainable end of an endless journey. (1994, 61)

Whereas cultural and chronological relevance may be called into question by modern readers accustomed to historicist hermeneutics, the cosmographic paradigm appears to reveal that certain human traits (and, often, monstrous forms) bridge the past and the present through a continuity of analogical resemblance. Montaigne's call for a rustic, simple reporter is, perhaps, the philosopher's desire to disavow the cosmographic ordering principles that filter difference before it can be understood.

Les singularités is a collection of curiosities in which analogy creates the basis for subsequent categorization. Thevet embarks upon his project by relating the remarkable things he sees and hears as a collage of topics, but then he proceeds to systematize and evaluate his observations. Thevet's methods, especially his tendency to amass examples of strange things—a gathering of "singularités"—represents a conventional cosmographic style of description (Hodgen 1964, 161–63). However, Thevet also introduces his own novel categories, based on his own analogically reduced understanding of the essential similarities linking things. In *Cosmographie Universelle*, for example, he places the sloth that he first describes in *Les singularités* under a category entitled "things which live on air"; the reason for this category is apparently that they live high in the trees and do not appear to eat (1983, 122). Despite recognizing the "newness" of the American continent, Thevet uses an "outdated analogic system ('reseau analogique') to position new discoveries in a pre-established, stable, hierarchic system" (Reeser 2006, 220). So fond is the cosmographer of this paradigm that he sometimes devises his own families of analogical resemblance in order to demonstrate his findings.

De Léry first mentions the "savages" in his fifth chapter. In his brief preview of the Brazilians he describes four tribes that, with difficulty, cooperate with one another, by living in proximity and trading together (1994, 154). De Léry appears to begin his "history" in a similar fashion to Thevet's: he compares one tribe of fast runners, the "Ouetaca," to the Basques because they both speak strange languages and run quickly (1994, 155). This familiarization of a strange group with a region closer to France bridges the distance of the Atlantic. As a gloss that suggests that perhaps things are not as strange across the ocean as one expects, it mimics the generalizations developed by previous travel writers, but this is where the similarities end. Further into *Histoire d'un voyage*, it becomes clear that de Léry knows almost nothing of the Ouetaca he first mentioned because, as readers discover, the Ouetaca does not interact with the Tupis and their allies (the French). De Léry is not immune to drawing general analogies when his experience is scant. However, when he begins describing the Tupinambas (chapter 8), de Léry no longer relies on simple analogies to equate the Tupis to Europeans. Instead, things become "non moins estrange que difficile à croire a ceux qui ne l'ont veu" (1994, 212–14) (no less strange than difficult to believe for those who have not seen it [trans. Whatley in de Léry 1990, 57]). This rapid change in tone, and the change in style it sparks, is clearly a result of direct experience overturning established modes of writing about alterity. The topographer risks going down the path of the analogical, comparative descriptions of cosmography if it weren't for his confrontation with a reality that could no longer be described by the kind of glosses deplored by Montaigne: analogies that create a semblance of similarity where very little exists. De Léry assumes the role of a topographer as soon as he relates his direct, visual experience. The author goes from a familiar place to an unfamiliar topos (and, eventually, back again). The process of deterritorialization—what Michel de Certeau sees as a temporal and spatial displacement toward exteriority (the other) and a subsequent return to interiority (sameness)—functions as a basic structure for the narrative (1988, 218–26).

Detailed narrativized descriptions become de Léry's main technique of writing about the Tupis. In one example, he attempts to explain to readers something quite foreign to them: the making and mounting of the penis sheath used by older Tupi men. De Léry considers the possibility that they wear the implement for modesty or to hide deformity but remains cautiously inconclusive.

> Combien que je ne m'en sois point autrement enquis, j'ay plustot opinion que c'est pour cacher quelque infirmité qu'ils peuvent avoir en leur vieillesse en ceste partie-là. (1994, 216)

> Although I have not made closer inquiry, I am still of the opinion that it is rather to hide infirmity that their old age may cause in that member. (translation by Whatley in de Léry 1990, 58)

His descriptions are often guided by a kind of functionalist logic that seeks to uncover the purpose of certain customs. A sense of utility guides de Léry in his choice of topics and the ensuing explanations (de Certeau 1988, 224). However, many of de Léry's observations are not offered from the perspective of utility. De Léry can surprise modern readers when he refuses to render judgment on matters that he deems aesthetic. The topographer allows for doubt and speculation when interpreting customs. One such case is the description of the lower lip piercing that Tupi men keep to wear a decorative jade piece:

> Que si au reste quelques fois quand ces pierres sont ostées, nos Toüoupinambaoults pour leur plaisir font passer leurs langues par ceste fente de la levre, estans lors advis à ceux qui les regardent qu'ils ayent deux bouches: je vous laisse à penser, s'il fait bon voir de ceste façon, et si cela les difforme ou non. (1994, 217)

> Sometimes when these stones are removed, our Tupinamba amuse themselves by sticking their tongues through that slit in the lip, giving the impression to the onlooker that that they have two mouths; I leave to you to judge whether it is pleasant to see them do that, and whether that deforms them or not. (translation by Whatley in de Léry 1990, 58)

By taking such a relativistic position early in his portrayal of the Tupi, de Léry sets the tone for reading *Histoire d'un voyage*. The topographer shows that the customs that shape aesthetics have no reason in themselves but are, on the contrary, quite arbitrary and open to subjective judgment. Moreover, de Léry's descriptions of the Tupis are devoid of analogies and cosmographic generalizations. A particular custom, the piercing of the lower lip, is not placed within a hierarchical (universal) system of values. Thus, the suspension of evaluation (relativism) opens a window for a positive description of otherness. Moreover, by making appearance a relative matter, a possibility arises that strangeness of appearance is merely superficial and unworthy of being considered as the basis for true "difference." The topographer has the advantage of having familiarized himself with the bodily appearance of his Tupi hosts—the pierced lower lip would be both strange and familiar to the author, facilitating his relativistic position.

Comparatively, Thevet is more likely to render judgment on the qualities he describes, be they negative (the vast majority) or positive. The Franciscan almost never defers judgment to his readers, leaving less room for them to participate in an active understanding of the subject. De Léry's *Histoire* is, for the most part, less argumentative and more likely to call for the reader's reflection than *Les singularités*—the ethnographic descriptions are freer of comparison to other historical and geographical contexts. However, the adventure into the land of the Tupi is framed by a narrative of Calvinist righteousness appealing to a Protestant ethos that seeks no further justification. De Léry's *Histoire d'un voyage* is a text that bears witness to a time and place where the author was an active observer. The topographer teaches himself to write in a new way in order to record his observations while also providing interpretative freedom to readers.

Thevet writes with a certain detachment that makes his knowledge less corporeal and more transcendental (Lestringant 1999, 67). His preference for belief over custom results in the inclusion of mythological and legendary stories that are attributed to Tupi cosmology. The Catholic friar translates Tupi mythological narratives into stories familiar to a Christian audience (Whatley, *History of a Voyage* xxxi). One such case is found in chapter xxiv, the first dedicated to the Tupis.

Thevet begins with the myth of the arrival of the sweet potato (*hetich*). By starting with a creation story, the cosmographer appears to retell what he heard directly from the Tupis. According to Thevet, the cannibals claim that the hetich was brought by a deified ancestor. Before the arrival of the hetich-bearing ancestor, writes Thevet, the Tupis ate grass "like wild beasts" (1983, 50–51). Therefore, the first details that readers receive of the "savages" are that they believe in many gods yet honor one deified ancestor above others for bringing hetich (1983, 50–51). Thevet begins not by describing the people—especially their physical appearance—like de Léry, but rather addresses their mythology and the food that nourishes them. Although the cosmographer seems to have avoided analogical reasoning, he has, in fact, already chosen it for the purpose. The cosmographer *collects* the creation story, but not without altering it. The details are structured to reflect a Renaissance hierarchy of beings: a divine power grants humans the life forms that sustain them. Thevet can be very skilled in introducing new stories, using familiar narratives and recognizable Christian motifs; Christian metaphysical assumptions are central to his translation and recording of Tupi myths, despite the incongruence of Catholic theology with Tupi cosmology (De Castro 2011, 13–15, 47). Lacking other methods of inquiry with which to explore Tupi mythology, Thevet relies on his analogical reasoning to create a syncretistic mythos. While analogies usually illustrate a resemblance or an essential quality linking the pairs, sometimes Thevet's seem to serve no purpose other than to indicate that there is a precedent for the singularity or to emphasize its perceived importance. In one such case, Thevet states that the Tupis worship a deity he names "Grand Caraïbe" in the same way as the Turks worship Mohammed (2011, 40). The analogical connection in this case is overly general—Thevet could be speaking about the frequency of prayer, the degree of piety, the movements of the body during prayer, or any other quality of "worship." His lack of precision fails to explain the nature of resemblance.

Aemulatio is the primary logical basis for Thevet's analogical comparisons. The Tupi belief in a mythical flood is quickly recognized as an emulation of the biblical flood. The Franciscan links Tupi belief to Christian doctrine by showing how the former mirrors the latter, albeit imperfectly. *Aemulatio* is a flexible tool of comparison because one thing need only distantly reflect the other. Thevet uses the flood myth to suggest that durability and truth are on the side of the Bible (and written culture), whereas the corrupt and twisted reflection of the myth is the oral version told by the Tupis:

> Or l'eau fut si excessivement grande en ce déluge, qu'elle surpassait les plus hautes montagnes de ce pays: et ainsi tout le peuple fut submergé et perdu. Ce qu'ils tiennet pour asseuré, ainsi que nous tenons celuy que nous propose la saincte escriture. Toutefois il leur est trop aisé de faillir, attendu qu'ils n'ont aucun moyen d'escriture, pour garder la mémoire des choses, sinon comme ils ont ouï dire à leurs pères. (183, 126)

> The water was so overwhelming in the flood that it surpassed the highest mountains of that country, thus all the people were submerged and lost. This [account] they believe with certainty, just as we believe [with certainty], what is proposed to us by Holy Scripture. However, it is quite easy for them to be wrong since they have no writing with which to keep the memory of things, other than what they have heard from their fathers. (translation mine)

The reported flood myth has little to do with the Tupis; it is, rather, for Thevet an affirmation of the veracity of the Bible. The imperfect accord between the Tupi myth and Genesis is attributed to the absence of writing. Difference of belief is thus also proof of the error of the "savages" on account of their inability to record memory through writing. Readers are frequently reminded that the Catholic friar considers the Bible to be the ultimate revelation of truth. Unlike the historians who "raconte" (tell), "la Sainte Ecriture" (Holy Scripture) "témoigne" (attests) (2011, 60–61).

Like Thevet, de Léry holds writing in high esteem. The topographer does not have better things to say about the illiterate people he lived with, but he certainly has *more* to say. Having had a chance to study their reaction to writing, de Léry records the Tupis as they struggle to comprehend the process by which writing records information and conveys meaning.

Semblablement ignorans la creation du monde, ils ne distinguent point les jour par noms, n'y n'ont acception de l'un plus que de l'autre: comme aussi ils ne content sepmaines, mois, ni années, ains seulement nombrent et retiennent les temps par les Lunes. Quant à l'escriture, soit saincte ou prophane, non seulement aussi ils ne savent que c'est, mais qui plus est, n'ayans nuls caracteres pour signifier quelque chose: quand du commencement que je fus en leur pays pour apprendre leur langage, j'escrivois quelques sentences leur lisant puis apres devant eux, en estimans que cela fut une sorcelerie ils disoyent l'un à l'autre: N'est ce pas merveille que cestuy-cy qui n'eust sceu dire hier un mot en nostre langue, en vertu de ce papier qu'il tient, et qui le fait ainsi parler, soit maintenant entendu de nous? (1994, 379–80)

Likewise being ignorant of the creation of the world, they do not distinguish the days by name, nor do they give one day preference over another, any more than they count weeks, months, or years; they only number and retain time by moons. They know nothing of writing, either sacred or secular; indeed they have no kind of characters that signify anything at all. When I was first in their country, in order to learn their language I wrote a number of sentences which I read aloud to them. Thinking that this was some kind of witchcraft, they said to each other, "Is it not a marvel that this fellow, who yesterday could not have said a single word in our language, can now be understood by us, by virtue of that paper that he is holding and which makes him speak thus? (translation by Whatley in de Léry 1990, 134–35)

Readers of *Histoire d'un voyage* are made aware of the large disparity between their own literacy and the condition of the Tupis. De Léry views writing as the ability of language to keep records of time. Thus the Tupis only measure moons because they do not have the written accounts necessary for greater divisions of time. Writing and history are closely associated for de Léry; not only is writing important for the long-term, chronological organization of events, but it is the continuous link between the beginning of the world (creation) and his own history. The power of written letters is such that the Tupis express awe when their newly-arrived guest is able to orally reproduce their language in a comprehensible form by reading a transcription. De Léry suggests that writing and reading are imbued with a power that seems to surpass human capacities of simpler, oral communication. The ethnographer takes on the role of an honest reporter who passes on the views of the people he meets. For de Léry, the experience with the Tupis leads to a better understanding of his own society:

> Parquoy, je di que, qui voudroit icy amplifier ceste matiere, il se presente un beau sujet, tant pour louër et exalter l'art d'escriture, que pour monstrer combien les nations qui habitent ces trois parties du monde, Europe, Asie, et Afrique, ont de quoy louër Dieu par dessus les sauvages de ceste quatriesme partie dite Amerique: car au lieu qu'eux ne se peuvent rien communiquer sinon verbalement: nous au contraire avons cest advantage que sans bouger d'un lieu, par le moyen de l'escriture et des lettres que nous envoyons, nous pouvons declarer nos secrets à ceux qu'il nous plaist, et fussent-ils esloignez jusques au bout du monde. Ainsi outre les sciences que nous apprenons par les livres dont ces sauvages sont semblablement du tout destituez, encore ceste invention d'escrire que nous avons, dont ils sont aussi entierement privez, doit estre mise au rang des dons singuliers que les hommes de par deçà ont receu de Dieu.

> Here is a fine subject for anyone to who would like to enlarge upon it: both to praise and to exalt the art of writing, and to show how the nations that inhabit these three parts of the world—Europe, Asia, and Africa—have reason to praise God more than do the savages of that fourth part, called "America." For while they can communicate nothing except by the spoken word, we, on the other hand have this advantage, that without budging from our place, by means of writing and the letters that we send, we can declare our secrets to whomever we choose, even to the ends of the earth. So even aside from the learning that we acquire from books, of which the savages seem likewise completely destitute, this invention of writing, which we possess and of which they are just as utterly deprived, must be ranked among the singular gifts which men over here have received from God. (translation by Whatley in de Léry 1990, 135)

De Léry begins to exalt writing without entirely leaving his main subject. The topographer's conscious understanding that writing comprises one of the principal differences between the Old and New Worlds seems to follow from his realization that the Tupis attributed magical qualities to his written sentences. Thus, the "savages" are effectively teaching de Léry a lesson about his own society and the significance of written communication.

THE LOCAL AND THE COSMIC

De Léry begins his report on Brazil by focusing on the place (the land around Guanabara Bay) and proceeds to describe the Tupi inhabitants in detail. The topographer describes their bodily appearance and corporeal decorations as well as how they make flour and *caouin* (sweet potato beer). The observations are not randomly ordered; instead, they indicate the first things that de Léry finds noteworthy as a traveler entering a Tupi village. Moreover, they are not a collection of individual "singularities"; rather, they show a distinct literary organization that reflects the observations made by an outsider when he first seeks to know the Tupis. By focusing on processes of alteration and cultivation (of body and of food), the topographer displays his interest in cultural phenomena.

It is noteworthy that the topographer does not begin by describing beliefs and material objects, but, rather, customs. He does not introduce the hetich of the Tupi through a mythological narrative; instead, he invites the reader into a Tupi village to see people altering their cherished root staple. The reader is told of the abundance provided by the prolific growth of the many root vegetables (1994, 241). After a detailed description of the growth, harvesting, and grinding of the root, de Léry creates a literary portrait of the making of *caouin*. As if to demonstrate the readers' unfamiliarity with the fermented beverage, de Léry describes how naked girls prepare a pulp by chewing the ground root. The discussion includes a comparison that invites readers into more familiar territory: the contemplation of similarities between wine and *caouin*. Indeed, it is through the same process of purification, argues de Léry, that one can understand how the mastication of root vegetables by young women does not pollute the final drink. De Léry responds to the disgust of his compatriots and fellow travellers at first seeing how the brew is produced—from the partially-chewed pulp of roots spat into containers to ferment—by reminding readers that grapes are also crushed by the bare feet of French farmers, yet wine is drunk without worry of contamination. Comparing the two fermentation methods, de Léry writes, "Je respons que nostre *Caou-in* se purge aussi, et partant, quant à ce point, qu'il y a mesme raison de l'un à l'autre" (1994, 256). (I reply that our *caouin* is purged the same way, and that therefore on this point the one custom is as good as the other [trans. Whatley in de Léry 1990, 77]). The purpose of this relativistic statement is to displace the reader's positionality: to invite the reader to briefly experience an emic perspective. The topographer writes of "our" *caouin* for the purposes of this comparison. Asking the reader to imagine *caouin* as their own drink may bring about a temporary estrangement to wine—a distance needed to analyze each custom objectively. The idea that both fermentation methods are equally valid is an indication of de Léry's movement toward a relativistic perspective. The topographer pursues this comparative and relativistic approach throughout the text. Further in, de Léry uses the same strategy to compare cannibalism to the violence of France in the midst of violent religious strife.

> Parquoy qu'on n'haborre plus tant la Barbarie des Sauvages Anthropophages, cest à dire mangeurs d'hommes: car puis qu'il y en a de tels, voire d'autant plus detestables et pires au milieu de nous qu'eux, comme il a esté veu, ne se ruent que sur les autres nations qui leur sont ennemies, et ceux-ci se sont plongez au sang de leurs parens, voisins, et compatriotes, il ne faut pas aller si loin qu'en l'Amerique ni qu'en leur pays pour voir choses si monstrueuses et prodigieuses. (1994, 377)

> So let us henceforth no longer abhor so very greatly the cruelty of the anthropophagous—that is, man-eating—savages. For since there are some here in our midst even worse and more detestable than those who, as we have seen, attack only enemy nations, while the ones over here have plunged into the blood of their kinsmen, neighbors, and compatriots, one need not go beyond one's own country, nor as far as America, to see such monstrous and prodigious things. (translation by Whatley in de Léry 1990, 133)

De Léry's experience, bolstered by a dual perspective that compares his own customs to those of the Tupis, leads him to conclude that the nature of ritual cannibalism among the Tupis and their rivals is both different from and the same as the religious wars in France. To reach a similar conclusion as Thevet, that the Tupis are brutally violent (2011, 207), would show a lack of reflexivity for the Calvinist topographer, who is aware of both the ceremonial nature of cannibalism among the Tupis and the vehement hatred that his fellow compatriots had shown to one another. The relativistic position employed by de Léry is a testament to his understanding of Tupi ritual practice as well as his ability to penetrate the mindset of a victim of cannibalism (i.e., to be proud of being slaughtered, considering it the best way to die). By contrast, his Huguenot compatriots were slain with unimaginable brutality. Montaigne employs a similar relativistic position in "Of Cannibals," arguing that the "savages" should not be considered more barbarous than other nations (2003). De Léry's experience among the Tupis could have provided Montaigne with an emic perspective—a way of becoming accustomed to strange customs through an imaginative displacement of the self into the mind of the other. Despite the fact that de Léry finds cannibalism abhorrent, the topographer, like Montaigne, is able to think like a cannibal. De Léry familiarizes himself with the practice of cannibalism and is able to exchange positions with the Tupis in order to understand the act as they do. By comparing cannibalism to the violence in France, he deduces that anthropophagy is not as violent as some of the Catholic-Huguenot skirmishes in France. Reflecting on anthropophagy in another instance, de Léry concludes that cannibalism is preferable to usury (1990, 375). In other cases (especially in matters of faith and belief) the Tupis are compared unfavorably to the French, despite the equation of Tupi idolatry to "popish" worship. Yet de Léry's ability to use his understanding of Tupi practices to reflect on those of the French makes the *Histoire d'un voyage* a particularly gripping account, for his contemporaries and modern readers alike. By exploring the particularities of the Tupi culture, de Léry is able to see that all customs "have reason" within their cultural contexts. Moreover, all customs have the *same* reason—they work to achieve something of intrinsic value within the society in which they are found. The outsider will often see these same customs as "savage" and "barbarous," but someone who is familiar with them will understand that this is not the case (at least for de Léry and Montaigne).

As opposed to the local focus and relativistic viewpoint preferred by de Léry, Thevet makes repeated comparisons between the Tupis and other nations to display his cosmographic expertise. The Franciscan relies on these comparisons to show that singularities reappear throughout the world and are always connected by general laws or patterns that give them meaning. The singularities collected from observing the Tupis are connected analogically to other such singularities, thereby annulling their distinct occurrence. Thevet charts his observations into categories that make up the entire known world (Lestringant 1999, 66). By comparing one nation to another, the Catholic author creates spatial (and temporal) links that project a unity and predictability of the world. This "rounding" by analogy allows singularities to be arranged in a map-like projection that operates in conjunction with the desire to map the surface of the world on a larger scale (Conley 2011, 192). When discussing the nakedness of the Tupinambas, for example, Thevet mentions other nations of people who go about naked but also cover their "shameful" parts:

> ce qui est sans comparaison plus tolérable que chez nos Amériques, qui vivent tout nus ainsi qu'ils sortent du ventre de la mère, tant hommes que femmes, sans aucune honte ou vergogne. (1983, 52)

> a thing which is without comparison more acceptable than that of the Americans, who live naked, just as they came out of their mother's bellies, men and women alike, with no shame or embarrassment. (translation mine)

The shock for Thevet is that there is "no comparison" to total nudity. A complete absence of clothing fails to resemble other civilized nations and contravenes Christian morality. Ironically, the strict judgment "without comparison"—even as a rhetorical phrasing—is entirely dependent on (analogical) comparison. In fact, Thevet uses a variety of comparisons in order to contemplate a hierarchy of dress in which being totally nude is the lowest (and most bestial). As soon as Thevet compares an aspect of Tupi appearance or custom to its analogical resemblance, he creates an arrangement that assigns degrees of a quality, as well as the hierarchical valuations that are inseparable from any ranked order. Thus, appearing on the lowest rung of dress makes the Brazilian cannibals particularly monstrous, even if they show glimpses of civilization elsewhere in *Les singularités*. By using an analogical model of comparison, Thevet *reads* the Tupis through a pretext which has already judged them. In his imagined teleological ontologies, the Tupis, for the most part, reflect undeveloped, bestial qualities.

The "singularity" of nudity remains singular only for a brief instant, and is summarily integrated into a cosmographic paradigm to illustrate a point. In this particular case, Thevet uses nudity to move into a general discussion of degrees of undress among past and contemporary peoples. By moving further away from the Tupis (and the topic of nudity), Thevet tries to use the example as proof of an ideal (covered) body. At this point the Tupi are barely relevant to the analysis, because the cosmographer is simply discussing the merits of nakedness and clothing. This movement from the particular to the general—or from the concrete to the abstract—is a frequently recurring strategy, central to Thevet's cosmographic paradigm; the tendency to make connections that are far removed from the place he purports to study is thus a principal cosmographic method in *Les singularités*. In his extensive analogies, Thevet uses geographic and historical variances to illustrate "nudity": while Canadian natives cover themselves in pelts, early Europeans were completely nude. The friar does not forget to mention Adam and Eve's expulsion from Eden, which, having changed the significance of nudity, makes it a serious heresy to advocate undress. Thevet continues his analysis by referencing the nude statuary of Roman temples and the Romans' avoidance of hats and wigs. The cosmographer even mentions the comb-over practiced by Caesar as an attempt to cover his baldness and natural shame of nudity (1983, 53–4). This extreme digression, while entertaining, serves not so much as a description of *Tupi nudity*, but rather an argument against nudity. He shows that the purpose of *Les singularités* is not just to describe "Antarctic France," but also to attempt to describe the entire world—how it is as well as how it should be. In this respect, Thevet follows the model set out in Muenster's *Cosmograph-*

ia—to collect strange customs and arrange them according to certain principles (Hodgen 1964, 163–65). Thevet provides an analogy on the basis of emulation, seeking to locate this instance of nudity on a temporal and spatial map. Thevet is not just writing about the nude Tupi body; he is also drawing a historical-spatial atlas of nudity (Lestringant 1999, 67). This method of linking a particular observation to other instances creates the genre of "cosmography." The term "singularity" can be misleading, by suggesting that something is unique unto itself, but this is not the case in *Les singularités*. The so-called singularities of Tupi customs, as well as the strange plants and animals of the region, are merely singular examples of universal genera of other such singularities.

Thevet views the Guanabara Bay region inhabited by the Tupis as a microcosm. This microcosm is always related to and defined by the macrocosm: the region, Antarctic France, and the greater world. For Thevet, the global occurrence of nudity is more significant than its topographic manifestation. The nudity of the Tupis acquires meaning only as it emulates other cases of nudity and the general concept. Lestringant calls this mode of comparison "synecdoche": the specific speaks for the general (1990, 209). Thevet's observations, his "singularities," are not freely existing; they are curiosities or aberrations at the microcosmic level—i.e., not capable of overturning the logic of the (macro)cosmos. Foucault writes of the synecdochal relationship in sixteenth-century epistemic models as a binding of local diversity to a (presumed) universal whole.

> [H]owever immense the distance from microcosm to macrocosm may be, it cannot be infinite; the beings that reside within it may be extremely numerous, but in the end they can be counted; and, consequently, the similitudes that, through the action of the signs they require, always rest one upon another, can cease their endless flight. They have a perfectly closed domain to support and buttress them. Nature, like the interplay of signs and resemblances, is closed in upon itself in conformity with the duplicated form of the cosmos. (1994, 35)

By using analogy to make comparisons across time and space, and by following a teleological understanding of the cosmos via synecdoche, Thevet finds significance in universal categories of being. The cosmographer relies on literary authorities who define a single universal order—especially Aristotle—to interpret a "singularity" as part of a hierarchy of universal values.

Unlike the cosmographic method used by Thevet, de Léry very rarely relies on analogies to illustrate particular cases. He is also less likely to narrowly define particular Tupi words. For example, the role of the medicine men ("pagés") and shamans ("caraïbes") is never as definite with de Léry as it is with Thevet (Lestringant in Thevet 1983, 71n2). This is a consequence of the topographer's reliance on understanding particular events instead of placing people in unambiguous categories. While the cosmographer creates resilient categories of comparison that view Tupi customs as a single manifestation of all global possibilities, the topographer looks within his *topos* to find relevance. When describing the appearance of the Tupis, de Léry is straightforward and to the point; he acts as a reporter or storyteller instead of as a "philosopher" whose aim is to explain the phenomenon. Where the cosmographer looks to analogies to explain the singularity, the topographer looks within the occurrence for its meaning. This is demonstrated by each author's treatment of the myth that Amerindians are hairy. De Léry writes:

> Et cependant tant s'en faut, comme aucuns pensent, et d'autres le veulent faire accroire, qu'ils soyent velus ny couvers de leurs poils, qu'au contraire, n'estant point naturellement plus pelus que nous sommes en ce pays par deçà. (1994, 214)
>
> And yet, contrary to what some people think, and what others would have one believe, they are by no means covered with hair; in fact they are not by nature any hairier than we are over here in this country. (translation by Whatley in de Léry 1990, 57)

Thus, de Léry writes simply to contradict the (unfounded) claim. Thevet, by contrast, devotes all of chapter 31 to write "contre l'opinion de ceux qui estiment les sauvages sont pelus" (against the opinion of those people that believe the savages are hairy [trans. mine]). The cosmographer shows a greater interest in addressing the "opinion" than in describing the Tupis as he sees them; the tone is argumentative rather than descriptive. He begins by urging readers to not believe the portraits of painters and the stories of poets who exaggerated and caricatured various other "races." Thevet's interest is in shaping the way others think about all people in the world, rather than merely describing the Tupis:

> [L]es escrits des poètes [sont pleins] de ces satyres, faunes, nymphes, dryades, hamadryades, orcades, et autres manières de monstres, lesquels ne se trouvent aujourd'hui comme au temps passé. (1983, 59)

> The writings of the poets are full of satyrs, nymphs, dryads, hamadryads, orcs, and other kinds of monsters, which one does not find today as [one did] in times past. (translation mine)

The cosmographer dispels the myth of monsters and denies the possibility of fantastical creatures in the present. Thevet proposes a rational and theological reason for the lack of monsters and hairy Amerindians alike, not only to dispel a wrong assumption about hairiness but to also establish a theory that will preclude unsubstantiated claims from being made in the first place. Fantastical monsters are replaced with various kinds of teratologies and deformities which the cosmographer argues arise as a matter of "accidents of nature":

> S'il advient une fois entre les autres qu'un enfant sorte ainsi velu du vêntre de la mère, et que le poil se nouurisse et augmète par tout son corps, comme l'on en a vu quelque-uns en France, cela est un accident de la nature, tout ni plus ne moins que si l'un naissait avec deux têtes, ou autre chose semblable. (1983, 59)

> If there comes a time that a child is born from the belly of the mother covered in hair throughout its body, as has been observed in France, this is an accident of nature; no more or less than if a child is born with two heads or any other similar thing. (translation mine)

Thevet's argument against hairiness is also an argument in favor of a mechanism that causes natural deformities. Moreover, the Catholic author sees ancient monsters as false figures that were produced by the devil in order to deceive humanity, but to which God has put an end through his compassion:

Lorsque l'esprit malin s'efforçait par tous les moyens de décevoir l'homme, se Transformant pour cela en mille figures. Mais aujourd'hui que Notre Seigneur par compassion s'est communiqué à nous, ces esprits malins on été chassés, nous donnant puissance contre eux, ainsi que temoigne la Sainte Ecriture. (1983, 59–60)

The evil spirit strove by all means to deceive humankind, Transforming for that reason into thousands of figures. But now that Our Lord by his compassion has made himself known to us, these evil spirits have been chased away, giving us power against them, as it is written in Holy Scripture. (translation mine)

The Catholic cosmographer is not merely interested in describing the Tupis as they appear to him; his intent is to bind their singularities to the laws of nature (ascertained through reason) and to the rule of God. The appeal to reason and to scripture is important for Thevet's positivist position as a rational scientist. Not only is the true likeness of the Tupis (i.e, their lack of hair) known to him, but it can be no other way—reason and God have decreed that there are no monsters, only deformities resulting from "accidents of nature." All ontological possibilities are thus occupied by what can be ascertained through human reason and divine revelation.

Just as de Léry uses writing to compare himself to the Tupis, Thevet contrasts his own rational analysis to the Tupis' irrationality. The cosmographer bluntly and repeatedly calls attention to the superstitious "savages" who are incapable of relying on science and the Bible for their reasoning. De Léry, contrastingly, considers the tragedy of the Tupis to be their lack of access to the gospel and thus their state of deprivation of grace. For Thevet, the minds of the Tupis and other Amerindians are occluded permanently by their inability to demonstrate reason. Thevet finds in the Tupis an ignorance of divine law, human law, and science. While Léry's relativism finds reason within Tupi customs, for Thevet their customs serve as negative examples of what is right, as a corruption of the ideal. The cosmographer implores his countrymen to avoid falling into the errors he finds among the Tupis.

Que nous sert l'Ecriture sainte, que nous servent les lois, et autres bonnes sciences, dont notre Seigneur nous a donné connaissance, si nous vivons en erreur et ignorance, comme ces pauvres Sauvages, et plus brutallement que bêtes brutes? (1983, 75)

Of what value and utility are Holy Scripture, laws, and other good sciences of which our Lord has given us knowledge, if we live in error and ignorance, like these poor Savages, and more brutally than brutal beasts? (translation mine)

Thevet appeals to his readers to grasp the importance of a cosmographic paradigm reliant on reason to explain, in turn, the virtues of reason. Thus, the mission of cosmography is to elevate Holy Scripture, law, and the sciences as hallmarks of civilization.

By contrast, the topographer's mission is more modest: to describe things as they were observed with minimal distortion. In de Léry's writing "there are no extrapolations, analogies, or learned quotations; instead there is a kind of reporting that claims to be based exclusively on the author's experience" (Hollier 1989, 242). The way this reporting takes place is through sustained narrative that is rarely interrupted to bring in "singularities" and the theories that explain them. The topographic aim is to provide a fuller representation of particular manifestations; de Léry is aware of the need to explain what he observes in minute detail. By returning later in the chapter to the claim that the "savages" are hairy, de Léry recognizes that fanciful stories based on superficial observation can be discredited by his own truthful descriptions rather than through theoretical injunctions.

> Davantage nos Ameriquains ayant quantité de poules communes, dont les Portugais leur ont baillé l'engeance, plumans souvent les blanches et avec quelques ferrementes, depuis qu'ils en ont, et auparavant avec des pieces trenchantes decoupans plus menu que chair de pasté les duvetz et petites plumes, apres qu'ils les ont fait bouillir et teindre en reouge avec du Bresil, s'estans frottez d'un certaine gomme, qu'ils ont propre à cela, ils s'en couvren, emplumassent, et chamarrent le corps, les bras et les jambes: tellement qu'en cest estat ils semblent avoir du poil folet, comme les pigeons, et autres oyseaux nouvellement esclos. Il est vraysemblable que quelques uns de ces pays par deçà, les ayant veu du commencement qu'ils arriver-

ent en leur terre accoustrez en ceste façon, s'en estans revenus sans avoir plus grande cognoissance d'eux, divulguerent et firent courir le bruit que les sauvages estoyent velus. (1994, 220)

Our Americans have a great deal of ordinary hens, which the Portuguese introduced among them and for which they have a use that I will now describe. They pluck the white ones, and after they have boiled the feathers and the down and dyed them red with brazilwood, they cut them up finer than mincemeat (with iron tools since they have acquired them—before that with sharpened stones). Having first rubbed themselves with a certain gum that they keep for this purpose, they cover themselves with these, so that they are feathered all over: their bodies, arms, and legs all bedecked; in this condition they seem to be all downy, like pigeons or other birds newly hatched. It is likely that some observers who upon their arrivals saw these people thus adorned, went back home without any further acquaintance with them, and proceeds to spread the rumour that the savages were covered with hair. (translation by Whatley in de Léry 1990, 59)

De Léry uses his careful investigation of Tupi corporeal feathering as a way of correcting the rumors that arise from insufficiently close observation. By explaining how it might appear that the Tupis are hairy, de Léry, like Thevet, offers readers a probable cause for the prevalent stories of the hairy, "savage" American Indian that were circulating in Europe. The direct observation of the topographer gives him the authority to contradict the hearsay that others mistake for a true report. Thevet argues that extreme hairiness is a rare deformity and not a normal appearance; De Léry states that through closer observation he can demonstrate that, by covering themselves in feathers, the Tupi only *appear* to be covered in hair. The topographic method of close observation not only provides proof of a positive quality attained through human arts, but it also negates alternate explanations by seeking to contradict their premises. Moreover, de Léry conducts a thorough observation of his hosts and also provides a brief sketch of the historical developments of Tupi customs as a result of contact with Europeans; the chickens and tools that the Tupis acquired from the Portuguese and the French allow them to dress themselves in feathers. Readers are shown that Tupis construct their appearance through deliberate, manufactured corporeal decorations. The sequential descriptions of the feathering process elicit a series of images in the reader's mind, as if observing the Tupis put on costumes. These composite images simultaneously make it possible to deconstruct the opposing (fantastical) explanation that the Tupis are naturally covered in fine red hair. Topography and history combine in *Histoire d'un voyage* to provide an account of close observation that reveals the processes (customs and genealogies) that produce final outcomes (appearances). With de Léry there is no theory that describes universal categories of human appearance, or aberrations due to deformities. For the topographer, the way to understand a strange appearance is through close, patient observation, not the detached speculation of deductive reasoning. Appearances are deceiving not because other travelers lack reason, but because they are superficial observers. Experience is thus proven to be the primary tool for understanding the "savages." Topography, through the observer's peering gaze, seeks the specific, local custom—what would now be characterized as an "emic" perspective—that escapes the bounds of the norms imposed on a unique culture through comparison.

TRANSLATING EXPERIENCE INTO TEXT

Relying on language to communicate the culture of unfamiliar peoples is a monumental task; the burden is even greater when one wishes to depict them vividly and accurately. At times, de Léry recognizes that no matter how many sketches he produces, his tools are limited by language as well as by his own literary abilities.

> Finalement combien que durant environ un an que j'ay esté en ce pays là, j'aye esté si curieux de contempler et les grands et les petits, que m'estant advis que je les voye tousjours devant mes yeux j'en auray toute ma vie l'idee et l'image en mon entendement: tant y a neantmoins, parce que leurs gestes et contenances sont du tout dissemblables des nostres, que je confesse estre malaisé de les bien representer ni par escrit, ni mesmes par peintures. Ainsi pour en avoir le plaisir, il les faut voir et visiter en leur pais. Mais, me direz vous, la planche est bien longue. Il est vray et partant si vous n'avez bon

pied, bon oeil, craignans que vous ne tresbuchiez, ne vous jouez pas de vous mettre en chemin. Nous verrons encore plus amplement ci apres, selon que les matieres que je traiteray se presenteront, qu'elles sont leurs maisons, utenciles de mesnage, façon de se coucher et autres manieres de faire. (1994, 233–34)

During the year or so when I lived in that country, I took such great care in observing all of them, great and small, that even now it seems to me that I have them before my eyes, and I will forever have the idea and image of them in my mind. But their gestures and expressions are so completely different from ours, that it is difficult, I confess to represent them well by writing or by pictures. To have the pleasure of it, then, you will have to go see and visit them in their own country. "Yes," you will say, "but the plank is very long." That is true, and so if you do not have a sure foot and a steady eye, and are afraid of stumbling, do not venture down that path. (translation by Whatley in de Léry 1990, 67)

De Léry's reflection on the challenges of describing the Tupis through writing reveals his awareness, as the author admits his limitations as a writer and illustrator of the very people he is describing. To be true to his promise to tell of things only as he has seen them, through multiple narrative portraits, de Léry acknowledges that his recollection of the experience is insufficient for writing a vivid and accurate description. This recognition of the limited human ability of capturing "true" appearances would have appealed to Montaigne, a thinker acutely aware of the limitations of the eye and the mind (Conley 2010, 24). De Léry's topographical account explicitly acknowledges epistemological limits in order to suggest that things are not always as they seem, despite the writer's desire to share how things seem to him.

De Léry shows an awareness of literary techniques used to capture the likeness of the unfamiliar. He has "a quite unusual capacity for putting himself in the mind of a European who has never crossed the Atlantic and is forced to envisage the New World from travellers' accounts" (Elliott 1970, 22). Andrea Frisch argues that the problem of representing the Tupis comes "not from a sense that language and painting are inherently estranged from reality, but from a sense that 'they' are intractably different from 'us'" (2014, 91). However, in *Histoire d'un voyage*, de Léry is explicitly concerned with his own memory and the capacity of language and pictorial depictions to capture difference. Although de Léry regards the Tupis as different in many ways, he does not express "difference" as a barrier to comprehension; the topographer specifically refers to certain gestures and expressions which are difficult to describe through language and pictures. Moreover, the problem of explaining and differentiating between "us" and "them" is the same as the problem of representation (these two concerns are too intimately linked to isolate in de Léry's text). An ineffable thought is not only too different to be captured by existing concepts, but the signifying capacity of language itself lacks the power to express it.

De Léry's reflection on the failure of representation also leads to the creation of spatial and temporal frames which are important to the structure of *Histoire d'un voyage*. Whereas, as a noble adventurer, the author seeks to close the distance between himself and the narrator to make himself the only subject of his experience, as an historian, ethnographer, and storyteller, the author admits he is no longer the protagonist of his story. Thus, to have knowledge of the Tupis and to reflect on the difficulty of expressing that knowledge reveals the passage of time between the experience and the act of writing about it. The true likeness of the Tupis is accessible only to the protagonist who has direct access to the lived experience; the writer has to overcome the stumbling block of language in order to reproduce it. These dual positions are highlighted by changes in the narrator's voice—at times engaged in expressing active observation, at other times reflecting on the artifice of written description. When addressing the reader, the narrator uses a didactic voice when speaking about the Tupis. However, when retelling certain events or when citing dialogue, the narrator assumes the voice of the traveler speaking to or with his collocutors.

De Léry's passage from the text to the experience suggests that he inhabits two temporally distinct frames—the writer's persona as narrator, and as explorer in Brazil—which are linked by a mnemonic relationship. The Calvinist storyteller transmits his memory as if he were listening to the story of his own internal narrator while writing it down for the reader. The two chronotopes established by the narrative are not evoked only for rhetorical effect; they are quite real for the author (i.e., the faraway place is not *imaginary* even though it is *imagined* for the sake of the dialogue within the narrative). To move from one chronotope to the other, the author descends into memory. De Léry uses the metaphor of a plank to describe the distance between the (imagined) reader in late sixteenth-century France and the transatlantic traveler in Brazil. The topographer encourages his readers to contemplate the two frames of reference—one inhabited by the author addressing the reader and the other by his own protagonist, face-to-face with the cannibals—and invites them to consider how one could physically move from one frame to the other by crossing the plank, which represents both a ship crossing the Atlantic and the topographer who transfers knowledge across distance. De Léry offers a subtle warning that seeking direct, unmediated contact with the world of the Tupis is a possibility, but only through a radically different and much more dangerous method of inquiry. Therefore, the topographer's role is to provide an alternate, and less threatening, plank for the reader seeking knowledge about a distant place.

Treating the same topic several times, de Léry writes a history that constructs meaningful depictions of the Tupis through a kind of "thick description" that Clifford Geertz could appreciate. This apparent excess of description, a constant deferment of related and relevant information, provides both depth and difference for readers (de Certeau 1998, 222–25). The richness of description is too great for a superficial or straightforward reading of the text; as a result, readers are encouraged to approach it in their own imaginative ways: "Le lecteur, par ceste narration les contemple comme il luy plaira" (1994, 233). (Let the reader, by this narration, contemplate them as he will [trans. Whatley in de Léry 1990, 66]). The topographer understands that the impressions created by his account will depend on the audience. Moreover, de Léry's descriptions of the Tupis are not contained by rigid chapter divisions, but revisited in later chapters. The topographer's experience embroiders the chapters with motifs that escape narrow definitions; for example, the Tupis' rapidly changing nature can be located in almost all of the ethnographic chapters. These motifs do not arise from direct comparison and causal linkage; rather, they emerge through the narrative, showing that de Léry's *Histoire d'un voyage* is connected to his thoughts and experiences as he comes to understand the Tupis as both a visiting traveler and a writer. Tom Conley writes that the topographic method is like the sensation and movement of a snail going through a dark maze, simultaneously exploring and moving along the surface (2010, 3).

A thorough reading of both *Histoire d'un voyage* and *Les singularités* requires readers to retain earlier details so that information can be seen in a different light in later chapters. Of the two texts, *Histoire d'un voyage* is more contingent upon readers actively recalling earlier details. For instance, de Léry returns to a previously covered topic to remind his readers that he is fulfilling his promise to continue to develop it:

> [S]uivant ce que j'ay promis ci-dessus, quand j'ay parlé de leurs danses en leur beuveries et *caouinages*, que je dirois aussi l'autre façon qu'ils ont de danser: à fin de les mieux representer, voici les morgues, gestes et contenances qu'ils tenoyent. (1994, 401)

> Now since I promised earlier, when I spoke of the dancing at their drinking bouts and *caouinages*, that I would also tell of their way of dancing, *the more fully to represent them* (emphasis mine). I will describe the solemn poses and gestures that they used here. (translation by Whatley in de Léry 1990, 142)

By returning to the topic of dancing, de Léry encourages readers to compare the new variant—a solemn dance (figure 1)–to the jovial dance performed during drinking bouts. The comparison suggests both similarity and difference between the two scenes. If de Léry had said everything about dancing in one uninterrupted description, that description would rupture the coherency of each distinct performance. Meaning is developed not just by presenting two different descriptions, but by the way these distinct images are juxtaposed. De Léry explicitly differentiates one performance from the other to indicate that they are linked to separate events—the result of careful topographic observation. By maintaining a separation between the two descriptions, the topographer shows that the two instances of dancing are thematically related, but temporally and contextually distinct. Thus, de Léry high-

Fig. 1. Two Indians with a parrot and monkey. Jean de Léry. Histoire d'un voyage fait en la terre du Brésil autrement dite Amérique. 1580. p. 246. Source: Gallica; Bibliothèque nationale de France. 8 December 2015. Web.

lights the importance of a recurring movement between two chronologically discrete events in order to show that dancing can be either ceremonial or recreational. De Léry avoids drawing analogical parallels to other kinds of dancing—Tupi dancing does not have one meaning, but many. The deferment of each image allows readers to reimagine the Tupis in a different position, setting, or context. Each portrait has its own place in the narrative, but its overall meaning is drawn from the development of the narrative.

De Léry describes some of the events which give his portraits meaning in order to retell his intimate experiences with his subjects. The spontaneity of these events is often affirmed by laughter as well as other forms of affect, as in the case of the locals who find themselves awestruck when de Léry changes his name to "Léry-oussou" ("big oyster").

> [I]l me falloit accomoder de leur nommer quelque chose qui leur fust cognue: cela (comme il me dit) estant si bien venu à propos que mon surnom Léry, signifie une huitre en leur language, je leur dis que je m'appellois Léry-oussou: c'est à dire une grosse huitre. Dequoy eux se tenans bien satisfaicts avec leur admiration Teh! se prenans à rire. (1994, 450–451)

> I had to accommodate by naming something that was known to them. Since by a lucky chance my surname "Léry," means "oyster" in their language, I told them my name was *"Léry-oussou,"* that is, big oyster. This pleased them greatly; with their *"Teh!"* of admiration they began to laugh. (translation by Whatley in de Léry 1990, 162)

In this short vignette about his new name, meaning emerges from a distinct event tied contextually to others in the narrative. The name is not only relevant because of the Tupis' difficulty in pronouncing *Jean* (which they pronounced *"Nian"*), but also because de Léry had previously written that the Tupis give each other the names of animals, often followed by "oussou" ("big"). In so doing, De Léry simultaneously shows his understanding of convention and his desire to accept it. By acquiring a "familiar" name for the Tupis, the author (briefly) becomes *Léryoussou*—that is, a new character in his own story. This seemingly minor anecdote does not just present information, but also displays de Léry's intimate interactions with the Tupis, to the point of temporarily *becoming* one of the "savages." De Léry reports the laughter of his Tupi associates as he reintroduces himself in their language while also including their *Teh!* (an exclamation of surprise, wonder, and amazement) (1990, 162). The humorous episode speaks to his ethnographic ability as well as his skill as a storyteller.

Thus, for de Léry, the mechanism that creates meaning is not a single, symbolically laden image, but rather an excess of detail, from seemingly minor anecdotes that often become polysemic as they converge. The richness of meaning resembles the proliferation of the *maniot* and *aypi* roots that de Léry admires (1994, 241). Meaning requires the reader to actively follow the narrative as a collaborator who can recall and relate de Léry's descriptions; the layered and imagistic text urges the reader to approach *Histoire d'un voyage* as a complex work which must be read in its entirety. The narrative folds into itself in order to allow for both repetition and progression, as certain themes continue throughout the narrative while being altered by particular episodes.

By contrast, Thevet's descriptions are divided into topics which culminate in analogical parallels to extrinsic, related examples. Although many rich details are revealed when the cosmographer enters into description, Thevet's exploration of the Tupis (and others) is limited by his desire to classify social and cultural traits. Unlike de Léry's focused and recursive descriptions, Thevet's observations are a collection or collage of singularities mounted on a cosmological structure. These singularities are retained and evaluated by an Aristotelian epistemology that thoroughly shapes Thevet's narrative and its central message.

For the Franciscan cosmographer, the Tupis are but one of many nations ranked by their values and political power; the goal of the cosmographer is to provide the whole image that disciplines each particular by keeping it bound within its category. As Denis Hollier describes, this process of integrating the "curiosities" of the New World into the knowledge of the Old World became a standard way of writing about new discoveries: "The strangeness of the New World was integrated without upsets into the system of traditional knowledge" (1989, 241–42). Thus, one can easily find in Thevet a curiosity to discover new things that is curbed by an equally powerful urge to systematize those discoveries.

The New World becomes at once the source for novel written material (*singularities*) and for the physical materials (*curiosities*). The cabinet of curiosities and cosmography reflects a common desire to collect material evidence of different, strange cultural and natural environments. The late-Renaissance collections of curiosities blurred the lines between natural and artificial in the pursuit of acquiring previously unseen, singular objects (Evans et al. 2006, 13). Similarly, Thevet's *Les singularités* seeks to acquire the novelties of the Americas and to bring them back to France. This process culminated in the transportation of several Tupinamba men to the court of Henry II as physical living proof of the singularities of the Americas. Renaissance curiosity was a new "desire to know" demonstrated, at least in part, by an interest in collection as well as in the "types of enquiry" taking place (Evans et al. 2006, 13). Like cosmography, the aim of the private cabinets of curiosities taking hold in Europe in the sixteenth century was to be "a veritable 'microcosm,' a 'compendium of the universe'... to take in the entire universe at a single glance, as this universe had been reduced to the scale of the human eye" (Pomian 1990, 49). Thus, the assortment of singularities was not meant to be kept unsystematised and open to various interpretations, but rather to be prepared for integration into previous knowledge. Frisch states that, for the cosmographer, "experience serves to confirm previous knowledge (or belief) and thus minimize 'singularity'" (2014, 64). It is useful to trace Thevet's development from *Les singularités* to the *Cosmographie universelle* (and later publications) to see the cosmographer's progression toward a wholly systematic presentation of his earlier singularities by relying on Aristotelian models of thought.

One of Thevet's most renowned literary and pictorial sketches is "Quoniambec," a chief first mentioned in *Les singularités* (chapter 54). The chief is described as a great ruler and strong man in Thevet's first publication; after a series of embellishments Thevet has Quoniambec firing cannons mounted on his shoulders and appearing beside other kings and emperors. Thevet's *Vrais Pourtraits* restyles Quoniambec as a European monarch through its symbolic allusions to monarchy, in order to "dress" the naked Quoniambec in the accoutrements of European rulers (Lestringant 1987, 45). Where de Léry's sparse portraits function as descriptive convergences that summarize the text, Thevet's portraits develop an iconic quality; they rely heavily on extratextual symbolism for their meaning. The aim for Thevet is not to explore the meaning of his earlier singularities or to keep them arranged as a collage of observations, but to find in them new analogical and allegorical resemblances. Thevet's later works (*Vrais Pourtraits* and *Cosmographie universelle*) solidify the analogical paradigm operating in *Les singularités*. The cosmographer, unlike the topographer, is not interested in a visiting traveler's view of daily life (a perspective maintained throughout *Histoire d'un voyage*); rather, he seeks to conduct a spatial survey of the globe in order to analyze and rank its many nations. Lestringant writes that powerful figures are, for Thevet, a sign of the political and social organization without which civilization could not exist (1987).

> Lack of government is synonymous with lack of humanity—and in this case Thevet places himself in the school of Aristotle for whom man is, of course, above all a political animal. (1987, 37)

Through the invention of a universal political order in which every nation has a figurehead (a king), Thevet shows that his Aristotelian interpretation misunderstands Brazilian (and other American Indian) cultures in order to make them "understandable."

The cosmographer's heavy reliance on Aristotelian modes of thought is also exhibited by his praise of certain virtues and his condemnation of immoderation. Thevet's *Les singularités* and other works are problematic because they use Aristotle as a basis for evaluating and ordering the New World (Reeser 2006, 218–19). Therefore, Montaigne's skepticism of cosmography could have also been a rejection of the Aristotelian models of social and political organization preferred by Thevet. Montaigne declares "that the Americans live 'sans les precepts d'Aristotle' ('without the precepts of Aristotle')" (Reeser 2006, 218)—the same precepts cherished by the cosmographic friar.

Thevet's mission is to reveal and describe the people of Brazil as much as it is to assign to them certain essential, indexical qualities that place them in a natural order in relation to their neighbors and the various nations named by prior cosmographers. In *Les singularités*, readers are told, for instance, that beyond Guanabara Bay lives another nation of even more bestial cannibals:

Cette canaille mange ordinairement de la chair humaine comme nous ferions du mouton, et ils y prennent encoure plus grands plaisir. Et vous pouvez êtres assurez qu'ils est malaisé de leur ôter un homme d'entre les mains quands ils le tiennent, pour l'appétit qu'ils ont de le manger comme les lions voraces. Il n'y a de bête aux déserts d'Afrique ou d'Arabie si cruelle et qui appète si ardemment le sang humain que ce peuple sauvage plus que brutal. (1983, 156–7)

These rogues usually eat human flesh as we would sheep, and they take even greater pleasure in the act. And you can be sure that it is not easy to free one of their captives, for they have the appetite of ravenous lions. There is no beast in the deserts of Africa and Arabia so cruel that would feast so ardently on human blood than these more-than-brutal savages. (translation mine)

This description is simultaneously an observation about another group of American Indians and Thevet's evaluation of the order of these people on a universal cosmographic hierarchy. The adjacent nation of cannibals thus descends to a lower rung of human sociability and civility as soon as they are mentioned. Interestingly, Thevet parallels de Léry's note of caution that seeking firsthand experience is dangerous. Thevet writes, perhaps sarcastically, that those that want to engage in trade might do well to bring them human captives (1983, 157).

Thevet's perspective suggests that he writes from "the point of view of the sailor" (Frisch 2014, 53). Although it can be argued that in *Les singularités* Thevet provides a chorographic point of view (that of a traveler passing through a large region), his perspective remains more removed and distant than that of de Léry, that of a sailor turned cosmographer: the singularities observed by the sailor are ordered and increasingly marginalized by the authority of the cosmographer. Conley summarizes Thevet's double-natured text as "a narrative mass that is at once unified and scattered" (2011, 192). The scattered singularities are the product of the sailor's gaze, for which newness is always beyond the horizon, even though it cannot be reached; the Catholic cosmographer displays the severity of an epistemological paradigm which subordinates difference even as it claims to document it (Reeser 2006, 221).

WRITING WITH NOSTALGIA, WRITING "IN PASSING"

Topography, unlike cosmography, requires a retracing and a revisiting of the subject. Despite the chapter divisions, which attempt to cut the *Histoire d'un voyage* into digestible portions composed of single core topics, de Léry frequently elaborates his prior observations with new details. This method of returning to a topic to cover it in greater detail is reaffirmed by de Léry's longing for a return to the site of experience: "Je regrette souvent que je ne suis parmi les sauvages" (1994, 508). (I often regret that I am not amongst the savages [trans. mine]), de Léry writes when recounting his return to France. Lestringant notes that "toute l'*Histoire d'un voyage* est ... empreinte de cette nostalgie" (1990, 80) (the entire *Histoire d'un voyage* is marked by this nostalgia [trans. mine]). The desire for a return to the land of the Tupis speaks to the misery the author would find upon his return to France. Yet what is more remarkable is that de Léry's wish to be among the Tupis has no comparison in *Les singularités*. A desire to return to the *topos* makes de Léry's account both a "history"—the description of a time in the past—and an intimate topography. The motif of "return," stated explicitly, and implied by nostalgia, suggests that de Léry found a homely place among the cannibals. The literary process of returning to the inception of a memory is necessary for the topographer to make himself, as author, the protagonist of his own story.

> Depuis mon retour par-deça m'estant trouvé en un lieu où on en faisoit, ce flair me fit ressouvenir de l'odeur qu'on sent ordinairement és maisons des sauvages, quand on y fait de la farine de racine. (1994, 238)

> After I came back over here, whenever I happened to be in a place where starch was being made, the scent of it made me remember the odor one usually picks up in the savages' houses when they are making root flour. (translation by Whatley in de Léry 1990, 69)

The topographer who used his senses to investigate the Tupis through "autopsy" also describes how his senses retain an affinity for their root flour; he continues to remember the smell of their houses despite the passage of some twenty years. De Léry's nostalgia points to action from a distance: the resurgence of a chronotope via a memory rekindled by a sensation. Moreover, the desire to reunite the sense organ and the stimulus reveals the intimate method of observation in topography and its aim to refer to direct experience. The expression of memory through sensory stimuli—especially taste and smell—is a motif also used by Marcel Proust. As Jeff Malpas recognizes, memorialization is always connected to the place where that memory was first created. "Proust presents such topoanalysis as an exploration of our own selves as well as an exploration ... of place—in Proust we find topophilia writ large" (1999, 6). Involuntary memory guided by the senses serves as a bridge that unites temporalities and locales, if only for a brief instant. De Léry's recollection of the starchy smell of Tupi houses leads the author—by the nose—to a place which he once knew; nostalgia sparks the return of happy memories that move the author from his writing desk to the Tupi hearth. Despite the fondness that de Léry shows for the land of the Tupis, his nostalgic tone is also a product of the upheavals in France which he experienced firsthand after his return (Lestringant 1990, 80).

Like de Léry, modern ethnographers express nostalgia for their first sites of study. Lévi-Strauss, for example, was acutely aware that he, like de Léry, also felt a longing to revisit the place he was writing about in *Tristes Tropiques* after a fifteen-year hiatus (Silver 2001, 125). The nostalgic return of the author is a keystone of the topographic (and ethnographic) mode because it reveals a sincere appreciation for a formative experience (i.e., the author's literary return reflects the desire for a corporeal return). When the writer "reunites" with the people and places that once formed an experience there arises a "consciousness vital to the sensation of an event a 'nexus of prehensions'" (2010, 68). The recollection of sensory experience, and the nostalgic tone that it sets, is not just an effective rhetorical device, but also the topographic method of closing the distance between the time and place of the author and that of the protagonist.

In sharp contrast to de Léry's desire to return to Brazil, Thevet writes in a style that conveys passage, and a recounting from a distance which grows continuously larger. The cosmographer does not return to the topic through nostalgia and sensation, but through a rationalizing analysis which reorders his observations into previously defined categories.

Thevet frequently describes peculiar things by starting with the phrase "en passant" ("in passing"). "En passant" appears to reflect Thevet's experience and claim to knowledge as a traveler to the New World. Whereas de Léry stays in one place for a duration and thus becomes intimately acquainted with his environment, Thevet passes through, collecting "singularities" and then moving on to other lands. The collection of singularities, like a collection of curiosities, is the action of a sixteenth-century European traveler "passing by" a place to take note or acquire something "curious." The singularity described "in passing" is also a rhetorical announcement that Thevet directly observed what he describes in the text. The linear movement implied by the phrase further suggests that while *Les singularités* covers many places, it does not have a particular place to return to (other than France). Frisch argues that this linear movement developed by textual "passage" is an indication that a significant number of Thevet's singularities are of a fleeting nature (2014, 63).

"En passant" is a cosmographic method for adjoining curiosities that are circumstantial to the main topic of a chapter but still related by some measure of *convenientia*, an association of things due to their physical proximity (Foucault 1994). Observations made within the bounds of a roughly defined locality are connected "in passing" to show that they exist in physical proximity to one another; thus, what is not related analogically to universal examples is adjoined "en passant." By indicating his willingness to tack on observations "en passant," Thevet also demonstrates his lack of focus on a distinct place. Thevet writes as if to suggest that "the description of Brazil is an extra, a word tacked on in passing" (Frisch 2014, 61). In this way, the phrase "en passant" reveals the style of *Les singularités:* Thevet's main topics are evaluated through analogies by following an Aristotelian model of organization, while lesser observations are marginalized by the author even though he cannot escape their geographic copresence. "En passant" responds to the perceived *convenientia* of the people, flora, and fauna that the cosmographer observes throughout his travels.

The introduction of something "in passing" gives the impression of an authentic "passage"—a chronological or geographic movement—but the phrase is mostly a way of appending the descriptions of things linked by proximity. By writing "en passant," Thevet appears to balance the perspectives of the Aristotelian thinker and theologian with that of the itinerant traveler. However, the cosmographer's distinguishing phrase does not allow readers to mobilize his observations with the same sense of coherency as *Histoire d'un voyage*. "En passant" is a rhetorical expression for creating longer lists rather than a reflection of physical and temporal movement. *Les singularités* does not provide readers with moments of reflection, because even lengthier descriptions are abruptly cut by a conclusion introduced "en passant"; nor does the addition of fleeting observations adjoined to main topics help to elaborate on an earlier description. The cosmographer, unlike the topographer, does not discuss how observations are related to one another. Unlike de Léry's multiple descriptions and textual portraits, Thevet's observations are not grounded by a context and are difficult to imagine as coherent events. "En passant" and other frequently used adverbial clauses that indicate passage and digression, are an integral part of the poetics of *Les singularités*.

Thevet's authority as a cosmographer comes from a paradigm of comparison in which curious phenomena are part of a larger macrocosm; passage is necessary not just to relate connected observations but also to move from the singularity to the universal. The cosmographer demonstrates that he is the first to bring knowledge of a custom, a tree, or a bird by virtue of their "singular natures." The tone set by Thevet's indirect and displaced mode of description is in stark contrast to de Léry's nostalgia. The ever-growing list of singularities, like Thevet's passage through "Antarctic France," prevents the articulation of a central *topos*. Thevet's passive treatment of a particular location leads to a dissonance in the text; for instance, he writes: "Et pour le surplus, nous avons délibéré d'écrire en passant un mot de la terre du Brésil" (1983, 150). (As for the rest, we have deliberated to write, in passing, a word about the land of Brazil" [trans. mine]). The "word" that Thevet claims to write "in passing" takes up roughly one third of *Les singularités*. The understatement on the part of the author is not due to modesty, but rather to a desire to keep moving, to distance himself from a particular place in order to focus on the cosmographic whole. The linear progression away from the "current" topic suggests that the place Thevet seeks is always beyond the horizon. Unlike de Léry's longing for reentry into a Tupi home to smell the starchy root flour for a second time, Thevet concludes his description of Brazil dispassionately. The cosmographer is not attached to a place; his concern is the description of space—the region, the world, and its universal forms. Therefore, the use of the adverbial phrase "in passing" allows for the collection of deracinated curiosities encountered in the Americas. The itinerant cosmographer seems to describe strange things that belong to a cosmic order, yet it is precisely by not becoming fully acquainted with any place in particular that his ordering gaze is given leave to "gradually convert the Brazil of the cannibals into another Europe" (Lestringant 1987, 41).

In contrast to Thevet, de Léry does not write "in passing" to adjoin his observations, nor does he abandon a description hastily in order to move forward. De Léry returns to previously treated subjects to give them a second look, and to introduce new information that casts a new light on previous descriptions. For instance, the topographer returns to a description of religion after expressing his own theological arguments: "Ainsi pour retourner à mon principal sujet, qui est de poursuyvre à declarer ce qu'on peut appeler Religion entre les Sauvages de l'Amerique" (1994, 393). (Let me return to my principal subject, and pursue the consideration of what might be called religion among the savages of America [trans. Whatley in de Léry 1990, 139]). De Léry does not cease describing the Tupi even after he has brought his own views into the discussion. Therefore, *Histoire d'un voyage* is a recursive text—the author always seeks to return to the *topos* that first formed his experience. By contrast, Thevet mostly employs the phrase "en passant" to expedite a description in order to avoid further reflection and the internalization of the strangeness of the other.

CONCLUSION

The descriptions of similarities and differences between cultures is always a fraught process. Difference can only be explained by finding a middle ground between familiar tropes—for the sake of making an account intelligible to one's audience—and experimenting with new techniques of representation. De Léry's topographic account estranges readers from their familiar settings only to refamiliarize them; chronology and spatial differences are preserved in multiple descriptive portraits to show that customs and appearances are not set in their meaning, but variable and subject to interpretation. De Léry's vignettes draw readers into the world of the Tupis through a curious pull of the author's nostalgia and previous lived experience. Thevet attempts to use a cosmographic approach to immediately juxtapose Tupi customs to those recorded in other parts of the world. This broadly comparative method relies on preexisting categories to find meaning in "new" ideas and details that capture the perceived characteristics of the other. Unfortunately, the cosmographer struggles to find meaning in the overwhelming strangeness he describes—the break is too great. Moreover, the reader is led away from the site and its people by a dispassionate analysis that uses hierarchies developed across the Atlantic to judge the corruption of the "savages." Montaigne's warning that cosmography attempts to explain more than any person could lay claim to knowing via direct experience justly applies to *Les singularités*.

Jean de Léry and André Thevet show that the search for meaning in intercultural experiences is a concern that predates the scientific methodologies of anthropology, ethnography, and ethnology. Contemporary ethnographers continue to encounter the problem of translating social and cultural phenomena into a familiar language (Darnell 1999). Despite the evolution of epistemological paradigms in the past four centuries, the literariness of topography and cosmography can still shape one's understanding of ethnographic production. Considering that Malinowski problematizes the relationship between the scientific "facts" and the experience on the ground (Young 2004, 432), it is worth expanding one's concept of "ethnography" in order to study the interpretative techniques and the effect of various epistemological paradigms on the representation of otherness throughout recorded history. The roots of ethnography may run deeper than Enlightenment science.

REFERENCES

Boemus, Joannes, Nicolaus, Jean De Léry, Damião De Góis, and Joseph Juste Scaliger. 1611. *The Manners, Lawes, and Cvstomes of All Nations*. Edited by Edward Aston. London: Printed by G. Eld.

Castro, Eduardo Batalha Viveiros De. 2011. *The Inconstancy of the Indian Soul: The Encounter of Catholics and Cannibals in Sixteenth-Century Brazil*. Chicago: Prickly Paradigm.

Certeau, Michel De. 1986. *Heterologies: Discourse on the Other.* Translated by Brian Massumi. Minneapolis: University of Minnesota Press.

———. *The Writing of History.* Translated by Tom Conley. New York: Columbia University Press, 1988.

Conley, Tom. 2010. *An Errant Eye: Poetry and Topography in Early Modern France.* Minneapolis: University of Minnesota Press.

———. 2011. *The Self-Made Map: Cartographic Writing in Early Modern France.* Minnesota: University of Minnesota Press.

Cosgrove, Denis. 2000. *Extra-Terrestrial Geography: Cosmography Before and After . . . Escholarship.* Accessed August 21, 2016. http://escholarship.org/uc/item/7g79h5k9.pdf.

Darnell, Regna. 1999. "Translation." *Journal of Linguistic Anthropology* 9 (1–2): 251–54.

Elliott, J. H. 1970. *The Old World and the New: 1492–1650.* Cambridge: Cambridge University Press.

Evans, Robert John Weston, and Alexander Marr. 2006. *Curiosity and Wonder from the Renaissance to the Enlightenment.* Aldershot, England: Ashgate.

Foucault, Michel. 1994. *The Order of Things: An Archaeology of the Human Sciences.* New York: Vintage.

Frisch, Andrea. 2014. "Passing Knowledge: André Thevet's Cosmographical Epistemology." *Journal of Early Modern History* 18 (1–2): 49–67.

Hodgen, Margaret T. 1954. "Sebastian Muenster (1489–1552): A Sixteenth-Century Ethnographer." *Osiris* 11: 504–29.

———. 1964. *Early Anthropology in the Sixteenth and Seventeenth Centuries.* Philadelphia: University of Pennsylvania Press.

Hollier, Denis, and R. Howard Bloch. 1989. *A New History of French Literature.* Cambridge MA: Harvard University Press.

Kenny, Neil. 2008. *An Introduction to Sixteenth-Century French Literature and Thought: Other Times, Other Places.* London: Duckworth.

Lestringant, Frank. 1987. "The Myth of the Indian Monarchy: An Aspect of the Controversy between Thevet and Léry (1575–1585)." In *Indians and Europe*, edited by C. F. Feest. 37–60. Gottingen, Germany: Herodot.

———. 1990. *Le Huguenot Et Le Sauvage: L'Amérique Et La Controverse Coloniale En France, Au Temps Des Guerres De Religion (1555–1589).* Paris: Aux Amateurs De Livres.

———. 1994. *Mapping the Renaissance World: The Geographical Imagination in the Age of Discovery.* Berkeley: University of California Press.

———. 1999. *Jean De Léry, Ou, L'invention Du Sauvage: Essai Sur L'Histoire D'un Voyage Faict En La Terre Du Brésil.* Paris: H. Champion.

Léry, Jean De. 1990. *History of a Voyage to the Land of Brazil, Otherwise Called America*. Translated by Janet Whatley. Berkeley: University of California Press.

Léry, Jean De, Frank Lestringant, and Claude Lévi-Strauss. 1994. *Histoire D'un Voyage Faict En La Terre Du Brésil (1578)*. Paris: Le Livre De Poche.

Malpas, Jeff. 1999. *Place and Experience: A Philosophical Topography*. Cambridge: Cambridge University Press.

Martin, John Jeffries. 2007. *The Renaissance World*. New York: Routledge.

Montaigne, Michel De. 2003. *The Complete Works: Essays, Travel Journal, Letters*. Translated by Donald Murdoch Frame. New York: A. A. Knopf.

Neto, Jose Raimundo Maia, Gianni Paganini, and John Christian. Laursen. 2009. *Skepticism in the Modern Age: Building on the Work of Richard Popkin*. Leiden, Netherlands: Brill.

Nushaj, Driton. 2016. *Cosmography and Topography: A Comparison of André Thevet's "Les Singularités De La France Antarctique" and Jean De Léry's "Histoire D'un Voyage Faict En La Terre Du Brésil."* Scholarship@Western. Accessed August 19, 2016. http://ir.lib.uwo.ca/etd/3701/.

Pomian, Krzysztof. 1990. *Collectors and Curiosities: Paris and Venice 1500–1800*. Cambridge, England: Polity.

Reeser, Todd W. 2006. *Moderating Masculinity in Early Modern Culture*. Chapel Hill NC: North Carolina Studies in the Romance Languages and Literature.

Silver, Susan. 2001. "Cannibalism, Nudity, and Nostalgia: Léry and Lévi-Strauss Revisit Brazil." *Studies in Travel Writing* 15 (2): 117–33.

Thevet, André. 1983. *Les Singularités De La France Antarctique: Le Brésil Des Cannibales Au xvie Siècle*. Paris: La Découverte.

———. 2011. *Le Brésil D'André Thevet: Les Singularités De La France Antarctique (1557)*. Edited by Frank Lestringant. Paris: Éditions Chandeigne.

Verdon, Michel. 2006. "The World Upside Down: Boas, History, Evolutionism, and Science." *History and Anthropology* 17 (3): 171–87.

Vermeulen, Han F. 2015. *Before Boas: The Genesis of Ethnography and Ethnology in the German Enlightenment*. Lincoln: University of Nebraska Press.

Williams, Wes, Alexander Marr, and Robert John Weston Evans. 2006. *Curiosity and Wonder from the Renaissance to the Enlightenment*. Aldershot, England: Ashgate.

Young, Michael W. 2004. *Malinowski: Odyssey of an Anthropologist, 1884–1920*. New Haven CT: Yale University Press.

CHRISTIAN FEEST

2

Faded Tracks of Austrian Anthropology
*Hans Sidonius (von) Becker (1895–1948)
and Some of His Contemporaries*

In his pathbreaking volume on anthropology under Nazi rule, Hans Fischer (1990a, 181) asserted that of all anthropologists in the Third Reich, only two had been deported to concentration camps: the West Prussian writer, amateur anthropologist, and impostor Hellmuth Draws-Tychsen (1904–1973)—apparently primarily as a troublemaker—and the Austrian Africanist Marianne Schmidl (1890–1942), as a Jew. Hans Becker (who was deported twice) went unnoticed by Fischer; forty-two years after his death, he had already by and large passed into oblivion. In Peter Linimayr's book on anthropology in Vienna during the period of national socialism, Becker figures as a concentration camp inmate and resistance fighter, but remains rather faceless in the twilight of the available sources (Linimayr 1994, 166, 168). Whereas Draws-Tychsen and Schmidl have since been dealt with extensively (Fischer 1990a, 131–60; 1990b, 2: 339–62; Kraft 2009; Geisenheiner 2005), there is still no comparable account of Becker, who, in recent anthropological writings, is at best noted as the husband of Etta Becker-Donner (1911–1975), the first woman to become director of an anthropology museum in Europe. This blank in the collective memory of the discipline is largely the result of a biography, in which cultural anthropology played an insufficiently documented (and also not the most prominent) part.[1] Although Becker held a PhD in anthropology and published in the field, he was never employed as an anthropologist and was thus regarded by the profession as an outsider. His biography nevertheless sheds light on Austrian and German anthropology of his period, and on the period itself.[2] It may also be read as a contribution to the ethnography of Austria during the first half of the twentieth century.

It may have been primarily Becker's versatility—a full range of hardly connected interests and activities—that led to his lack of recognition and prevented him from attaining a posthumous reputation. He is still most frequently remembered for his role in combatting national socialism before and after the German occupation of Austria in 1938 and for his account of this resistance (Becker 1946a). Somewhat curiously, nearly all of his writings on ethnological subject matter, which were hardly in line with the prevailing political ideology, were published during the period of Nazi rule.

Becker's versatility is also one of the reasons for the scattered source materials and the unsatisfactory state of research. Potential biographical documents resulting from a variety of activities (including journalistic writings in Austria and South America) still remain to be discovered. Many records, including, notably, his ethnographic field notes and correspondence prior to 1941, were lost in the course of his relocations between the continents or during the period of his first detention. Best documented are his activities in the anti-Nazi resistance movement, from the beginning of his work for the *Vaterländische Front* (Patriotic Front)—the political arm of the Austrofascist movement in the 1930s—until the end of World War II and the short postwar period. The presently available sources permit a better reconstruction of some aspects of his biography than they do of others; however, they offer insights into a network of relationships with some of his contemporaries that help to locate him physically and ideologically in his time, and which will therefore be given special consideration.[3]

BEFORE ANTHROPOLOGY, 1895–1922

Johann Sydonius Ritter von Becker was born on 22 September 1895 as the youngest of five children of the Rear Admiral Alois Johann Heinrich Ritter von Becker (1842–1900) and his wife, Emma Caroline (née Wickerhauser, 1856–1918), in Pola (now Pula, Croatia), the main naval station of the Austro-Hungarian monarchy. Two years earlier, Alois von Becker had returned from the trip around the world undertaken in 1892–93 by Archduke Franz Ferdinand von Austria-Este on the cruiser

Kaiserin Elisabeth commanded by Becker, which had resulted in the accumulation of the largest ethnographic collection of the present Weltmuseum Wien. Becker's grandfather, Moritz Aloys Ritter von Becker (1812–1887), had been director of the Habsburg Family Fideikomiss Library and one of the tutors of Crown Prince Rudolf von Habsburg. Moritz was a prolific writer, especially in the fields of local history and ethnography of Lower Austria, an honorary member of the Imperial and Royal Geographical Society, and—in the words of an obituary—he "took a lively part in the life of political parties and during elections, especially in the combat with democrats" (Anonymous 1887). Emma Wickerhauser was a daughter of Moriz Wickerhauser (1815–1874), a professor of oriental languages at the Oriental Academy in Vienna, and of Augusta von Rosthorn (1827–1871), a member of a prominent family of industrialists in Lower Austria; one of Emma's second cousins was the sinologist and diplomat Arthur von Rosthorn (1862–1945), who, in the period between the two World Wars, inhabited an official residence in what was formerly the Imperial Castle and is now the Weltmuseum Wien.[4] The fact that Emperor Franz Josef was bearing all costs for the education of Becker's eldest son Moritz at the Naval Academy in Fiume after the rear admiral's early death illustrates the family's close ties to the House of Habsburg (Gotschim-Jauk 1990, 5n3).

Johann Sydonius (or Hans Sidonius) grew up as a semi-orphan in comparatively modest circumstances. His brother Moritz—seventeen years his elder—acted as a substitute father prior to the beginning of his naval service, while his mother promoted his interests in the fine arts and music. Hans attended the naval primary school and, subsequently, the state gymnasium in Pula, where he was exempted from tuition fees. His final report card in 1913 shows him to have been a good student with excellent grades in German, geography and history, philosophy, physical education, and free-style drawing, and a single D in Greek (Gotschim-Jauk 1990, 5–7).[5]

In a later memoir Hans expressed his gratitude for a destiny that had "permitted him to grow up at the intersection of Romanic, Germanic, and Slavic cultures" and thus granted him the privilege of a live experience of the multiculturalism of the Austrian Empire, making him cognizant of the fluidity of the concept of nationhood. He was proud of the fact "both parents had imparted [to him] a living tradition of the knowledge, arts, and integrated culture . . . of the peoples of Europe from Spain and England to Turkey."[6]

He would have preferred to become an artist. His decision to enter the University of Vienna in the fall of 1913 to study law may have been informed by his mother's wish that he secure a decent livelihood as a civil servant. This, however, did not prevent him from also attending classes on painting and architecture as an external student at the *Kunsthochschule* [arts college] (Gotschim-Jauk 1990, 8). Becker's teachers at law school represented a remarkable spectrum of intellectual and political currents, which must have significantly shaped the student's worldview. In his first semester he studied Roman law with Moriz Wlassak (1854–1939); constitutional law with Edmund Bernatzik (1854–1919), the father of anthropologist Hugo Adolf Bernatzik; Austrian legal history with Sigmund Adler (1853–1920), the younger brother of Viktor Adler, the founder of the Austrian Social Democratic Party; and German legal history with Robert Bartsch (1874–1955), a turncoat who, with equal enthusiasm, served the Empire, the fascist Corporative State (*Ständestaat*), and the Third Reich. In his second semester he studied economic history with Carl Grünberg (1861–1940), a pioneer of Austromarxism and one of the founding fathers of the Institute for Social Research at the University of Frankfurt.[7]

Hans's studies were abruptly interrupted after one year by the outbreak of World War I. In the wake of the general war fever Hans Becker enlisted on 8 September 1914 as a one-year volunteer, was inducted into the Tyrolian mountain troops (*Gebirgsjäger*), and graduated from the Reserve Officer Candidate School in Innsbruck. Beginning in January 1915 he served as platoon and company commander on the Russian front and won his first honors for special bravery. After a severe illness he was deployed between October 1915 and September 1916 on the southwestern front as commander of the Third Machine Gun Detachment of the First Tyrolian Rifle Regiment (*Kaiserjäger*), distinguished himself once again, and was promoted to lieutenant of the reserve (Gotschim-Jauk 1990, 10–16).

Despite these accomplishments, the challenges of service in the infantry were apparently not enough for Becker. While on furlough, during which he took the state exam in legal history at the University of Vienna in October 1916, he requested—much to the regret of his superiors—to be admitted to the Pilot Officer School in Wiener Neustadt and was subsequently detailed to the Imperial and Royal Aeronautic Troops, where survival chances were significantly below those of other military units. After the end of his training he served as observation officer in the exploration and bombing of enemy positions, especially in Galicia (western Ukraine) and on the Piave (northern Italy). In February 1918 he was promoted to First Lieutenant and in September 1918, following the completion of his combat pilot training, began to serve as a fighter pilot. Finally, on 29 October 1918, when the Danube Monarchy was already in a state of dissolution, one day before the constitution of the Republic of German Austria, and six days before the signing of the armistice, the highly decorated Hans von Becker was admitted to service as a career officer (Gotschim-Jauk 1990, 16–25).

The prospect of a lifetime post, however, went as quickly as it had come. On 31 January 1919 Becker was relieved from active duty, returned to the reserve, and compensated with a payment of 3,397.25 crowns (approximately eight thousand U.S. dollars today), which, in the subsequent years, were reduced to literally nothing by rampant hyperinflation.[8] In August 1922 the exchange rate of the paper crown for the gold crown was 14.400 to one, and Becker's compensation (if still existent) would have valued just a quarter of a gold crown.

Fortunately, Becker had never abandoned his studies and, in spite of his duty on the front, had been enrolled at the University of Vienna's School of Law from the winter term 1917/8 to the summer term of 1919. On 14 October 1919 he received his absolutorium and was able to sign up for final exams on the 25 October.[9] It is unknown why he never took these exams. He may have finally admitted to himself that he wanted to be an artist rather than a lawyer. Perhaps his mother's death in 1918 had liberated him from a moral obligation. In typical Becker fashion he now followed a dual strategy and, in 1919, took courses at the Academy of Applied Arts and enrolled as a guest student at the Technical University in Vienna in order to take a course in surveying (Gotschim-Jauk 1990, 32).[10]

There was another change in Becker's life. On 3 April 1919 the Austrian parliament passed a law abolishing the privileges of nobility, including titles such as "von" or "Ritter" [Knight]. Thus, as of 10 April, Hans Sidonius Ritter von Becker became Hans Sidonius Becker. His pride in his extraction, however, turned out to be stronger than his respect for the law that deprived him of an essential part of his identity and heritage; while in Argentina and Paraguay in 1922-27, far from the arm of the Austrian law under which the use of nobiliary particles was punishable with a fee of 20,000 crowns or a prison term of up to six months, Becker regularly used the "von." This practice had to come to an end after Becker's return to Austria, but only until the establishment of the Corporative State in 1934, when the law was not rescinded but demoted from constitutional law, and never strictly enforced. In any case, the "von" returned to Becker's name even in official documents.[11] The legal situation did not change in principle in 1938 after the annexation of Austria by Germany, where, after 1918, titles of nobility had become part of a person's proper name, since the titles of nobility once lost in Austria were not restored by virtue of the enforced naturalization of the Austrians (Wikipedia 2015a). In real life, however, this was hardly ever observed, and Becker's doctoral certificate was made out in the name of "Johann Sydonius Ritter von Becker." Only a few documents of the period—including a Nazi diatribe of 1938 that sneered at the detained officials of the Patriotic Front, and the certificate of his release from the concentration camp in Mauthausen—refer to him as "Hans Becker."[12]

Becker's insistence on the use of his nobiliary particle was later interpreted by Viktor Matejka (1901–1993), his friend and communist fellow inmate at Mauthausen, as an indication of legitimist inclinations ("unreformed monarchist") (Gotschim-Jauk 1990, 104). Looking back on his experiences with "various kinds of republics and dictatorships" between 1919 and 1945, Becker was indeed reluctant "to take an unconditional oath on the republic," yet had found "truly evolved democracies . . . in Europe only in Switzerland, England, the Netherlands, and the Scandinavian states"—in other words (and with the exception of Switzerland), in constitutional monarchies. He therefore saw in the Habsburg monarchy, whose bad reputation he blamed on its negative representation in the writings of the "Prussian historians," primarily a model for a "future solution of the European question" in the sense of "a collaboration of peoples" (Becker MS, 15–16). Becker's conservative friend Franz

Pessler, who knew him both during the days of the Patriotic Front and in the concentration camp, asserts, in contrast to Matejka, that Becker "considered monarchist propaganda a mistake. The attempts of this kind made in 1937 had not been justified" (Pessler 1949, 9).

By 1920 at the latest, Becker's compensation for the termination of his military career had finally been spent. Hans Becker was twenty-five, and had not completed any professional or vocational training; neither did he have a job. Nevertheless, on 20 May he found employment in what was, for him, a completely new line of work. The *Deutschösterreichische Zentralstelle für den Devisenverkehr mit dem Ausland* (German-Austrian Central Office for the Exchange of Foreign Currency with Abroad) hired him for a monthly salary of 200 crowns, plus 400 crowns as compensation for inflation. Becker, however, soon made use of his one-month right of termination and left the organization, which attested him to have been "in every respect a capable, diligent, and ambitious clerk," and on 20 September moved to Gefex, a foreign trade organization, which he left (again at his own request) on 1 February 1921 after having worked there "very beneficially" in office and field service. His next "permanent" position, which lasted from 1 December 1921 to 30 September 1922, was with Treuga, a corporation for the fiduciary management of property, where he performed to the "complete satisfaction" of his employer, who deeply regretted Becker's departure at his own request.[13]

In addition to these jobs, Becker was actively pursuing his artistic and literary interests. On 23 October 1922 the commercial artist Otto Dely, who was primarily working for the light music business, certified that Becker had "splendidly solved the task set to him, both in terms of the drawing and the typography." Under the same date the Association of Austrian Banks and Bankers acknowledged that Becker had worked for their publishing division for several months as a writer, publicist, and translator.[14] His unsteady professional life was accompanied by a frequent change of address; between 1919 and 1922 Becker lived under at least three different addresses in various districts of Vienna.

Becker's closest friend during these years was Hermann Heinrich Schefter (1895–1979), who in 1916-17 had been his classmate at aviation school. The two were the only members of their class to have survived the war (Gotschim-Jauk 1990, 18–19). Schefter's father was the owner of a silk factory in Hohenstadt in Moravia (Zábřeh, Czech Republic, today) (Šebestová 2008, 16; Engelmann 2015) and in Vienna operated a sales company for textiles, in which his son served as manager before taking over the factory in 1923. In 1948 Schefter, who was also a creative writer, reminded Becker of a joint visit to the Salzburg Festival "about 25 years ago" (between the inception of the festival in 1920 and Becker's departure for Argentina in 1922). They had frequented the Café Bazar, a noted hangout for artists, and sat at a table with the famous actor Alexander Moissi (1879–1935), who had played the lead role in *Everyman*, the regular key event in Salzburg, and with the painter Anton Faistauer (1887–1930).[15] Already, in its early years, the Salzburg Festival had been a stomping ground for "the rich and the beautiful."[16] In view of Becker's precarious financial situation, it is likely that his friend helped him out, although, during the same period, Becker also undertook journeys to Spain, Portugal, France, Romania, and Bulgaria.[17]

In 1925 Schefter visited Hans Becker in Paraguay and remained in close contact with him until Becker's death.[18] Like Becker, Schefter later entered politics and became chairman of the German Democratic Party in Moravia (a task involving the protection of German minority rights in the postwar Czechoslovak Republic); like Becker, he was detained by the Nazis as an opponent of the regime after the German occupation of the Sudetenland in 1938 (Anonymous 2003).

One can only speculate about Becker's reasons for looking for work in the banking and commercial sectors. An explanation may be found in his acquaintance at that time with the sisters Helene and Anna Lieser, members of a wealthy Jewish family in Vienna. Their father, Justus Lieser, was part-owner of the First Austrian Burlap Spinning and Weaving Company. After their parents' divorce in 1905, their mother, Henriette Amalie ("Lilly") Lieser (1875–1943), whose own wealth surpassed that of her husband, cultivated contacts in Vienna's music scene, was acquainted with the composer Gustav Mahler, and after his death became a close friend of his widow, Alma Mahler, who prompted her to give financial support to the dodecaphonic composer Arnold Schönberg (Suchy 2008). In Breitenstein, south of Vienna, Lilly built herself a villa on a property next to Alma's house, where she kept her art collection, including everything from Michelangelo to Rembrandt and from Klimt to Kokoschka. The relationship between the two women cooled down in 1915, when Alma, who is believed to have detected the lesbian inclinations of her friend, married the architect Walter Gropius. Because of the friendship between Alma's daughter Anna and the two Lieser girls—both of whom quit the Jewish religious community in the early 1920s—the families (later including Hans Becker) remained in touch until the 1940s, when both Alma Mahler-Werfel and Anna Lieser were living in exile in Beverly Hills.[19]

In 1919 Helene Lieser (1898–1962) had attended courses at the law school at the same time as Becker, and in 1920 was the first woman at the University of Vienna to receive a doctorate in political science, with a dissertation on the monetary literature of the early paper-money period in Austria (Olechowski et al. 2014, 196, 200–203). In 1920 her sister Anna ("Annie," 1901–1972), a student of the dance artist Grete Wiesenthal (1885–1970), had become prima ballerina at the "Volksoper" [People's opera] in Vienna and began a career as a solo dancer. In 1920 the writer Joseph Roth (1894–1939), the chronicler of the doom of the Danube Monarchy, went to see two of her performances—in February, in the great hall of the Vienna Concert House, and in November, in Berlin—and reviewed them both for Berlin newspapers. In Vienna, there was whispering in the audience about the wealth of her father, who apparently had arranged for a bouquet of flowers the value of a dancer's annual salary to be brought to the stage at the end of the performance. Roth (1994, 81–82) described her frame as that of a "masculine heroine" and her dancing as "devoid of all eroticism." Nine months later in Berlin his assessment was considerably more favorable: "If, as it must be assumed, she has herself composed the choreography of her dances, then the ability and taste of this nineteen-year-old are remarkable. . . . Annie Lieser promises much."[20] The prominent playwright Arthur Schnitzler (1862–1931), who had also attended the performance in Vienna (without recording any comments), was a close friend of Helene, who, for example, paid him an unannounced visit on New Year's Day in 1921 (Schnitzler 1993, 26, 64, 124). It was this circle of Viennese artists, musicians, literati, and their admirers that Hanks Becker obviously frequented as well.

In 1927, shortly after her marriage to Hans Becker, Annie, in a letter to her friend, the actress Luise ("Luzie") Korngold (1900–1962)—wife of composer Erich Wolfgang Korngold (1897–1957)—reminded her, "You also know him and have witnessed part of our story."[21]

"ESCAPE TO SOUTH AMERICA"

In 1922 Becker decided to emigrate to Argentina,[22] which he later described as his "escape to South America."[23] In his case, it was not so much the economic depression that prompted him to take this step—after all, he never had a problem finding permanent employment—but his quest for change, the restless curiosity reflected both in his professional career and his divergent, simultaneous studies of the law, surveying, art, and architecture. One cannot well imagine the fighter pilot of World War I, a man given to "thirst for adventure and risk-taking" (Gotschim-Jauk 1990, 15), striving to become a clerk of an Austrian bank in times of peace. Thus, Becker's "escape" was from the his limited perspectives in a country shrunken from a dual monarchy to a small republic, where the inflation rate had reached its high point in August 1922.

The quest for new challenges, however, was accompanied by a strategy of risk reduction. Characteristic of this dual agenda is his self-designation as "artist and clerk" in the Vienna address book of 1921/2 (Lehmann 1921/2, 2: 65). In this respect he differed from those Austrians who emigrated to Argentina "in order to found a new existence" in a country recently profiting from an economic upswing, and whose numbers had reached a peak in 1923 with 2,267 migrants (Blaschitz 1992, 35, 38, 46).

From a recently published book by the German emigrant Hans Schmidt in 1922, one could learn how the hopes and aspirations of emigrants to Argentina or Paraguay were all too often shattered, causing many of them to return to Germany. The risk was especially high for those who wanted to settle as farmers, but had neither sufficient knowledge of the language and local conditions nor independent means. Schmidt's best experiences had been in administrative work for international corporations, and this is exactly what Becker had in mind, and what regional studies of the period were suggesting: "The Germans are notably wanted as clerks, scholars, and doctors . . . likewise as merchants and engineers" (Regel 1914, 170). Of special importance in this context was the expansion of the railroad network in the country's north and northwest, primarily undertaken by British and North American corporations (Regel 1914, 113–16).

Becker may have chosen Argentina because several of his cousins had already moved to South America (Gotschim-Jauk 1990, 35). He succeeded in receiving an appointment as permanent contributor in South America (with a status and pension claim comparable to that of a civil servant) by Edward Ludwig (1883–1967), the head of the Federal Press Service ("*Bundespressdienst*") within the Department of Foreign Affairs,[24] whom he was "occasionally to supply with reports of a journalistic nature."[25] Ludwig, who would come to play an important role in Becker's life, speaks of him in a letter to the liquidated Austro-Hungarian consulate in Bueno Aires as a "painter and journalist . . . well known to the Federal Foreign Ministry, Federal Press Service." He likewise notes that Becker was required to submit reports from Argentina to two major Viennese newspapers (*Neue Freie Presse, Neues Wiener Tagblatt*).[26] So far no reports by Becker either to the Federal Press Service or to the two newspapers have been found.

Becker's visit with Ludwig took place on 23 October 1922, the same day the laudatory employment reference letters by the Association of Banks and by Otto Dely had been issued, which referred to Becker's qualifications as a writer and graphic artist. Still, Ludwig would hardly have received and commissioned the unemployed young man without a personal recommendation. Even if Becker was now well connected within Viennese society, it seems likely that such a recommendation came from Ambassador Rosthorn, his mother's cousin. Becker must have been very sure of the results of his conversation with Ludwig; his passport, valid for "all states of Europe without Russia, South America, Dutch colonies," was issued on 28 August 1922, the visa for Argentina was granted on 10 October, and already on 28 October the traveler had passed the Austrian border at Passau on his way to Hamburg and, from there, to Argentina.[27]

In retrospect, Becker's immediate employment in the Argentinian railroad industry reveals that his previous activities, such as the study of surveying and perhaps also his changing jobs in the finance and business world, were part of a purposeful strategy. Thanks to these skills he was hired shortly after his arrival in Buenos Aires in November 1922 by Bradbury and Street, a British construction company, which sent him to northwestern Argentina as project manager of the railroad line from San Miguel de Tucumán to Salta and also put him in charge of the construction of the new line from Salta to Antofagasta in Chile. He must have acquired the necessary language skills quickly, perhaps partly during his previous travels in Spain. Once again, however, his employment lasted for less than a year. Malaria, contracted in the subtropical lowlands, was given as his reason for terminating the contract, but at that time he was already stationed in Salta—where, on 1 October 1923, he was hired by the provincial government of Salta as a surveyor—at the foot of the Andes, at an elevation of four thousand feet. He was also employed there as a supervisor of construction, and worked as an architect (Gotschim-Jauk 1990, 37–38).

In Salta Becker quickly connected with a circle of artists and intellectuals headed by Juan Carlos Dávalos (1887–1959)—one of the best-known Argentinian writers of the twentieth century—who met for a weekly "symposium." Dávalos came from an old Saltensian family, devoted himself extensively to the collection of folk traditions of his homeland, and probably encouraged Becker, who for this purpose learned to speak Quechua, to follow in his footsteps.[28] Becker also contributed fifteen illustrations, the cover design, and chapter initials to Dávalos's book *Los casos del zorro* (1925), a collection of animal tales of the region, adapted for the use of children.

As an artist Becker must have been fascinated with the spectacular mountain deserts in the Calchaquí valleys west of Salta. At the site of Incahuasi ("house of the Inca," in Quechua) in the region of Tacuil, where the Dávalos family owned vineyards, a bronze ornamental plaque dating from the Diaguita (or Calchaquí) culture of the last centuries prior to the Spanish conquest was discovered by Dávalos in 1923. The short report written by the poet and published in 1924 by the newspaper *La Nación* (Buenos Aires) was illustrated with a drawing by Becker (Becker 1946c, 164). This engagement with the archaeology and folklore of the province of Salta provides the earliest evidence for Becker's growing interest in the indigenous cultures of South America.

Drawings by Becker from Salta and the Calchaquí valleys were published in 1926 in the first volume of *Deutsche Blätter*, a German biweekly for culture, politics, and business published in Buenos Aires, to which Becker also contributed an obituary for the Austrian poet Rainer Maria Rilke and an essay on the history of the colors of the German flag (Becker 1926a, 1926b, 1926c).

After only nine months in the service of the government of Salta, Becker turned his back on Argentina and in July 1924 signed on as head of the construction and road department of the Compañía Internacional de Productos in Asunción in Paraguay.[29]

CHACO, 1924–1927

Becker's new job provided him with an opportunity to develop an additional extraprofessional field of interest: ethnography. Other than in the province of Salta, there were no spectacular archaeological remains to be found in the northern Chaco region, but instead a distinctive folk culture and numerous indigenous populations, who, despite centuries of contact with the neo-Paraguayan settlers, had largely preserved their respective languages and ways of life. Becker's interest in the local customs is apparent in an essay published in the German-language daily *Argentinisches Tageblatt* (Buenos Aires), describing as "a funny buffoonery" a bullfight witnessed on 21 December 1924 in Paraguarí, southeast of Ascunción, at the feast of Saint Thomas, the local patron saint (Becker 1925).

His special attention, however, was focused on the indigenous peoples. His obligations as construction manager of the Compañía included port expansions, the erection of factories for the extraction of tannin, and the construction of railroad lines crossing the territories these peoples inhabited.[30] He thus became an agent in the apparently unstoppable endangerment of their traditional ways of life, which nobody deplored as much as he did. Just like some of the other agents involved in this process, including missionaries and government officials, Becker felt the urge to document for posterity the cultures of the aboriginal inhabitants prior to their disappearance.

Except for his doctoral dissertation, which was published two decades later, a few articles written for Viennese newspapers after his return to Austria, and various, often conflicting résumés, few documents remain to shed light on Becker's research activities in Paraguay. In any case, in July 1924 Becker arrived in Puerto Pinasco on the Rio Paraguay, a "gathering place of various Indian tribes," and found a mentor for his ethnographic work in José de Alarcón y Cañedo, who was in charge of "Indian affairs . . . a man popular among the Indians." Alarcón's own ethnographic notes on the tribes of the northern Chaco were published (even if "only in a very abbreviated and biased manner") in the same year in Italy in a book prefaced by the Salesian missionary among the Lengua, Riccardo Pitti, who intended to express the Catholic aspirations for a speedy triumph over traditional manners as well as encouraging donations to support the missionary labors (Becker 1941b, 358; Alarcón y Cañedo and Pittini 1924; Chesterton 2013, 91–93). For his own work, Becker benefited from Alarcón's "advanced knowledge" (Becker 1941b, 358).[31]

A mission station operated among the Lengua since 1889 by the Anglican South American Mission Society was located to the south of Becker's primary field of activity (Becker 1941b, 362; see also Chesterton 2013, 82–87). Becker cites the book by the former head of this station, W. Barbrooke Grubb (1911), but apparently had no personal contacts with Grubb's successor, Andrew Pride.

In Puerto Pinasco Becker was able to meet members of various Mascoy-speaking tribes (Lengua [Enlhet, Enxet], Sanapaná, Angait), the Mataco-speaking Ashuslay (Sujin [Nivaclé, bzw. Chulupi]) and Macá (Toozli), the Guaykurú-speaking Toba [Qom], and the Kaiotuguí.[32] In the course of his surveys, which took him nearly two hundred miles to the west and into Bolivia, he was dealing principally with the northern Lengua and Kaiotuguí, from whom he collected a wealth of ethnographic data, even if his professional chores did not leave him enough time "to make this collection complete"; a planned visit to the Toozli was not accomplished (Becker 1941b, 358, 359). Whereas his contacts with the Lengua extended over the whole period, his investigations in Kaiotuguí territory were undertaken only in 1926 and 1927. The fragmentary data on the Sanapaná, Angaité, and Toozli were recorded either in Puerto Pinasco or from indigenous members of his work crew; a deserted camp of the Moro [Ayoreo] was investigated in 1926 (Becker 1942a, 78, 87, 88, 91).

By far the largest part of Becker's ethnographic data was obtained in the course of interviews and observations. It cannot be determined whether information was also received from other fieldworkers or knowledgeable people apart from Alarcón. It is, however, very likely he was in contact with Iwan (Juan) Beliaeff (1875–1957), a Russian officer who, after the October Revolution, had come to Paraguay in 1924 by way of Bulgaria and Argentina, undertaken in the following years thirteen exploratory and cartographic expeditions for the government, and established especially close relationships to the Maca. It was almost inevitable that the surveyor Becker and the cartographer Beliaeff, who shared an interest in the indigenous populations, would come to know and interact with one another. In his dissertation Becker cites only two of Beliaeff's publications of 1930 and 1931, because the majority of them were published only after 1941, but he also refers to Beliaeff in other contexts (e.g., Becker 1942a, 91).

For a reconstruction of Becker's fieldwork we have to depend upon his own, rather sketchy indications. His gift for languages enabled him to quickly apprehend Guarani, used in Paraguay as a lingua franca and also mastered by many members of the various indigenous communities. His knowledge of the Lengua language was sufficient for him to follow the recitation of their stories (Becker 1941b, 359). Field notes have not been preserved, but must have existed, in view of the mass of detailed information included in his dissertation. In 1944 the Austrian anthropologist Martin Gusinde, S.V.D. (1886–1969) questioned Becker as to whether his Lengua texts had ever been published; Becker's reply has not been preserved, but in his response Gusinde deplores the fact that "you had such bad luck with your Lengua texts."[33] Informants are only occasionally named in Becker's published records, but the impression is that at least on certain subjects Becker interviewed more than one person. He was quick to recognize a major obstacle for fieldwork: "Curious questioning is unknown [among them], and they are also reluctant to answer such questions. Systematic interrogation rarely results in correct data, because the acquired restraint is accompanied by suspiciousness and aversion against concentration and deliberately misleading information is given. Only once a relationship of trust has been established, the Lenguas are eagerly offering information, often even endeavoring to satisfy all requests to their best abilities" (Becker 1941b, 404).

Becker's musical training enabled him to record at least two examples of Lengua and Kaiotuguí music in musical notation (Becker 1941b, 414; 1942a, 87). Some of his field photographs are known from his dissertation and from newspaper articles (Becker 1929, 1932c, 1934a). Others had been lost prior to 1941 (Becker 1941b: 359; see also below); since then, the rest have also disappeared.

As an artist Becker also made drawings of ethnographic subject matter. His dissertation features line drawings of Lengua face paintings, the typical shapes of Lengua, Kaiotuguí, and Toozli pots, copies of drawings on decorated gourds, and a detailed sketch of the mode of stringing the bow (Becker 1941b, 370, 374, 412; 1942a, 89). Since there is no evidence he ever collected artifacts or studied museum collections, these drawings must have been made in the field. Ethnographic drawings also appear in one of his newspaper accounts (Becker 1929) and have been preserved by his family.[34] Others were exhibited in Vienna in 1928, and as late as 1943 he was offering for sale to a German collector "landscapes and types from South America (Brazil, Paraguay, the Andean region, Argentina)," and sold some of them to the *Museum für Völkerkunde* (Museum of Ethnology) in Vienna (Gotschim-Jauk 1990, 150). The earliest published drawing of this kind—the portrait of a young Lengua man—graces the cover of Hermann Schefter's book *Yankees und Indianer*, dedicated to "My friend H. S. v. Becker (Asunción)" (Schefter 1927).

As many ethnographers before and after him, Becker invokes the importance of his investigations by referring to the impending disappearance of the indigenous groups or the loss of their "traditional" culture, which, of course, even in the 1920s was exhibiting distinct traces of the historical changes since the time of the first encounter with western civilization (Becker 1941b, 359). In fact, Becker makes no attempt to offer a sanitized account blanking out all visible evidence of culture change, in the style of "memory ethnography," and indeed the conditions have further changed substantially during the past ninety years, especially as a result of the increasing amalgamation of indigenous communities in Paraguay. As prognosticated by Becker, the Chaco

War between Paraguay and Bolivia, which erupted after the end of his sojourn, dramatically affected the cultural landscape of the region.

Becker's Kaiotuguí data are of special interest, because this group was never described either before or after him and has since been absorbed by the neighboring populations. He characterizes these neighbors and enemies of the Lengua as hunters and gatherers, who, like the Zamuco-speaking Chamacoco and Ayoreo, "practice just about no horticulture, and fishing only to a limited extent. Pottery is primitive, weaving unknown." Following Loukotka (1968, 57), who exclusively refers to Becker, the linguistic literature assumes the Kaiotuguí to have been Lengua speakers. Other than in the Lengua chapter, Becker does not provide terms in the section on the Kaiotuguí, with the exception of their self-designation "Inzlit." The Lengua's reference to them as "'hostile' but not explicitly foreign" and their designation with the derogatory term "Kispang" may indicate that they were secondary speakers of a Mascoy language, although not necessarily of Lengua. In an undated note Becker reported that, according to the Lengua, the Kaiotuguí "did not speak their language, but a related one" (Becker 1941b, 365; 1942a, 70).[35]

When he was not working on the railroad line or was stationed in Puerto Pinasco, Becker enjoyed the "civilized" sociability of Asunción. The center of his network of social contacts was the city's botanical garden, at the terminal station of Becker's railroad. Attached to the "Jardín Botánico" (known as *yboty rendá*, "flower shop," in Guarani) were a zoo, an agricultural experiment station, and a museum, which included anthropological collections. The garden had been established in 1914 by the Hamburg botanist Karl Fiebrig (1869–1951) on the grounds of the summer residence of the former dictator Francisco Solano López (1826–1870). Because of ill health, Fiebrig had never been able to finish his studies in Germany, had gone to Paraguay in 1904 to collect plants for European museums, and was appointed professor of botany at the University of Asunción in 1910 (Obermeier 2012). Becker kept in touch with "Don Carlos" Fiebrig up to the time of his own death.

At the botanical garden Becker encountered the Austrian agronomist Alexander (Alejandro) Langer (1899–?), who in 1921 had emigrated to Brazil and in 1923 had been hired by Fiebrig as head of the cotton experiment station (Langer 1935). It is unlikely that Becker and Langer had known one another in Vienna, because Langer had lived in Czechoslovakia from 1919 to 1921 (Agstner 2015, 406). In his dissertation Becker (1941b, 359) refers to "Alejandro Langer" as his "friend, who at that time was staying at the Mennonite colony Casado" and helped Becker with Lengua photographs after Becker's own had been lost. The Mennonites, primarily from Canada, arrived in Puerto Casado (today La Victoria) in 1926, and in 1927 began to settle in several villages in the colony Menno in the territory of the northwestern Lengua, close to Becker's railroad tracks (Chesterton 2013, 97–101). Between 1928 and 1931, near the hamlet Hoffnungsfeld, the Corporación Paraguaya—a Mennonite support group—operated an ultimately failed agricultural station headed during the first two years by Langer (Ratzlaff 2011: sub https://menonitica/lexikon/?V:Versuchsstation_Hoffnungsfeld).

Fiebrig's circle likewise included the agriculturist Friedrich Christian Mayntzhusen (1873–1949), also from Hamburg, who in 1907 had founded the primarily German colony Capitán Meza and who is today remembered largely for his meritorious research on the language and culture of the Guayakí. In 1941–42 Becker was interested in publishing a voluminous manuscript by Mayntzhausen that was formerly in Fiebrig's possession, and which unfortunately had been lost in the meantime.[36]

Becker may also have met the Swiss botanist Emil Hassler (1861–1937), who was living in San Bernardino close to Asunción and was closely connected with Fiebrig and his Paraguayan vice director. In the late nineteenth century Hassler had assembled the world's largest collection of ethnographic material from Paraguay, which has since found its way into numerous museums in Europe and North America (Feest 2014, 94–95).

According to Becker's own account, he painted a portrait of the president of Paraguay, which was hung in the latter's residence (Gotschim-Jauk 1990, 42). Becker's sitter was José Eligio Ayala (1879–1930), under whose liberal presidency (1923/4 and 1924–28) the country experienced a rare period of stability and an economic boom. Ayala had studied for some time in Heidelberg, spoke German, and was therefore favorably disposed toward German-Paraguayans such as Fiebrig. His death a few years later, in a shoot-out in the house of his mistress, would have been an apt example of the impetuousness of feelings and the little respect in Paraguay for the life of other and of one's own—as later described by Becker in one of his newspaper accounts (1932b).

Becker definitely had no contact with the German anthropologist Herbert Baldus (1899–1970), whom he praised in his dissertation as "an accurate and observant researcher" and who was staying in Brazil and Paraguay at the same time as Becker, pursuing his fieldwork in the northern Chaco from Sastre, "two steamboat stops north [of Puerto Pinasco]" (1941b, 359). Baldus had first come to the Chaco in 1923, before Becker arrived at Puerto Pinasco, as a member of an Italian film expedition, and he only began his systematic fieldwork in 1928, when Becker was already back in Vienna. Like Becker, Baldus had been an Air Force officer in World War I and had emigrated to South America, as an adventurer, in 1921; like Becker, he undertook his ethnographic research in the Chaco without the benefit of academic training, but with great aptitude. Baldus returned to Europe one year after Becker to study anthropology, but was obviously given more support by his Austrian teacher Richard Thurnwald (1869–1954) than Becker later received from his German teachers Wilhelm Koppers and Wilhelm Schmidt. Thanks to Thurnwald, Baldus was able to publish the results of his fieldwork in 1931 under the title *Indianerstudien im nordöstlichen Chaco* (Indian Studies in the northeastern Chaco), which was extensively reviewed by Becker in *Anthropos* (Baldus 1931a; Becker 1932a). The subtitle of Becker's dissertation, probably written soon after, was "*Indianerstudien im Chaco Boreal*" (Indian Studies in the Chaco Boreal), a clear reference to Baldus.[37]

Becker and Baldus shared their opposition to national socialism. Baldus, however, emigrated to Brazil in 1934, where he became one of the founding fathers of modern Brazilian anthropology (Becher 1970, 1972; Fischer 1990a, 176). Unlike Becker, Baldus was also successful as a creative writer. His novel *Madame Lynch*, about the mistress of the dictator Solano López and the horror vision of a "total war" against both the neighbors Bolivia and Brazil and the people of Paraguay, was followed (under his wife's name) by *Im Herzen Südamerikas* (In the Heart of South America), which fictionalized some of the experiences of the film expedition of 1923 (Baldus 1931; Baldus-Hasselpflug 1933).

RETURN TO AUSTRIA, 1927–31

By the end of 1926 Becker had already been working for two and a half years for the Compañía Internacional de Productos, much longer than in any other previous job. It seems he was feeling at ease and was ready to stay on, but then something unexpected happened. At the end of September 1926 Annie Lieser wrote to her good friend Luzie Korngold: "On 26 November I am going to South America and will be staying for six months. What will happen to me afterwards, I don't know, I believe much will have changed for me!"[38] Indeed, on 24 January 1927, before the magistrate of Buenos Aires, she entered into marriage with "Johann von Becker."[39] No effort was made to involve clerical institutions on this occasion.

This development had obviously come as a surprise for Becker, and its consequences had hardly been reasoned out. As she had planned, Annie returned to Austria after six months—probably just in time to attend the funeral of her father, who had died on 18 June 1927. In expectation of her inheritance she may not have had a good reason for a swift return to South America, and continued to perform as a dancer.[40] Hans Becker requested from his employer a leave of several months for a trip to Europe, which was granted on August 20, together with an expression of confidence in his return at the earliest possibility.[41]

Becker took a ship to Europe and at the beginning of October 1927 arrived in Hamburg, where Annie was waiting for him and where they went to see the world premiere of Erich Korngold's opera *Das Wunder der Heliane* on 7 October.[42]

On their way to Vienna they made a stop in Munich, where Becker twice had the opportunity to see Adolf Hitler at close range, once at a public gathering and once at the private dinner given by an industrialist. The first impression was "to invite laughter.... In front of me there was a caricature of Charlie Chaplin." However, it soon became apparent that this man—"who in Austria could only have become a circus clown," who appeared to consist "merely of his skin filled with a supersaturated lotion of hubris and craving for recognition," and whose success as a speaker derived from his ability to inflate his audience consisting of "those roughly treated by fate, failed, or limping...

like shriveled rubber animals with self-confidence and pride"—was "an especially dangerous demi-fool" (Becker MS: 2–3).

Back in Vienna, Becker found that Austria had not changed for the better: "For one used to the personal freedom in America it was already notable how tightly knit were the nets of prohibitions, the inordinate interference with any personal initiative in the field of economy. . . . The strange torpidity of political life contrasted sharply with the still fluid changes of the post-war period." In Becker's view this was particularly true for the Social Democratic Party, "in which had developed a party and trade union bureaucracy in no way second to that of the imperial-royal period." The tone of the political debate in the press was little more than a "torrent of abuse" and "did not eschew the use of personal invectives." Even the *Arbeiter-Zeitung*, the Social Democratic Party daily, "once one of the best-edited papers, which not only had tremendously contributed to the elevation of the intellectual level of the Austrian workers, but had also become an inevitable supplementation and amplification of knowledge for the intelligentsia," had now "under the leadership of Dr. Bauer and Austerlitz adopted that piqued-offensive tone, which at the time also evoked my astonishment" (Becker MS, 4–5).[43]

The newlyweds moved into an apartment in the house of the branch office of the hemp-spinning company Lieser and Duschnitz, near the city center.[44] On 17 November Becker enrolled as an external student at the Technical University of Vienna, either to upskill himself (Gotschim-Jauk 1990, 49–50) or to sound out the job market, and on 15 January 1928 applied for employment at the A. Spritzer construction company, where he was appointed on 1 March 1928 as "technical foreman with an assignment as engineer."[45] His driver's license, acquired in February apparently for this purpose, allowed him convenient access to the construction sites he maintained, including the hydroelectric power plant at Fischamend, on the Danube.[46] When thirteen months later he left the Spritzer company at his own request, the employment reference letter praised him as an "extraordinarily reliable, technically and commercially well-versed employee."[47]

In the meantime Becker had also started to position himself in Vienna in other fields of interest. Already on 25 November 1927, hardly six weeks after his return, he gave a lecture on "The Republic of Paraguay," illustrated with photographs and drawings, at the prestigious *Österreichische Politische Gesellschaft* (Austrian Political Society).[48] The short-term nature of the invitation by a society usually featuring ministers, deputies, ambassadors, professors, and distinguished foreign visitors as speakers, points to his recommendation on the part of somebody of influence, most likely Eduard Ludwig, who must have been informed about the return of his protégé, who—at least formally—was still employed by the Foreign Ministry.

In January 1928 the *Neues Wiener Tagblatt* published the first of several articles by Becker on his experiences in South America (1928a, 1929, 1930a, 1930b). Two of his South American paintings were exhibited in 1928 at the *Künstlerhaus*, an exhibition hall operated by a conservative association of artists, while in December of the same year he participated as a guest in the fifty-seventh exhibition of the more liberal Hagenbund, with which he remained closely associated over the subsequent years (Gotschim-Jauk 1990, 59; Husslein-Arco 2014, 215, 223, 430). "H. S. Becker as well one likes to see again," a critic in the conservative *Reichspost* remarked. "His South American watercolors, technically brilliant, are atmospheric pictures of exquisite delicacy of color."[49] In 1929 he joined the *Zentralverband der Bildenden Künstler Österreichs* (Austrian Central Union of Fine Artists).[50]

Becker claims to have given lectures at the same time about the opportunities for exporting Austrian companies to South America.[51] This may have brought him to the attention of Tomáš Baťa (1877–1932), an enthusiastic amateur pilot and owner of the internationally famous shoe factory in the Moravian town of Zlín.[52] In March (or May) 1929 Baťa hired Becker to head his division for exports to South America and to help with the expansion and reorganization of the network of branch offices and of advertising. In addition, Becker became involved in the interior design of the branch offices (Gotschim-Jauk 1990, 50–52). He quickly applied for and received a visa for Argentina, but never took the trip, partly because he left Baťa—again at his own request—in November 1929.[53] Immediately after leaving Baťa, Becker gave a lecture at the *Politische Gesellschaft* [Political Society] about "The Bata System," focusing on the innovative marketing organization and rationalization strategies of the company.⁵⁴ Two months later a slightly modified version of this lecture met with great interest at the Trade Association of Business Graduates.⁵⁵

That Becker was introduced at the meeting of the Business Graduates as "Ing. [Engineer] Hans S. Becker" illustrates the perception that a professional or academic title was necessary to gain social respectability in Austria. Becker had still not completed any higher education; although by now he could look back at several years of highly qualified practical work in the construction business, the only exam he had ever taken in this field was the one qualifying him as surveyor in the province of Salta. From now on, however, the "Ing." increasingly appears as Becker's title in newspaper accounts and, after 1934, also in official documents.⁵⁶

In the winter term of 1929–30 Becker expanded his commercial knowledge by attending a course on advertising law taught at the *Hochschule für Welthandel* [School of Global Trade]— the precursor of the present Vienna University of Business and Economics—by his former law professor Robert Bartsch, followed in 1930 by a course given by Erwin Paneth (1895–1998) on "Theory and Technique of Advertising." Both were part of a training program in advertising sponsored by the *Gewerbeförderungsdienst*, an organization of the Department of Trade and Transportation, and by the Austrian Society for the Science of Management.⁵⁷

Becker's departure from Baťa and his participation in the advertising course coincided with significant changes in his private circumstances. Justus Lieser's will had been probated and his daughter Helen was now able to buy a house, the *Villa Gottessegen* (Villa God's Blessing) in the suburban district of Ober-Döbling. In 1929 Hans and Annie Becker also moved into this house, together with the retired Yugoslavian colonel Čot-Srnič and Marianne Thalmann (1888–1975), the second woman ever to be habilitated in the field of German literature at the University of Vienna. Thalmann moved to the United States in 1933 to take a position at Wellesley College (Keintzel and Korotin 2002, 740–41), but retained her apartment in Lieser's house until 1938. It was probably their exceptional positions at the university which brought Thalmann and Lieser together.

In view of the financial security provided by Annie's share of her father's estate, Hans Becker could now afford to give up wage labor and start his own business. These changes are reflected, with some delay, in his entries in the Vienna city directory. Listed as a "clerk" until 1931, the entry was changed to "artist" in 1932 and would remain so until 1939, including the period of his work for the Patriotic Front (Lehmann 1930, 1: 67; 1932, 1: 77; 1939, 1: 57). According to his own later account, he was running an office for market analysis and advertising, giving advice on matters of production and marketing (Gotschim-Jauk 1990, 64). If so, his office never appears to have been officially registered.

In 1929 Becker joined the Masonic lodge *Zukunft* (Future). His sponsor was the lodge's Worshipful Master, the social democratic councilman Viktor Hammerschlag (1870–1943), who later perished in the concentration camp Theresienstadt (Kodek 2009, 34–35; Patka 2010, 68, 114, 116), but the person who brought him into the lodge was actually Hermann Schefter, who had joined the Zukunft in 1926 and had been elevated to the second degree in 1927 (Kodek 2009, 301). Becker's adhesion to the Masons may first of all be regarded as his acknowledgment of a global humanity, tolerance, and fraternity at a time when the world appeared to be increasingly dominated by intolerance, inhumanity, and partisan politics.[58] His own nonpartisan impartiality and contacts with people of diverse political views is illustrated by his pencil portrait—made in the same year, 1929—of the Austrian Chancellor Johann Schober (1874–1932), a German-national liberal politician (Gotschim-Jauk 1990, 60).

Becker joined the Hagenbund in 1931 and remained a member until its liquidation by the national socialists in 1938, but contributed to their exhibitions only until 1933 (Husslein-Arco 2014, 226, 229, 232, 233, 293, 408, 430), probably because his work for the Patriotic Front (PF) was increasingly demanding his attention.[59] He certainly continued to maintain his contacts with other members, particularly since the cultural policies of the PF were focused on the promotion of a distinctive Austrian modernity at a time when many artists drifted into the illegal Nazi camp (Klamper 2014, 351, 352).

It was during this period, 1930–31, that Becker was visited in Vienna by his friend Alexander Langer. While Langer's motivations for temporarily returning to Austria are unknown, the results changed the course of his life. He had brought with him a large ethnographic collection, mostly of Lengua objects, but also featuring material from other indigenous groups of Paraguay, which he offered for sale to the Museum of Ethnology. The museum was financially in dire straits, but its director, Fritz Röck (1879–1953)—supported by the expert opinion of his predecessor as head of the Anthropological-Ethnographic Department of the Natural History Museum, Viktor Christian (1885–1963)—succeeded in getting the purchase funded by the Department of Education. Moreover, Langer offered to assemble additional collections for Vienna and other museums in German-speaking countries after his return to Paraguay.[60] It is doubtful whether Becker, who had not himself engaged in collecting, was instrumental in establishing contact between Langer and Röck, since at that time his interests were not focused on anthropology. More likely, his enthusiasm for this subject was rekindled by Langer's visit.

During his sojourn in Vienna Langer stayed with Viktor Strasser (1899–?) in the house owned by Strasser's father, the Jewish real estate mogul and art collector Alfred Strasser-Sánczí (1854–1937). Strasser-Sánczí was part of the same group of Jewish super-rich art lovers in Vienna as the Liesers (Sandgruber 2013), whereas Langer was of modest means and hardly well-connected in Vienna. It may well be that Hans and Anna Becker had arranged for Langer to stay with Strasser. In any case, Langer fell in love with and married Viktor's sister Clarisse and in 1931 returned with her to Paraguay.[61] Instead of having to devote himself to the painstaking task of collecting ethnographic material, he was now able to use his wife's money to buy a country estate near Villarica (Agstner 2015, 406).

Toward the end of his stay in Vienna and aided by his newly acquired connections, Langer paid a visit to the secretary of agriculture, Andreas Thaler (1883–1939), who for some time already had been pondering the idea of establishing an Austrian colony in South America, to rescue the impoverished Tyrolian peasants from their plight. Langer was able to convince Thaler of Paraguay as potential goal for emigration—at least he believed he had done so—and Becker reported about Thaler's plan to move to Paraguay, without mentioning Langer, in a Viennese newspaper (Anonymous 1931; Becker 1931). Thaler resigned as secretary in

1933 in order to implement the project—not in Paraguay, but instead in the colony Dreizehnlinden (Treze Tilias, Santa Catarina) in southern Brazil, selected by Walther von Schuschnigg (1899–1966), a cousin of the later Chancellor Kurt Schuschnigg (Prutsch 2012).

As a reward for his effort (and perhaps with a little help from a friend) Langer was appointed Austrian honorary vice consul in Villarica on 16 October 1931 and held this position until December 1936, when he returned to Asunción for business reasons (Agstner 2015, 222, 406) and subsequently moved to Argentina because of the anti-German sentiments in Paraguay after the Chaco War.

STUDENT OF ANTHROPOLOGY AND JOURNALIST, 1931–33

When Becker returned to Vienna in 1927, there was neither a museum of ethnology in the city, nor a department of cultural anthropology at the university.[62] A few months later, however, in May 1928, the Museum für Völkerkunde was opened in the former and now deserted imperial palace, combining the ethnographic collections of the Museum of Natural History and the material collected by Archduke Franz Ferdinand on his world tour of 1892–93, which for Becker was associated with the memory of his father (Feest 1978; 1980, 13–34; 1995, 114–15, 122–26). One year after the appointment of Father Wilhelm Koppers, S.V.D. (1886–1961) as professor of ethnology, a department of ethnology ("Institut für Völkerkunde") was established in the same section of the imperial castle in 1929 and soon became the center of the "Vienna School" of "culture-historical" ethnology dominated by Koppers's mentor Father Wilhelm Schmidt, S.V.D. (1868–1954) (Haekel 1956). Liberated from the need to be breadwinner, Becker decided soon after Langer's return to Paraguay to underpin his practical experiences as an ethnographer with academic training.

As someone who had done fieldwork, Becker was warmly received at the department, not least because neither Schmidt nor Koppers had worked in the field; Becker was later even listed among the "fieldworkers originating from the department" (Haekel 195, 7), although no department had existed at the time of Becker's work in Paraguay. Starting in the winter term 1930/1, Becker attended courses offered by Koppers, Schmidt, Robert Heine-Geldern (1885–1968), and Fritz Röck, and in his first semester also took a course on Heredity by the physical anthropologist Josef Weninger (1886–1959). In Röck's course, Quechua Texts, he must have stood out as the only actual Quechua speaker in the class; Schmidt's course on Culture Circles of South America, which extended over several semesters, may not have convinced him and left no trace in his own subsequent writings. Already in the third semester a ten-credit hour course offered by Koppers on "Work at the department" became his primary obligation and was devoted to advice on his PhD dissertation.[63] Although after 1934 Becker's full-time work for the Patriotic Front hardly made it possible for him to attend classes, he gained his absolutorium in 1936, but (as was the case in law school) did not take the final exams.[64]

In an undated manuscript of a lecture (probably written in 1934) he expresses his gratitude to "my teachers, Prof. Schmid [sic] and Prof. Koppers, whose fundamental systematic investigations only have made it possible for me to produce scientifically useful results from my rather exact local knowledge."[65] Whereas Koppers's role was primarily as Becker's thesis advisor, Schmidt's relationship with Becker may have extended beyond the field of academic anthropology. In an interview in 1991, the museum's former Africanist Annemarie Schweeger-Hefel (1916–1991) recalled that her father Ernst Hefel (1888–1974)—then a high official in the Department of Education—Wilhelm Schmidt, and Hans Becker had been members of a committee for the founding of a Catholic university in Salzburg (Linimayr 1994, 160). As a matter of fact, only Hefel and Schmidt (one of whose main interests was the establishment of an anthropology department in Salzburg) were part of this committee, while Koppers and Hefel were sounding out the potential interest of the Corporative State in the project (Rinnerthaler 1988, 48, 52). Becker may have belonged to the Vienna Circle of Friends of the University of Salzburg or been involved in the discussion as a prominent official of the Patriotic Front, but his relationship with Schmidt could hardly have been a close one.[66] After World War II Schmidt cites Becker's published memoir *Österreichs Freiheitskampf* in his own account of Austrian resistance against Hitler (W. Schmidt 1949, 227–56; Becker 1946a), but erroneously places him in the "left wing" of a monarchist resistance group formed after the Nazis' invasion of Austria—at a time when Becker was already detained in a concentration camp (W. Schmidt 1949, 223).

In the 1930s the number of anthropology students (majors and minors) in Vienna was about one hundred (Haekel 1956, 9); everybody knew everyone else. Among those whom Becker must have known were Hugo A. Bernatzik (1897–1953) and his wife Emmy (1904–1977).[67] Becker attended classes with him during his first year and with her during the following two years.[68] Hugo Bernatzik and Becker were of nearly the same age and had both widely traveled. Bernatzik's "pariah" status as a "liberal Protestant" in the thoroughly conservative and Catholic department (Byer 1999, 105) should not have been a problem for Becker, who was a liberal himself. Still among the students was also Josef Haekel (1907–1973), the later chairman of the department, who, as an Americanist who had never been outside Austria, must have been especially interested in Becker's experiences. After the arrest in 1934 of Koppers's assistant, Fritz Flor (1905–1939), for participating in secret negotiations with the Nazi party NSDAP (outlawed in Austria), Haekel was appointed to Flor's position. Christoph Fürer-Haimerdorf (1909–1995), Robert Heine-Geldern's assistant, was himself a member of the illegal NSDAP (Linimayr 1994, 43–45). The patriotic Austrian Becker must have been worried by the growing number of Nazi sympathizers, even among intellectuals.

In November 1931 Becker could not have missed the lecture given at the department by the Swedish anthropologist and Chaco specialist Erland Nordenskiöld (1877–1932). On this occasion, as well in two other lectures delivered in Vienna, Nordenskiöld talked about his recent fieldwork among the Kuna in Panama.[69] For Becker's own work, Nordenskiöld's earlier publications had provided a major inspiration, and he must have come to hear him.[70]

At present, it is impossible to verify whether Becker was a member of the venerable *Anthropologische Gesellschaft in Wien* [Anthropological Society in Vienna], founded in 1870 (Feest 1995, 119–22).[71] He attended at least some of its monthly meetings and in February 1932 participated in the discussion following a lecture by the Jewish historian of technology Hugo Theodor Horwitz (1882–ca. 1942) on the "Evolution of Rotary Motion," whose significance for cultural history

Becker, the engineer, may have grasped more quickly than the anthropologists in the audience.[72]

Strangely enough, Becker never gave a lecture at the Anthropological Society. Instead, he addressed the Geographical Society (Feest 1995, 115–16)—where his grandfather was still remembered—in November 1934, on the subject of "The Chaco Boreal and its Ethnographic Conditions" (Arthaber 1935, 314).

In September 1933 a woman, who, despite the absence of documentary evidence, must have crossed Becker's path, came to see Fritz Röck at the Museum of Ethnology. Wanda Hanke (1893–1958), born in Moravia, was two years older than Becker and had acquired a portfolio of doctorates in the fields of psychology (University of Munich, 1918), medicine (University of Würzburg, 1920), and law (University of Marburg, 1926). Thus she was the first woman in German-speaking countries to hold three doctorates and, as such, would have qualified for the circle of academic power women associated with Becker. Her medical practice had been interrupted by several hospitalizations in psychiatric clinics before her decision to enter the field of anthropology—this time without a doctorate or even a few semesters of academic training (Liener 2010).

According to a work plan submitted in 1933 to Fritz Röck and to the Austrian embassy in Rio de Janeiro, Hanke intended to undertake her investigations in the Xingú region. Either because of the lukewarm response from Rio or because of advice received in Vienna, she went instead to Buenos Aires in 1934, did fieldwork among the Caingua in the province of Misiones, and in 1935 proceeded to Paraguay to make an expedition to the Guayakí, which lasted until 1936, before being repatriated by the Austrian general consulate in Buenos Aires in a "sick and destitute" condition (Liener 2010, 18–22, 26–27). In the meantime she had called upon the Austrian consul in Villarica, Alexander Langer, and appealed to him for help. On 23 September 1936 Langer wrote to Röck that he had given aid to Hanke despite the fact (also reported by others) that she had not made herself popular in many places, had often acted awkwardly, and he had not found her particularly taking (Liener 2010, 47). Becker must have learned about Hanke, at the latest, after her visit with Langer. It would seem natural, however, for Hanke to have been sent to the Chaco-seasoned Becker for advice prior to her departure from Vienna, and perhaps Becker had even been responsible for her change of plans.

Hanke returned with a substantial ethnographic collection for the museum, from the Paraguayan Chaco (including fifty-eight Lengua objects) and from Bolivia. On 6 September 1937 she delivered a lecture, "On My Research Trip Through Paraguay and the Gran Chaco," at the Anthropological Society. Among others, Josef Haekel, Josef Weninger, and Viktor Christian participated in the discussion, with Becker most likely conspicuous by his absence.[73] Perhaps he was prevented from attending by urgent official business, but he may have merely been trying to avoid the embarrassment caused by many of her statements, which Herbert Baldus (1954, 292–94) was later to castigate ("lack of anthropological training," gross "ethnocentrism," "scholarly incompetence," "lack of scientific value").

Shortly after her return to Vienna Hanke was beginning to plan her next venture and in 1938 once again departed for South America. It turned out to be an unsteady existence, until her death in 1958: moving back and forth between Argentina, Paraguay, Bolivia, and Brazil, always out of money and looking for gainful employment. She returned to Austria only for a few months in 1956, after Hans Becker's second wife and widow, Etta Becker-Donner—whom she had met two years before at the International Congress of Americanists in São Paulo—bought from her additional collections for the museum in Vienna and was attempting to raise money to permit Hanke to continue her research (Liener 2010, 68–69).

Besides his activities as a business consultant, painter, and student of cultural anthropology, Becker found time to work as a journalist. He was an irregular contributor to several Viennese newspapers, especially the *Neues Wiener Tagblatt* and the *Neuigkeits-Welt-Blatt*, where he wrote about his South American experiences (Becker 1932b, 1934). Of a topical nature were his knowledgeable commentaries on the military conflict between Bolivia and Paraguay that culminated in the Chaco War (1932–34), in which a quarter of the 400,000 soldiers fighting on either side lost their lives. Like Herbert Baldus, Becker saw Bolivia as the aggressor against the much weaker Paraguay (Baldus 1931a, 5–8;

Becker 1928b, 1933b, 1934a). Paraguay's somewhat unexpected victory resulted in reprisals against its German-speaking citizens, because the Bolivian army for two years had been under the command of the Prussian general Hans Kundt (1869–1939). In the midst of this xenophobic turmoil Karl Fiebrig lost his job as director of the botanical garden and had to escape head over heels to Germany, where he found employment at the Ibero-American Institute in Berlin. Among the documents he had to leave behind was a significant collection of Becker's drawings.[74]

Becker's odd jobs for newspapers turned into full-time employment for the new Sunday paper *Jedermann*, founded in October 1933 and published by Lisl Goldschmidt (1894–1975). Goldschmidt, probably the only female newspaper publisher in Vienna, was the daughter of the Jewish publicist Benno Karpeles (1868–1938), who prior to 1918 had been one of the leading Austrian social democrats. He left the party after the death of Viktor Adler and on Easter 1932 converted to Catholicism, persuaded by the stigmata of the Bavarian mystic Therese von Konnersreuth (1898–1962). In 1917 he had published under the pseudonym "Dr. Franz Wahrhaft" ("Truthful") the book *Die neue Partei* (The New Party), which set forth the vision of a democratic postwar Austria and the solution of the nationalities question on the basis of equal rights for the peoples of Austria. In 1918 Karpeles founded the pacifist weekly *Der Friede* (The Peace) and, in 1919, the daily *Der neue Tag* (The New Day), whose list of contributors reads like a *Who's Who* of contemporary German-language (and even European) literature, and included such luminaries as Peter Altenberg, Erwin Kisch, Thomas Mann, Robert Musil, Joseph Roth, and Franz Werfel (Wikipedia 2014). At least one of the contributors, Leo Perutz (1882–1957), was one of Hans Becker's personal friends.[75] After the two journals closed down, Karpeles worked in the logistics business (his father had been the founder of the logistics company Schenker), before retiring to the home of his daughter Lisl Goldschmidt in Vienna. It was only a retirement of sorts.

Karpeles clearly was the mastermind of *Jedermann* and served as its regular columnist under his old pen name, "Dr. Franz Wahrhaft." In fact, the whole journal was little more than a reincarnation of the two formerly failed periodicals. Its editorial line was democratic, pacifist, left-liberal, and patriotically Austrian, which in the context of the 1930s also meant radically anti-Nazi. In contrast, the contributors represented a range of viewpoints, extending far into the bourgeois camp; some of them would soon even become national socialists. Many of them, including Alfred Polgar, Otto Soyka, and Richard Arnold Bermann (formerly coeditor of *Der Frieden*), had already worked for Karpeles in 1918–20; new to the team were Josef Weinheber, Richard Schaukal, Karl-Heinrich Waggerl, the prominent sportscaster Willy Schmöger, and the art historian Wilhelm Hausenstein. Raimund Keiter, formerly in charge of *Der neue Tag*, served as the editor-in-chief. *Jedermann* was in every respect an outstanding product and printed in lavish photogravure.

The L. Goldschmidt company was registered on 11 October 1932 at the commercial court in Vienna three days after the first issue had been published.[76] Hans Becker was hired on 16 November as "technical editor with a starting salary of 500 Austrian schilling" and was responsible for "the whole artistic and typographic design and for photo editing, including all preparatory work." Becker was to be paid separately for his own contributions as an artist; the publisher also secured for herself a preemptive right on Becker's written contributions.[77] Until the journal's discontinuation in March 1933, *Jedermann* published at least sixteen of Becker's drawings and three of his texts (Becker 1932c, 1933d, 1933a).[78]

One of the paper's distinctive features was its extensive coverage of exotic subject matter in a popular yet serious manner. Each issue included a two-page spread, "Stories of a Globetrotter," anonymously contributed by the well-known travel writer Richard A. Bermann (1883–1939), who also wrote for *Jedermann* under his pseudonym Arnold Höllriegel. Exemplary for this genre are his reports about the Taos Indian painter Albert Martinez Looking Elk (1888–1940) and the Canadian Sarcee Robert One Spot (Bermann 1932a, 1932b). Anthropologists also served as contributors. In addition to Becker, these included Father Paul Schebesta, S.V.D. (with two excerpts from his recently published book on the Congo pygmies), and Hans Becker's fellow student Hugo Bernatzik (Schebesta 1932a, 1932b, 1932c; Bernatzik 1933).

On 4 March 1933, hardly two weeks after "Dr. Franz Wahrhaft" had in a column castigated Austria as a "playground of unscrupulous demagoguery," the Austrian chancellor Engelbert Dollfuß (1892–1934) staged a coup d'état, eliminated parliamentary control, and instituted censorship of the press. *Jedermann* ceased publication on 26 March and on 4 July 1933 the L. Goldschmidt publishing company canceled Becker's health insurance and pension scheme at the Insurance Institution of the Press. Once again Becker's employment had only lasted for a few months, but it was the first time it had not been terminated at his own request.

CONFRONTATION WITH NATIONAL SOCIALISM, 1933–38

Immediately following the coup d'etat, the man who had been working for a newspaper critical of the regime was taken into the service of this very regime. According to Becker's later recollection, he was hired "in early March 1933" by virtue of a "request of the general director of the official *Wiener Zeitung*" as deskman beginning on 15 March 1933 and was, "this employment notwithstanding, at the same time delegated to head the publicity department of the Patriotic Front (PF)."[79] In fact, the *Wiener Zeitung* was merged with the Government Printing Office only in April 1933, when Pankraz Kruckenhauser, the former deputy editor-in-chief of the conservative *Reichspost*, was appointed first general director of the new unit, while Ferdinand Reiter (named as a witness by Becker) took over as editor-in-chief of the *Wiener Zeitung*.[80] The Patriotic Front was only founded on 1 June 1933. Strangely enough, Becker's mandatory insurance with the Insurance Institution of the Press was also only registered per 1 June, and as deskman of the *Österreichische Volkspresse*, another newspaper edited by Kruckenhauser,[81] with a monthly salary of 450 Austrian schillings.[82] The *Volkspresse* followed a line of appeasement with national socialism, and Kruckenhauser was recalled in August from his position as secretary general of the PF, probably because of this unacceptable policy (Kriechbaumer 2005, 107; Tálos 2013, 154).

By official instruction, Becker's employment at the PF was renewed on 1 January 1934. However, it was only on 16 July 1934, nine days prior to the failed Nazi coup d'état and the assassination of Chancellor Dollfuß, Becker was additionally hired as of 1 August as division head at the Federal Commissariat for Homeland Service (with a monthly salary of 200 Austrian schillings), which, after the establishment of a one-party system in Austria, was made part of the Federal Press Service at the Chancellor's Office.[83]

Becker, who held no membership in any political party and moved in politically highly heterogeneous circles, obviously owed his new and unexpected career once again to Eduard Ludwig (Urbanek 2011, 18), still head of the Federal Press Service, who after the Dollfuß coup had been charged with the reorganization of the *Wiener Zeitung* and of the Austrian media landscape in general. Becker's willingness to accept this offer from a regime he did not feel comfortable with was caused by the specific agenda of his new job(s), consisting—especially as far as the Homeland Service was concerned—primarily of the defense against subversive propaganda and, more particularly, in combating national socialism in Austria. According to his friend Franz Pessler (1949, 9), Becker was "not very keen on the Corporative State. He was very much aware of its weaknesses and felt there was not enough space in it for the workers." At the same time, Becker perceived national socialism as an immediate threat to the continued existence of Austria, and in the Corporative State—after the suppression of all other political institutions—the only remaining means of resistance against aggressive German policies (Becker 1946a, 3–4).[84]

Becker faced two practical problems in his new position in the PF and in the ultra-Catholic Corporative State. Membership in a Masonic lodge was considered un-Catholic and therefore undesirable; it was explicitly prohibited to civil servants (Patka 2010, 29–66). Although this regulation would appear to have applied to employees of the Homeland Service as well, Becker did not acquiesce to this demand. As late as January 1938 he was elected to the board of the Austrian League for the League of Nations, an organization supported by the freemasons and the Pan-European Union (both outlawed in Germany by the Nazis after 1933), which, after Germany's withdrawal from the League of Nations in 1933, was playing a growing role in the struggle against national socialism.[85] The other problem was his marriage with Anna Lieser in Buenos Aires, which had been without the blessings of the Catholic Church—a condition unacceptable for an official in the Catholic Corporative State. This omission was corrected on 16 July 1934, the day on which he was hired to work for the Homeland Service (Gotschim-Jauk 1990, 45).[86]

Within the governance structure of the Corporative State, which was no less bureaucratic than the Social Democratic Party and characterized by an "entanglement of offices . . . personal unions, double functions, and paradoxes" (Urbanek 2011, 16), Becker held two positions. As head of a division in the Federal Commissariat for Homeland Service he was responsible for the fight against national socialism and the dissemination of the ideology of the Corporative State. In the Patriotic Front he served as head of Section III (Publicity Service)—with the official title "Federal Chief of Publicity" after 1935—and had to oversee the production of advertising material, the organization of meetings, and the training of regional and local advertising representatives. The training was often done by Becker himself, because it kept him in touch with the grassroots. His closest collaborator, especially in the field of anti-Nazi propaganda, and his deputy in the Publicity Service, was the later vice-chancellor Fritz Bock (1911–1993). In both positions Becker initially reported to Walter Adam (1886–1947), until Adam, after the July Agreement with Germany of 1936, was replaced as secretary-general of the PF by Guido Zernatto (1903–1943) (Kriechbaumer 2005, 107–109; Tálos 2013, 157–58).

Publicity for the PF may have been Becker's most challenging task, not only because of his own doubts regarding the ideology of the Corporative State, but also because the PF, until the end, never had a clearly formulated program (Tálos 2013, 152–54; Kriechbaumer 2005, 53–81). The promotion of an affirmation of an independent Austria certainly was no problem for Becker and was immediately connected to the threat posed by Nazi Germany and the subversive activities of the illegal Austrian NSDAP. Publicity was also made difficult by the limitation of available resources—especially compared to Germany's—and by the timidity of the Austrian political leadership in its demeanor toward Hitler. In hindsight Becker regarded the ideological antibiotics applied by the Corporative State and the PF against the Nazi virus as "insufficient in substance and intensity" and also felt the Austrofascist repression had contributed to driving many (and especially the young) Austrians into the national socialist fold (Becker 1946a, 11).

The condition further deteriorated after the July Agreement with Germany of 1936, in which nonintervention in the internal political affairs of the other country and the sovereignty of Austria as a "German state" had been agreed upon. A secret supplementary agreement called for the inclusion of NSDAP-friendly politicians in the Austrian government and an amnesty for members of the Austrian NSDAP. Becker had opposed the agreement, and *Wiener Zeitung* now had to continue the anti-Nazi propaganda more or less underground. The small office created for this purpose within the Publicity Service in 1935 disappeared from public view and communicated exclusively with the chancellor and "Front leader" Kurt Schuschnigg (1897–1977) and with Eduard Ludwig (Urbanek 2011, 27–29; Becker 1946a, 7–8).

Among the numerous areas of conflict between the Corporative State and Nazi Germany, the film industry was of particular importance for cultural politics and the dissemination of ideologies. It was only marginally related to Becker's agenda as federal publicity chief, but was obviously a serious concern in the context of limiting Nazi influence on Austria. The controversy focused on the future fate of the Sascha Film Industry, a corporation which, after phenomenal achievements during the silent film era, had suffered a setback with the rise of talkies and in 1932 had been purchased by the Jewish businessman Oskar Pilzer and his brothers. The takeover was financed in early 1933 by the sale of a majority of shares to the Tobis syndicate, the largest German film company in the Third Reich, next to UFA. When the highly successful film *Maskerade*—produced by the Austrian actor and film director Willy Forst and starring Paula Wessely and Hans Moser—was being shot in 1934, Tobis attempted to enforce in Austria the German ban on the participation of Jews in film productions: a regulation finally included in the German-Austrian Film Commerce Agreement of February 1935. German laws prohibiting the transfer of capital to Austria got the Austrian Tobis-Sascha company into serious trouble, since most of its revenues were made in Germany. At the same time, the company's Viennese house bank, Creditanstalt-WienerBank, which was also a minority owner of the company, declined to extend their credit line and ultimately forced Pilzer to resign as president of the company at the end of 1936 and to sell his shares to the bank for one thousand schillings (which he probably never received) in January 1937.

The Corporative State reacted to this threat in December 1935 by establishing an Austrian Film Conference as an advisory group for the Department of Trade and Transportation. Becker was appointed as a member and in this matter was able to demonstrate his expertise. After Pilzer's withdrawal Becker was elected to the board of directors of Tobis-Sascha, and he kept this position up until the German occupation (or "repatriation") of Austria.[87] In July 1937 the former Secretary of Trade Eduard Heinl (1880–1957) became the company's new president.[88] The position of technical director was filled by Albert Göring (1895–1966), the younger brother of Reichsmarschall Hermann Göring (1893–1946). Albert, a declared opponent of the Nazi regime, was living in Austria in exile, and had adopted Austrian citizenship. He had been hired by Pilzer, whom he later helped to escape from the Gestapo. Like Becker, Albert Göring later maintained close contacts with the Czech resistance, although with different groups.[89]

In September 1936 Anna and Hans Becker became the parents of a son. His boss Guido Zernatto and Fanny Starhemberg (1875–1956), the mother of the vice-chancellor and Home Guard leader Ernst Rüdiger von Starhemberg (1899–1956) and herself head of the PF's women's organization, served as godparents: an illustration of Becker's standing in the hierarchy of the Corporative State.[90] Anna Becker was already thirty-five years old and would have preferred to continue as a dancer, rather than become a mother. Six months after her son's birth she cried on the shoulder of her friend Luzie Korngold: "I have already turned completely rancid here. By and large we are doing well. Hans has much trouble, much work, little money. Always the same old song. I am big and chubby, therefore grumpy and unbearable."[91] This is not what contentment sounds like, and it would later become apparent that her marriage with Hans was heading into a crisis.

DACHAU AND MAUTHAUSEN, 1938–40

In 1936 Becker had already predicted Hitler's plans for the annexation of Austria and had immediately started to make preparations for the necessary resistance to improve Austria's prospects after the inevitable collapse of the Third Reich (Pessler 1949, 9; Becker 1946a, 8).

It was therefore not much to his surprise when Hitler's troops finally marched into Austria, just as in the offices of the Patriotic Front final preparations were underway for a plebiscite on the country's independence, planned for 13 March 1938. After the enforced resignation of the

Schuschnigg government, the desks had to be cleared and incriminating documents destroyed prior to the massive wave of arrests. In Vienna alone, more than 76,000 persons—officials of the government and of the PF, social democrats, communists, monarchists, Jews, Catholic priests, and freemasons—were detained by the Gestapo (Becker 1946a, 9).

Becker was on the Nazis' priority list and was arrested the night of 12 March at the East Railroad station just as he was trying to make his escape to Hungary. He was taken to the police prison at Rossauer Lände, where a few days later he was forced to listen to a broadcast of the "screams of welcome" for Hitler by the people of Vienna (Becker 1946a, 9). It took until 5 May for the agency in charge of the liquidation of the Patriotic Front to cancel his statutory health insurance retroactively as of 31 March.[92] But there must be order!

On 1 April Becker was among the 151 political prisoners deported via Munich to the Dachau concentration camp in Bavaria.[93] There they were assigned to "commandos" with tasks ranging from work in the gravel pit, the demolition and construction of buildings, roadwork, or indoor service, including office work or the darning of stockings, to useless occupations such as shoveling a pile of dirt back and forth. In addition, there were "punitive measures," enforced by heavy beatings, such as pushing a heavily loaded wheelbarrow for many hours up to and beyond the limits of physical capability. Everything was accompanied by constant physical abuse at the hands of the SS guards, some of them raw recruits sent to Dachau to be trained in the perpetration of the most inhumane cruelties, up to gratuitous murder. In the case of an individual's attempted escape, the whole group was punished by having to stand at attention, often for more than twenty-four hours and even during the freezing cold of winter.

For some tasks the camp's administration made use of skills acquired by the inmates in their civilian occupations. In Becker's case these were his talents as a designer, and after an initial period of hard work he was assigned to the concentration camp's "museum," where images or casts of the heads of inmates with physical peculiarities, and a wooden model of the camp, were made and preserved.

Since most of the Austrian prisoners were kept together, Dachau also became, in Becker's words, a "college of political learning opportunities," where "Austrian politicians of all shades" (although dominated by former members of the PF) could develop a nonpartisan sense of Austrian community and together profess their "unconditional and total avowal of democracy." This discussion group not only laid the foundations for a liberated postwar Austria, but also for the underground resistance against the Nazi regime, in which the mutually complementary experiences of "communists . . . and Austrian police officers" provided "excellent training material" (1946a, 10).

While Becker and his fellow inmates were mistreated and humiliated in Dachau, the Nazi press had nothing but scorn and derision for the detained officials of the Corporative State. In April 1938 an illustrated story in the SS rag *Das Schwarze Korps* (The Black Corps) offered proof that "the pillars of the Schuschnigg system had not all of them more or less bit the dust." Their suspenders, neck ties, and razors had been taken away to prevent them from committing suicide. "Thus these worthy men are looking somewhat 'unshaved and far from home' . . . but they will later be grateful to the national socialists for their care to have kept them alive. . . . Hans Becker, head of division of the Patriotic Front, now also has sufficient opportunity to reflect about the senselessness of turning, before the eyes of the government and in public, against the agreement concluded between the Führer and Schuschnigg, against the Führer, and against the [national socialist] movement" (Anonymous 1938, 16).

In the meantime the "Gildemeester Initiative" had been launched in Vienna, which enabled the legal emigration from the German Reich of wealthy secular Jews and their non-Jewish spouses for a levy of seventy percent of their property. Becker's wife Anna, along with her husband, would have qualified under the Gildemeester Initiative, but her name does not appear among those who emigrated under this plan (Venus and Wenck 2004).

The Dutch philanthropist Frank van Gheel-Gildemeester was a colorful figure who, in 1935, had been under observation by the Federal Commissariat for Homeland Protection because of alleged ties to the illegal Austrian NSDAP (Venus and Wenck 2004, 122–31, especially 125). A petition by Gildemeester for the release of Becker (as well as of Walter Adam, the later Austrian chancellor Leopold Figl, and others) was declined in February 1939, although the Gestapo had no incriminating evidence against him apart from his activities for the PF. 137 Austrian inmates were granted early release in April 1939; Becker's name was among the fifty-three whose release had originally been proposed, but was ultimately rejected (Gotschim-Jauk 1990, 126–27; Pessler 1949, 9). In February 1939, at the time of Gildemeester's petition, Anna had received assurances from the Paraguayan embassy in London that her husband, as a former resident of Paraguay, would be welcome to return to this country.[94] When Hans Becker was not released at that time, Anna and her son Nikolaus emigrated with her sister Helene to Switzerland. While Helene stayed there, Anna and Nikolaus later moved to California. Her mother did not consider emigration, was deported in 1942, and died in 1943, most probably in Auschwitz.

After the beginning of World War II, Dachau was closed as a concentration camp, because the facilities were needed for the stationing of SS reserve troops. In late September 1939, after eighteen months in Dachau, the majority of the Austrians were moved to the concentration camp Mauthausen in Upper Austria, where conditions were even worse, if that was even possible. In any case, daily rations were smaller and up to twelve hours of work in the quarry spelled doom for those not sharing Becker's strong physical condition and will to survive. During the first five months in Mauthausen more than three-quarters of the prisoners transferred from Dachau died of dysentery, exhaustion, undernourishment, torture, or murder.

By the end of 1939, however, Becker succeeded in getting transferred to the camp's construction office, thanks to the combination of his qualifications and bribing a professional criminal who had been selected among the inmates by the SS as head of the punitive commando. The office was in charge of planning and supervising the building of additional barracks, crematories, and a gas chamber, as well as of the auxiliary concentration camp Gusen. In the course of time the Austrians no longer received the same attention of their henchmen as the more recently arrived Poles, Spanish communists, and Jews.[95]

ANTHROPOLOGY AND RESISTANCE, 1941–45

To his own surprise, Becker was released as a prisoner from Mauthausen on 1 January 1941. At the same time he was ordered to stay on until

31 March as "civilian staff ... up to the completion of plans for certain building projects."⁹⁶ During these first months of 1941 he was already able, from his hotel room in Mauthausen, to reestablish a correspondence with old colleagues and friends, including Karl Fiebrig in Berlin and Etta Donner in Vienna.

Becker's immediate return to anthropology after his release from Mauthausen was certainly due mainly to Donner, in whose apartment in the seventh district of Vienna he was able to find shelter. In the fall of 1928 Etta Donner had started to study linguistics and oriental history, but soon changed her focus to African languages and cultural anthropology (Plankensteiner 2011a, 10).⁹⁷ Beginning in the winter term of 1931/2, Becker and Donner sat together in at least one class per term; in the summer term of 1933 the number had grown to four, including Röck's Quechua Texts, which was of only marginal interest to Donner.⁹⁸

Like Becker, Donner never was a professional journalist and only wrote pieces for local journals (especially the *Kleines Blatt, Interessantes Blatt, Wiener Bilder,* and *Radio Wien*). She shared Becker's taste for adventure and in 1934, at the age of twenty-two, had gone to do fieldwork in Liberia, followed by a second trip in 1936/7. The young woman's expeditions to the "dark continent" caused a considerable stir in Viennese society (Plankensteiner 2011b, 25–49). Neither Becker nor Donner was overly interested in the theories and methods of the culture-historical "Vienna school." They were passionate fieldworkers for whom the interaction with live cultures was far more important than the explanation of their origins. Given the small number of students in the anthropology department, the two of them must have known one another and presumably discovered their shared interests. Becker, however, was relatively recently married and sixteen years Donner's senior. He had to devote all of his attention to his work for the Patriotic Front, while she was mostly traveling in Liberia. A closer relationship may have developed only in 1937/8 after her return from Africa and prior to his detention in Dachau.⁹⁹

In May 1941 the marriage between Hans Becker and Anna Lieser was annulled by the district court in Vienna. Wilhelm Fürer-Haimendorf, the brother of anthropologist Christoph Fürer-Haimendorf, had argued that the plaintiff had only "after his release from the concentration camp ... been enlightened about the harmfulness of a marriage with a non-Aryan woman. Thus, at the conclusion of the marriage he was in error regarding the circumstances of the other partner, and it has to be assumed he would otherwise not have entered into this marriage." The reason named for an alternatively requested divorce ("since the defendant without good cause had emigrated to America and had expressed her intention never to return") is equally bitterly cynical.[100] Becker's second marriage, to Etta Donner, took place on 18 September 1941 (Gotschim-Jauk 1990, 147), once again without the benefit of a Catholic ceremony.

To suspect Becker of antisemitism would be patently absurd. He probably had more Jewish than non-Jewish friends, and he certainly could not have cared less about how later race laws would classify his wife. All that mattered to him in 1941 was to terminate a marriage in name only as quickly as possible. Already in February Etta had studied the Marriage Act and "found two useful things, one more useful than the other.... In all likelihood the ordinary procedure would also be possible, but tedious and thorny because of endless bureaucratic obstacles, and I would be inclined to save these troubles—you already have enough of them."[101] Anna was never able to forgive him for annulling their marriage and in spite of several efforts on Becker's part refused him any further contact with Nikolaus.[102]

Beginning in January 1941 Etta supplied Hans with news about the changes in the anthropology department since 1938.[103] Schmidt, Koppers, and Heine-Geldern had all gone into exile, and Hermann Baumann (1902–1972) had recently been brought in from Berlin to succeed Koppers, despite valiant efforts by Hugo Bernatzik to use his Nazi connections to get the job (Gohm and Gingrich 2014).

In 1940 Donner had received her PhD in African languages as a student of Wilhelm Czermak and vigorously supported Becker's decision to get his degree. To do so, it was first necessary to rectify an omission. In the 1930s Becker had neglected his minors, and he now had to attend to prehistory, art history, and philosophy as quickly as possible.[104]

Becker's dissertation may have been more or less finished in 1936 at the time he received his absolutorium—the purely ethnographic part, in which no literature after 1931 is cited, perhaps even as early as

1934.¹⁰⁵ The culture-historical summary requested by Koppers cites a 1935 publication by Walter Krickeberg.¹⁰⁶ Notable insertions dating from 1941 include some comparative references to a Lengua animal tale (Becker 1941b, 409), which in part are not listed in the bibliography.

Etta Donner, who had a better grasp of the current academic requirements, read the text critically in February 1941 and offered some constructive suggestions. One of them concerned Günther Tessmann (1884–1969), who, like Becker, had done ethnographic fieldwork without the benefit of academic training, first in Cameroon and Equatorial Africa and later in the Peruvian part of Amazonia. "Your attitude toward Tessmann," she wrote, "and to what an extent you consider him a role model, needs to be discussed closely, and as already mentioned it would be good to occasionally talk about it with Baumann."¹⁰⁷ In the dissertation as submitted Tessman is no longer mentioned, but the result of the discussion is reflected a few months later in a letter to Fiebrig: "Just as everywhere, people with field experience and a knowledge of the language are generally no anthropologists—and the anthropologists more often than not do not understand their 'victims' and even in the course of fieldwork are lacking the time to establish the necessary contact. A good example would be Günther Tessmann, who investigated wholesale a whole group of Peruvian tribes."¹⁰⁸ In the first sentence Tessmann (without being named) stands for the field-experienced amateur (and Becker's "role model"); in the second he is the anthropologist hastily rushing through the field.

There was hardly any time to rewrite. The dissertation was submitted in June 1941 and examined by Baumann, whose report of 30 June was endorsed two days later by the prehistorian Oswald Menghin (1888–1973).¹⁰⁹ On 2 July Becker applied for admission to the oral exams, after which he was awarded his PhD on 14 July.¹¹⁰ For Becker it was the first and only of his several ventures into academia that was brought to a happy end. The swiftness of the procedure is remarkable, especially in view of the sufficiently known facts about Becker's former work for the PF and his detention in Dachau and Mauthausen (neither of which are noted in the résumé attached to his dissertation).¹¹¹

Despite a note in the university records stating that Becker's dissertation "had nothing to do with the culture circles doctrine of Schmidt-

Koppers" (Gotschim-Jauk 1990, 143), it is notable that a dissertation written under the supervision of Koppers was now rubber-stamped by Baumann without any significant changes. Indeed, there is no mention of culture circles in Becker's mostly ethnographic thesis, and the culture-historical digressions (as well as the tabulation of "culture elements") are rather in the tradition of the regional studies of Erland Nordenskiöld and similar approaches by Walter Krickeberg.

Hermann Baumann, formerly an Africanist curator at the ethnological museum in Berlin, had been appointed as Koppers's successor, specifically because "in a critical attitude toward the Vienna School he had liberated himself from its mistakes" (Gohm and Gingrich 2014, 187). The assertion made in Becker's application for admission to the oral exams, however, that his dissertation had been written at the suggestion and under the supervision of Baumann, points to a complicity between the two in obfuscating a now unseemly academic past. Since Baumann had never met Becker before, it is likely Etta Donner had prevailed upon Baumann to accommodate this problem case. Baumann had first met Donner in Berlin in 1937, when she sold her collection from Liberia to the museum, and she was now also doing work for him in addition to her job at the museum (Linimayr 1994, 165, 173).

The dissertation's bibliography includes two works by Wilhelm Koppers, both of which are not cited in the text, and, even more remarkably, words of praise for Herbert Baldus, whose German citizenship had been revoked after his emigration.[112] Such friendly references to well-known opponents of the regime provided no obstacle to the academic procedure.

In his written assessment of the dissertation Hermann Baumann is critical enough. He finds fault with the unprofessional citation method and points out shortcomings in the representation of the "spiritual and social culture," which Becker considered to be the best part of the thesis.[113] It may be surprising that Becker received an "A" under such circumstances, but it fits the reading of of a privileged treatment.

The orals consisted of three two-hour exams in anthropology, prehistory, and art history, as well as a one-hour exam in philosophy. The examining professors were all prominent exponents of national socialist ideas. In addition to Baumann the committee included the prehistorian Oswald Menghin, who had been secretary of education in the transitional Nazi government after the occupation of Austria in 1938; the art historian Hans Sedlmayr (1899–1984), who had prevented Etta Becker's colleague Annemarie Hefel from continuing her studies in art history because of her family's proximity to the Corporative State (Linimayr 1994, 160); and the philosopher Arnold Gehlen (1904–1976), who had recently been appointed to fill the position of a Catholic professor who had been removed from his office. It may have contributed to the especially amicable course of the exams that all examiners except for Menghin were younger than Becker. In any case, Becker reported to Fiebrig: "The orals were actually much fun, since they turned into discussions leading to the request by the philosopher that I should be writing a new aesthetics, whereas the art historian consulted with me on the origins of naturalism in art."[114] Since all of his exams were graded "A," Becker was awarded his PhD "with distinction."[115]

Despite the total absence of any even only formal expressions of devotion to the ideology of national socialism, the university regarded the dissertation as worthy of publication. A significant role in this process was played by the dean of the Philosophical Faculty (and string-puller in the anthropological field in Vienna at that time), Viktor Christian. "The dean," Becker wrote in August 1941, "promised me to have it published in the Vienna journal of anthropology [*Mitteilungen der Anthropologischen Gesellschaft in Wien*, the organ of the Anthropological Society], because all the publishing venues of the department of anthropology are currently blocked."[116] A few months later, Christian, who was also president of the Anthropological Society (the board of which included Baumann and Menghin), had changed his mind: "After talking to an office of the party [NSDAP] it appears to be preferable not to publish your work in the *Mitteilungen*, because the *Mitteilungen* are published by a press affiliated with a party organization. There may be no objections against publishing it elsewhere."[117] The unnamed "party organization" was none other than the infamous foundation *Ahnenerbe* (where Christian was head of a department) devoted to the exploration of the Aryan heritage of the German people. For the *Ahnenerbe* to publish a dissertation by Becker, the former anti-Nazi propaganda chief of the Patriotic Front and concentration camp inmate, would indeed have been preposterous.

Becker, however, had already started in August 1941 to look for alternatives for a swift publication of his thesis. He had asked Karl Fiebrig to put in a good word with Walter Krickeberg (1885–1962), then the leading expert in the field of American ethnology and archeology in the German-speaking world, and director of the Museum für Völkerkunde in Berlin. In March 1942 Becker wrote directly to Krickeberg—whom he had only known from his published work—introduced himself, and requested his advice regarding possible publication. By return mail Krickeberg suggested the *Zeitschrift für Ethnologie*, published by the Berlin Association for Anthropology, Ethnology, and Prehistory, "which (at least for now) is still being published." After receipt of Becker's manuscript, he investigated the situation at the *Baessler-Archiv*, the museum's own journal, but had to report in July that a backlog of contributions made it impossible to publish Becker's work in the foreseeable future. Instead, Krickeberg passed the manuscript on to the *Zeitschrift für Ethnologie*.[118]

In October 1942 Hans Nevermann (1902–1982), the editor of the *Zeitschrift für Ethnologie*, proposed an unabbreviated publication in two parts, starting in number 4–6 of volume 71 (1941), scheduled to appear in early 1943 and actually published at the end of 1943, after Krickeberg had assumed the position of editor. The delay in the production of the second part, in number 1–3 of volume 72 (1942), until late 1944/early 1945 permitted Becker to add a short section on the Toozli. Otherwise, the published text shows only minimal editorial changes and three new references to older literature.[119]

Even prior to the publication, Becker gave a lecture on "New Research among the Chaco Tribes" on 25 June 1942 for the Berlin Association at the *Museum für Vor-und Frühgeschichte* (Museum for Pre- and Protohistory) in Berlin, which had been arranged through the offices of Krickeberg (Gotschim-Jauk 1990, 150–51). The public announcement of this event alerted the Linden-Museum in Stuttgart to Becker, who was invited to lecture there on 13 November 1942 as guest of the Württemberg Association for Trade Geography, which operated the museum. His talk was focused on aspects of his research in the northern Chaco and "because of the danger of airstrikes in the later hours of the evening [had to be] limited to one-and-a-quarter or at most one-and-a-half hours."[120]

While he was still looking for a suitable venue to have his dissertation published, Hellmuth Draws-Tychsen entered Becker's life and opened for him the door to an unlikely literary career.

Actually, nobody could have taken much pleasure from coming into sustained contact with Hellmuth Draws-Tychsen. Those unable to avoid this fate, such as the German writer Marieluise Fleißer (1901–1974), who had to put up with him for four years as her fiancé, unanimously described his personality as "aggressive, arrogant, vain, self-directed, imaginative, and restless" (Fischer 2004, 159; Kraft 2009). Draws-Tychsen, a poet who preferred to refer to himself as an anthropologist, was an impostor who managed to gain advantages on the basis of a freely invented biography and the alleged influence of powerful friends. The focus of his anthropological endeavors—never taken seriously by experts—was the "autothalattian" origin of the Polynesians on the sunken continent Lemuria in the Pacific Ocean.

According to a later account by Draws-Tychsen, he had been preparing a "universal Polynesian exhibition" in connection with an "international congress of Oceanists in Vienna on the occasion of the centenary of the birth of Andreas Reischek in 1945."[121] Draws-Tychsen claimed to have lived in Vienna in 1939/40, after having been ousted by Hitler's remote command from an (imaginary) position as visiting professor of ethnomusicology in Budapest, and to have fled to Slovakia, where he ostensibly had supported "the Slovaks in their struggle for their just cause against Adolf Hitler and his ilk." From Slovakia he had supposedly been deported to Vienna in order to work as a Gestapo informer (Fischer 2004, 131, 142, 151). He was later remembered by the curator in charge of the Oceanian collections of the museum in Vienna, Dominik Josef Wölfel (1888–1963), who had been forced into retirement by the Nazis for refusing to divorce his Jewish wife but who kept an office at the museum in connection with a research project on the Canary Islands: "Here as well he was a denouncer and megalomaniac, but in this respect he has colleagues among present-day scholars" (Fischer 2004, 133).[122] Draws-Tychsen had also become notorious at the department of anthropology at the University of Vienna. At a time when Becker had already disappeared from his memory, Hermann

Baumann recalled Draws-Tychsen as a psychopath, but also as "the only anthropologist who was against the Nazis" (Fischer 2004, 136).

Becker must have encountered Draws-Tychsen after his release from Mauthausen in the spring or summer of 1941. Whatever the reasons may have been—perhaps Becker was interested in Draws-Tychsen's alleged activity in the anti-Nazi resistance, or maybe his new acquaintance claimed (as he later did during his own detention in a concentration camp) to be "conversant in some Indian languages of South America" (Fischer 2004: 140), or perhaps it was their shared love for the Spanish language—Becker gave Draws-Tychsen a copy of his unpublished paper on "*Die Vielstaatlichkeit des spanischen Südamerika*" (The Fragmented Statehood of South America).

On 9 September 1941 Becker received an unexpected letter from the editorial offices of the *Zeitschrift für Geopolitik* (Journal of Geopolitics) in Berlin. "Mr. Draws-Tychsen," it read, "has made available to us your paper . . . and suggests its publication in the *Zeitschrift für Geopolitik*. Both Professor Haushofer, the editor of our journal, and I [Kurt Vowinkel] have enjoyed the article and would like to publish it already in the next issue. . . . The remuneration is 15 reichsmark per printed page. . . . We would be very pleased if there could be a sequel to this first collaboration. We believe to be able to offer an effective forum for your local knowledge acquired in the course of years of personal inspection and your ability to captivatingly present the problems of South America from your own point of view."[123] This was the beginning of Becker's collaboration with the journal, which lasted nearly until the end of World War II.

The term "geopolitics"—referring to the "doctrine of the geographical contingency of politics"—had been coined in 1899 by the Swedish political scientist Rudolf Kjellén (1864–1922). It was received with special enthusiasm in Germany after World War I, in connection with the issue of war guilt, because Kjellén had declared the war to have been the unavoidable result of Germany's geopolitically predetermined aspiration to become a global power. A geopolitical approach, with diverse emphases on geography, political science, and historiography, is found in such disparate discourses as those of Fernand Braudel and the *Annales* school or Halford Mackinder's "heartland theory" of the rise of large empires in the interior of Eurasia. Among German geographers it was seamlessly combined with the ideas of the anthropogeographer Friedrich Ratzel (1844–1904), whose diffusionist theories had significantly shaped the culture-historical approaches of early-twentieth-century anthropology in German-speaking countries. As founder of the *Zeitschrift für Geopolitik* in 1923, the Munich geographer Karl Haushofer (1869–1946), who happened to be the teacher and friend of Hitler's deputy Rudolf Heß (1894–1987), became the most visible representative of geopolitical doctrines. Of these, especially the idea of "*Lebensraum*" as an inalienable right of a people to a sufficient land base was instrumentalized by national socialism for its own purposes. Both the journal and Haushofer, who was married to a "half-Jew," were profiting from this interest by the regime, which only began to decline after 1938 and was further reduced after Heß had defected to England in 1941. The execution of Haushofer's son and collaborator Albrecht as a confidant of the attempted assassination of Hitler on 20 July 1944 may have been the major reason for the journal's demise before the end of the war (Sprengel 1996, 15–38).

It was during the journal's last years when Hans Becker, former inmate of Dachau and Mauthausen, became one of its most regular contributors (Becker 1942b, 1943, 1944a, 1944b, 1944c; Sprengel 1996, 349) and thus found himself in highly unenviable company. Other contributors of this period not only included Draws-Tychsen, but also the Viennese travel writer Colin Roß (1885–1945), an intimate friend of the Nazi elite; Gustav Fochler-Hauke (1906–1996), then a member of the NSDAP, after the war a prominent geographer, and, like Roß, one of Haushofer's students; and the prominent anthropologist and pronounced national socialist Wilhelm Emil Mühlmann (1904–1988).

At the request of the editor, Becker wrote two further essays on Middle America (designated as "Caribbean culture area" by the journal) and Brazil to complement his article on Spanish South America. The word "geopolitical" appears only once in these texts, and on the whole Becker's lines of argumentation are not compliant with geopolitical or national socialist assumptions. Becker points to ethnic rather than geopolitical factors as the major impetus of historical developments ("the pointed contrasts within the pre-Columbian countries"); he praises the Paulistas ("Mamluks") for their role in the colonization of Brazil and the "tenacious efficiency of this jumbled bunch of bandits"; and he favorably comments on the "strong influence of an Indian and especially an African feeling for art" on the Brazilian baroque (Becker 1942b, 412; 1944a, 61, 62).

In his cover letter for his essay on Brazil, Becker specifically identifies two passages in his text which "are truthfully dealing with the racial liberalism of Brazil. I have no idea how these things are presently being regarded, and I would therefore request you to make whatever minor changes or deletions necessary." In this case, no editorial changes were made, and the only suggestion was to add a short paragraph noting the entry of Brazil into the war against Germany, since the lack of such a reference "would be found objectionable by the body of censors, who are pedantic in this respect."[124]

The German element, so prominent in various parts of South America and of interest to the national socialists as *Auslandsdeutschtum* (Germanness abroad), is only marginally referred to (Becker 1942b, 409). However, in the same issue as Becker's essay on Brazil, the journal published a contribution by the East Prussian teacher Gerhard Hargut (1901–1994) on Germanness in Brazil, which the editorial office had requested Becker to review and revise. Perhaps the closest Becker ever got to geopolitics was in connection with the immigration freeze decreed by the autocratic president of Brazil—and admirer of Hitler—Getúlio Vargas, which appeared to be the more remarkable as Brazil was (not in Becker's words) a "space without people," in contradistinction to the national socialist description of Germans as "a people without space."

Despite a reduction in the allocation of paper by fifty percent in April 1943, the *Zeitschrift für Geopolitik* continued to be interested in Becker's essays because "presently it is not so easy to get really valuable contributions."[125] There was even talk about publishing his collected articles on Latin America in book form.[126] Among possible but never realized essays suggested by Becker was "The Argentinian Gaucho," a subject already dealt with in a book by Juan Carlos Dávalos (1928); two other essays, however, were published.

"*Zur Frage der geschichtsbildenden Elemente*" (On the Question of Elements in the Formation of Historical Consciousness) departs from an observation made in Becker's dissertation and attempts to link the presence or absence of historical consciousness to different conceptions of death and the resulting relationship to the ancestors (Becker 1944b, 1942a, 100). The problems of "completely different historical results in spite of shared natural preconditions [race, climate, geographical and economic conditions], especially among neighbors" or of "completely divergent behavior of one and the same people in different periods of its history" shook the foundations of the geopolitical notion of the geographical contingency of politics, and Becker was quick to point out the significance of ethnological data for dealing with this issue (Becker 1944b, 113).

Whereas the first four contributions were written in a casual style, without notes and references, Becker cites the most recent research by the American botanist Paul Mangelsdorf (1899–1989), as well as archaeological and ethnographic works, in his "*Der Ursprung des Mais*" (The Origin of Maize). Since his remarks—which focused on culture-historical relationships between the Andean highlands and Mesoamerica—were so remote from geopolitical concerns, Haushofer felt it necessary, as editor, to preface the essay with a paragraph asserting the interest of geopolitics in "coincidence between phytogeographical and anthropogeographical, political and cultural boundaries" (Becker 1944c, 151), even if such coincidences cannot be recognized in Becker's text. Like his first contribution, on the political diversity of Spanish South America, the essay on corn was not written at the request of the journal and had in fact already been in the works as early as 1942.[127]

Becker's attitude toward geopolitics becomes apparent in his reference to Rudolf Heß as the "Führer's deputy, who was permitted to consort with chiromancers, astrologists, and geopoliticians" (Becker MS, 1). His publications in the *Zeitschrift für Geopolitik* primarily offered him an opportunity to distinguish himself as an author with anthropological and historical expertise; the number of periodicals still being published during the last years of the war was extremely limited, and the journal was probably unique in this field in being able to pay authors for their contributions. At the same time, it may have served as a convenient disguise for Becker's simultaneous activities in the resistance against national socialism: publishing in a journal that was at least until recently closely associated with the regime, without the least attempt at ingratiation.

Becker's cooperation with the monthly *Kunst dem Volk* (Art for the People), published in Vienna since 1940 by Hitler's favorite photographer and official photojournalist of the NSDAP Heinrich Hoffman (1885–1957), took him in a different direction (Schedlmayer 2010). At the end of 1942 Becker had sent a few sample essays to the journal, thereby triggered their interest in a collaboration with him, "since as a result of the many call-up orders we are presently extremely short of contributors having the necessary expert knowledge."[128] However, only one of his articles (on the Markos, a family of nineteenth-century Hungarian landscape painters) was published in the last issue before the journal was discontinued on account of the war.

Draws-Tychsen and Becker remained in touch after 1941. On 4 August 1943 Becker received a letter from the publisher Ernst Reinhardt in Munich, who was planning to publish a translation of the book *El mundo visto a las ochenta años: impresiones de un arteriosclerótico* (The World as Seen with Eighty Years: Impressions of an Arteriosclerotic), a late work of the Spanish philosopher Santiago Ramón y Cajal (1852–1934).[129] The translation had already been started by Draws-Tychsen, "who, however, as I have learned from him, has unfortunately been taken into protective custody and is now in the concentration camp Sachsenhausen near Berlin. As he now reports to me he has deposited with you the copy of the book, reviewed and annotated for the purpose of translation by the Reich Ministry of Public Enlightenment and Propaganda, and also thinks you would be in a position to finish the German translation." This project was abandoned when the publisher ultimately acquired an already existing translation.[130]

Another translation project was brought to Becker's attention by the Catholic publisher Schöningh in Paderborn (Westphalia). It concerned a translation into Spanish of one of five volumes of *Katholische Kirche und Kultur* (Catholic Church and Culture) by the historian Gustav Schnürer (1860–1941). In addition, Dominik Josef Wölfel had drawn up with Schöningh a translation program, which also included "your

Latin American [book]"—either the dissertation or, more likely, the collected essays from the *Zeitschrift für Geopolitik*. Neither of the two plans could be realized before the end of the war.[131]

At the beginning of January 1944 Becker held talks in Vienna with the owner of the Oswald Arnold publishing company in Berlin and with his representative Richard Kühn, himself the author of a biography of the Swedish-American actress Greta Garbo, as well as other books on historically significant women (Kühn 1934, 1935, 1942). These contacts led to a contract signed by Becker on 22 March,[132] whereby the author sold his copyright of three books still to be written for an advance payment of 2,000 reichsmark: a "small world history, a work about J[G]. G. Moreno, a work on aesthetics." In the subsequent correspondence the contents of these books become more apparent.[133]

The volume on aesthetics, obviously inspired by his conversation with Arnold Gehlen on the occasion of his PhD oral exams, was still "in a state of a confusing collection of notes on slips of paper," which first of all needed to be brought into conceptual order. The "small world history" was to be an alternative take on a subject already treated by H. G. Wells in *A Short History of the World* (1922), which in 344 pages had traced an arc from the origin of life on earth to the founding of the League of Nations. Wells's work was considered by Becker "today already so primitive in its historical-materialist concept . . . to make it easy to outdo it"—a statement illustrating Becker's healthy self-confidence. His goal was to demonstrate to the reader "that every historical deed, whether by a pygmy in the jungle or by the general staff of a modern empire, can only be made after having been intellectually shaped from a belief, knowledge, or hope, so that any kind of materialism is reduced to absurdity, given it is itself only an idea (generally not a good one)."[134]

For the Moreno project there was already a draft outline entitled "*Der Gottesstaat im 19. Jahrhundert*" (The Theocratic State in the Nineteenth Century), which, unfortunately, has not been preserved. Gabriel García Moreno (1821–1875) had been a conservative president of Ecuador, who established Catholicism as the state religion, restricted the freedom of the press, and outlawed secret societies (including the freemasons), although political parties were still allowed to exist. By historians favorable to his autocratic regime, Moreno is said to have been successful in promoting public education, economic development, and the fight against corruption until he was murdered by his political opponents. Obvious similarities with the Austrian Corporative State may not be accidental, and it would be interesting to know more about Becker's intentions when dealing with this parallel historical case. Soon after his death Moreno had become the subject of a German novel by Phillip Wasserburg (1827–1897)—a writer recently converted from communist to conservative and to anti-Prussian Catholic—as well as a historical study, either of which may have drawn Becker's attention to this subject (Berlichingen 1884; Laicus 1880).

After the contract had been signed, Kühn proposed to expand the subject to include other theocracies, such as those of the Jesuits in Paraguay, the Quakers in Pennsylvania, the Jewish theocratic state, and Saint Augustine's *Civitas Dei*. Becker was quick to agree that he did not regard "the type of an interesting biographical account suitable for my kind of treatment of the subject." At the same time he suggested the "bonding of the state and the divine" to be "an intention manifest throughout the whole history of humanity," and thus that the subject might be getting out of hand.[135]

One can only admire the publisher's courage to pay good money merely for the idea of three books. Perhaps the advance was intended as covert support from a Catholic source for Becker's stand against national socialism. Both the small world history and the book on Moreno were declarations of war against materialism, whose renunciation of any responsibility to a "superior spiritual power" had led to the criminal amorality of Hitlerism. It may not have been a mere coincidence for Kühn to encourage Becker to visit the German Catholic philosopher Alois Dempf (1891–1982) (compare Dempf 1954) in connection with the theocracy project. After Dempf had warned the Vatican in 1934 against a concordat with Hitler, he was unable to get an academic position in Germany. In 1937, at the suggestion of Wilhelm Schmidt and Wilhelm Koppers, he had been appointed to the vacant chair in philosophy formerly held by Moritz Schlick (1882–1936) at the University of Vienna, only to be removed from it in 1938 by the interim national socialist government of Austria and replaced by none other than Arnold Gehlen. He was now living in inner emigration in the palace of the Archbishop of Vienna. Becker instantly replied, "With Prof. Dempf I already had a very interesting conversation, which I will continue in the near future."

Becker's low opinion of the caricature of the theocratic state in clerical-fascist guise is illustrated by his statement to the American military administration in July 1945, identifying the "complete separation of church and state" as one of the two most important items on the agenda of the newly formed conservative *Österreichische Volkspartei* (Austrian People's Party, ÖVP) (Rathkolb 1985, 264). His former professor Wilhelm Schmidt, however, was in 1949 still longing for the renascence of a Christian (i.e. Catholic) world, at least as a metaphorical *Civitas Dei* emerging from the rubble of World War II (W. Schmidt 1949, 535–57).

After returning to civil life from Mauthausen, Becker saw his priorities in finishing his studies and in literary activities, but his self-assessment as an artist had not changed. In August 1941 he applied for admission as a "designer of furniture etc." in the Reich's Chamber of Fine Arts, which retroactively accepted his membership in April 1942.[136] He may have expected better opportunities for gainful employment as a designer than as a painter. His admission was facilitated by the favorable assessment of Leopold Blauensteiner (1880–1947), a member of the NSDAP and until 1941 the president of the Vienna Künstlerhaus who, toward the end of the war, had helped to save from destruction works of what in Nazi parlance was "degenerate art" (Gotschim-Jauk 1990, 75–76). As in the case of anthropology, professional loyalty proved to be stronger than political differences.

As a painter, Becker attempted to sell works from his stock (including drawings made in South America); there is evidence for the sale of two watercolors to the owner of a furniture factory in Bremen.[137] In 1942/3 the Museum of Ethnology in Vienna also acquired, probably by purchase and through the efforts of Etta Becker-Donner, a total of three watercolors with South American subject matter.[138]

During these difficult years Becker's most significant commissioner of painting was the Archdiocese of Vienna. Already in October 1942 Becker reported to Fiebrig: "I have heavily fitted out interior designs with murals and daubed a few halls with large figural things. In addition this method led me to try my hand in church paintings, which earned me a successful start with four evangelists three meters in height."[139] Unfortunately, neither the place of this painting, nor the circumstances of the commission, are known.

It may have been his first job for the Archdiocese of Vienna, and it is surprising that the Church would have chosen a freemason, who for many years had not been married according to Catholic rites; who had his marriage annulled only under civil and not also under canonical law; and whose remarriage not only excluded him from receiving the sacraments, but also from any employment by the Catholic Church (Rhode 2014, 23–24). Since no earlier examples of religious art by Becker are known, he is unlikely to have been hired because of a specific qualification.[140] Perhaps the archdiocese wanted to pay tribute to his suffering in the concentration camps and to his resistance against the regime, in which prominent churchmen were likewise active, including the prelate Jakob Fried (1885–1967), a key figure of political Catholicism in the Corporative State and in the resistance (Fried 1947; see also W. Schmidt 1949).

There were at least three commissions by the archdiocese to Becker, dating from 1943 and 1944. In the case of the parish church in Breitensee, Lower Austria, the murals were to show a cycle of representations of peasant life, the veneration of the Sacred Sacrament of the Altar, and symbols of the sacraments of marriage, confession, and baptism. After drafts submitted by another artist had been rejected by the head of the architectural department of the archdiocese, Vicar Alois Penall (1906–1968), the job was turned over to Becker. The paintings were executed in December 1943 and earned Becker 3,700 reichsmark.[141]

Already in June 1943 Penall had turned to Becker regarding a project concerning the parish church of Alberndorf, Lower Austria. Becker was asked to paint the ceiling of the church with symbols of the four evangelists, as well as the two lateral walls, with depictions of the harvesting of grain and grapes. After an inspection of the site, Becker and Penall agreed on an honorarium of four thousand reichsmark and a modified iconographic program; instead of scenes from peasant life, there were now to be heroic images from the life of the patron saint. According to the church chronicle, one could soon behold "on the ceiling ... St. Laurentius distributing his wealth to the poor, on one of the lateral walls St. Laurentius taking leave from the Pope, and on the other one the sacred martyr dying for his faith"; the four evangelists were featured in the corners of the vault.[142] Whereas the original plan may be seen as a perpetuation of the ideology of peasantry as one of the pillars of the Catholic Corporative State, the paintings executed by Becker were more timely, focusing on the fate of an upright churchman exposed to the arbitrariness of a despotic ruler.[143]

The last commission concerned the recently built church of the parish St. Hubertus and Christophorus at the *Lainzer Tiergarten* on the outskirts of Vienna, for which Becker submitted his drafts in January 1944. One of the lateral walls of the nave depicted the baptism of Christ, the other the Sermon on the Mount (John 6: 66–68) dealing with a question then current in 1944: "Lord, to whom shall we go?" (Anonymous, ca. 1986: 29, and color plate 1). The stipulated honorarium of 6,400 reichsmark was paid in monthly advance installments, usually of 1,000 reichsmark.[144] Given an equivalent purchasing power of one reichsmark to about three present-day U.S. dollars, the commissions by the Archdiocese of Vienna must have significantly contributed to the income of the Becker family, which, after the birth of two daughters, had grown to four.[145] The archdiocese is also said to have been instrumental in other clerical institutions commissioning work from the artist.[146]

At the same time Becker was working between July 1941 and 1945 as an interior designer for the architect Wilhelm Kattus, who was dissatisfied with Becker and, in September 1942, ready to dismiss him. Somehow, despite the mutual discontentment, the collaboration must have continued; in October 1942 Kattus called Becker "a complete ignoramus" who had "too many other interests," and noted that both of them had not done enough "to complement one another to the extent I would have deemed necessary."[147]

As far as the "too many other interests" are concerned, the architect certainly had a valid point. Becker's remark in a letter to Fiebrig, "I am abundantly stressed by my two jobs," was a gross understatement. In addition to his work as an anthropologist and architect, and as a painter and writer, he had also resumed his activity as a business consultant.[148]

After receiving his PhD, Becker re-enrolled as an external student at the University of Vienna to attend several courses on the languages, arts, and cultures of Africa, offered by Wilhelm Czermak (1889–1953), Etta Donner's dissertation adviser. Perhaps it was a continuation of the old Beckerian practice of continuing education in new fields of knowledge, or perhaps he was attempting to get into closer contact with Czermak, who kept his distance from the NSDAP and—despite his notorious antisemitism—was at least until 1942 blacklisted as an enemy of the national socialist movement (Gütl 2015, 506).

By his own account, as early as May or June 1941 Becker began to coordinate the activities of the various resistance groups active in Austria according to the ideas formulated in Dachau.[149] The spontaneous resistance that cropped up immediately after the annexation of Austria had been largely uncoordinated and quickly squelched by the brutally repressive regim (Becker 1946a, 12–13; compare W. Schmidt 1949, 223–27). Becker established an "office of operations" designed to steward the work of small cells, connected with one another only indirectly through the central office, in order to impede surveillance by the Gestapo. Among the immediate goals were to make Austrian conscripts unfit for military service, sabotage production essential to the war effort, agitate for the resistance movement in order to recruit new collaborators and to subvert the Nazi propaganda on the home front, cooperate with resistance groups outside Austria, and establish contacts with the allied powers (Becker 1946a, 13; Gotschim-Jauk 1990, 155–56).

For Becker these activities entailed high risk, since this former concentration camp inmate was closely watched by the Gestapo. He managed to keep a low profile, and even his neighbors were unable to report on him; he made appropriate donations to the various funding drives of party organizations, but was considered to be "still standing apart" and, according to an official assessment, "has as yet not found his way to the German people's community" (Gotschim-Jauk 1990, 156). His manifold activities contributed to his cover, since they made it easily possible to explain his travels and contacts. In a similar manner, the resistance used commercial or insurance agents as couriers to groups outside Vienna, because their movements did not raise any suspicion. Particularly remarkable is Becker's ability to organize the resistance next to all of his other professional obligations (Gotschim-Jauk 1990, 182).

The release of further political detainees in 1942 made it possible to enlarge the office of operations, which in the fall of that year was renamed "Central Committee Austria." Among his closest associates was now Raoul Bumballa (1895–1947), an old friend from the days of World War I who had served time with him in Mauthausen and had recently been released from the Buchenwald concentration camp (Gotschim-Jauk 1990, 182). Toward the end of 1942 contacts are said to have been established with the Czech resistance, even though the documented cases of cooperation date from subsequent years. Hermann Schefter's name is found on a list of contacts from these early years, compiled by Becker after the end of the war (Becker 1946a, 16; Gotschim-Jauk 1990, 121, 167–82, 188).

"The same period," Becker reports, "saw the expansion of small [resistance] groups in .. scientific institutions and museums—in the latter case primarily for the purpose of safeguarding the immeasurable works of art for Austria" (Becker 1946a, 15). One of the most important contacts in this connection was Hermann Michel (1888–1965), a mineralogist who had been removed by the national socialists from his position as the first director of the Museum of Natural History in Vienna, of which the Museum of Ethnology was still an administrative part. Under his leadership, Michel brought the resistance group into the fold of the Central Committee in 1943, and toward the end of the war played an important role in keeping the national socialists from destroying the works of art removed from Vienna to a disused mine in Altaussee in Styria.[150] At the Museum of Ethnology a resistance group had formed around the curators Robert Bleichsteiner (1891–1954) and Etta Becker-Donner, who also served as a courier between Michel and Hans Becker and who, thanks to Michel's sustained contacts to the bureaucracy, was even made a tenured civil servant.[151] Becker-Donner had probably also established the contact between Michel and her husband.

With the decline of the military fortunes of the German Reich in 1943 and 1944, the inflow of people to the resistance groups increased; as a result, the challenges posed by their coordination increased as well.

The Central Committee, originally dominated by bourgeois members formerly close to the Patriotic Front, was little by little augmented by representatives of social democratic, communist, and legitimist groups. A "Panel of Seven" comprising all parties was created in November 1944 as an executive board presided over by Becker, with Bumballa acting as his deputy. Contacts were stepped up not only with the resistance within the Wehrmacht and with Tito's partisans in Yugoslavia, but also with the American and British secret services and, later, with the Red Army advancing on Vienna. The liaison with Austrian exile groups abroad turned out to be much more difficult, which made it necessary to formulate political visions for Austria after the war without their input (Gotschim-Jauk 1990, 184–208).

The request, especially when made by the British, for visible evidence of an Austria-wide resistance, led to the creation of the logogram O5 (for OE, the first letter of the word Österreich written without an umlaut: O plus the fifth letter of the alphabet), which in large-scale nocturnal campaigns was scrawled on the walls of houses and soon became the new and catchy designation of the Central Committee. In December 1944 the O5 created a "Provisional Austrian National Committee" (POEN) replacing the "Panel of Seven" and constituting the united political arm of the resistance, while the general staff of O5 under the direction of the POEN was planning and supervising activities, attending to logistics and communication, and taking responsibility for propaganda (Gotschim-Jauk 1990, 184–208).

On 25 February 1945 Hans Becker barely escaped arrest by the Gestapo, but three days later he was seized in a trap that had been set up for him along with other POEN leaders and members of the resistance. Bumballa moved into Becker's position as leader of the O5, but arrests severely reduced the operability of the group and cut the lines of communication (Gotschim-Jauk 1990, 208–17).

Becker had to expect his immediate execution at the Gestapo's Vienna headquarters, but after weeks of interrogation he and fifty other members of the resistance were once again deported to Mauthausen on 1 April.[152] As a welcome they were given a good beating, after which the new arrivals had to stand naked and silent for two days in the camp's square before being released to daily routine. This routine was already showing signs of the system's disintegration. For example, service in the orderly room was primarily upheld by senior political prisoners. Even some members of the SS could see the end fast approaching and were willing to cooperate. As a "celebrity inmate" Becker was nevertheless highly endangered. When in the second half of April rumors about his impending execution began to circulate, the orderly room succeeded in moving him to the more or less uncontrolled sick bay, where he "died" as a French prisoner of war, and thus saved his life (Gotschim-Jauk 1990, 215–24).

POSTWAR YEARS AND ASSASSINATION, 1945–48

On 7 May 1945 the Eleventh Armored Division of the Third U.S. Army moved into Mauthausen and liberated the prisoners. Becker joined the "Austrian National Committee in the Former Concentration Camp Mauthausen," which consisted both of former members of the Patriotic Front and communists, and which took care of the specific needs of the Austrians in the camp. In this function Becker supplied the inmates returning home with papers certifying their detention in Mauthausen (Gotschim-Jauk 1990, 225–28).

At the same time he was working closely with the American Commission to Investigate War Crimes and took down the statements of the former inmates. After having won the trust of the Americans, he left Mauthausen on 16 May and proceeded to Salzburg to help the Counter Intelligence Corps (CIC) in an advisory function, to gain a better understanding of the conditions in Austria and of the role of the resistance (Gotschim-Jauk 1990, 228–37).

In Salzburg Becker was also involved in the formation of the local branch of the conservative Austrian People's Party (ÖVP) and returned to Vienna on 4 June expecting to find a central role in the federal ÖVP. This hope was bitterly disappointed, because all of the leading positions in the party had been filled after its founding on 17 April; the role of the resistance groups, such as the O5, in the postwar political order had declined in importance as a result of the growing clout of the social democrats returning from exile; and not least because Becker was simply not "from the same stable" as the seasoned politicians (Gotschim-Jauk 1990, 238–56). Moreover, in Becker's absence,

Bumballa had claimed the place of a representative of the resistance in the party's provisional executive board and thereby made it even more difficult for his old friend to find his place in politics.

The ÖVP was a conglomerate of three organizations representing the estates of businessmen, peasants, and employees. Becker did not feel at home in any of these groups and, together with the former O5 member Willy Thurn und Taxis, attempted to establish a "Free Union" as the party's fourth pillar (Gotschim-Jauk 1990, 257–58). Under the imprint of this group Becker published his perspective on the Austrian struggle for liberation from Hitler's Germany (Becker 1946a) and a similar booklet on administrative reform (Becker 1947), which drew in part upon his experience in Thomas Baťa's company and was to prove his competence in a central issue affecting the modern state.

Becker's activities on behalf of the "Free Union," which quietly disappeared from the political scene in 1947, were as futile as his endeavors to create an "apolitical front," which was to place the "well-being of Austria above party interests" (Gotschim-Jauk 1990, 258), and his attempt to unite on a permanent basis the members of the resistance in an "Austrian League of Democratic Freedom Fighters" in accordance with the lessons learned at the "Dachau college of political learning opportunities." For the league he also served as editor of the journal *Austria Rediviva*, of which only one issue was published in March 1946 before the organization disbanded (Gotschim-Jauk 1990, 259–63). Obviously such activities annoyed the party machine and further reduced Becker's chances for a political career.

The ÖVP delegated him in June 1945 to the political committee overseeing the public radio station RAVAG, expected him to write a popular commentary on the chapter about foreign policy in the party program, and counted on his support in the election campaign of 1945 (Gotschim-Jauk 1990, 253–54), but these were only crumbs instead of the anticipated loaf of bread.

To provide him with a basis of existence, he was appointed on 21 September by Eduard Heinl—his former boss at Tobis-Sascha and now once again secretary for Industry, Trade, and Transportation—as "future head" of an Austrian central agency for the promotion of tourism, but no salary was paid until February 1946, when he was given a monthly advance of 1,000 Austrian schilling, "subject to a later regulation of your income in accordance with your official position." On 1 October 1946 he was appointed honorary "head of the department for reconstruction in the office for the reconstruction of the Austrian tourism industry... regardless of your activity as a consultant for tourism." The "fictive date of the beginning of the employment" was specified as 15 March 1945, when Becker had been a prisoner of the Gestapo.[153] Bureaucracy, said to have been invented in its modern form by Empress Maria Theresia in the eighteenth century, had obviously survived the Corporative State and the Third Reich and was alive and well in the Second Austrian Republic. This appointment was certainly not what Becker had hoped for. In June 1946 he wrote to Karl Fiebrig, "I am presently active as representative for the reconstruction of tourism, have much trouble with it, and wish for a return to science."[154]

After the end of the war the reconstruction of the Museum of Ethnology in Vienna was largely and of necessity in the hands of Etta Becker-Donner and Annemarie (Schweeger-) Hefel. Fritz Röck and Walter Hirschberg (1904–1996) had lost their jobs because of their entanglement with national socialism, and Maria Horsky (1905–1950) had for the same reason gone into hiding. Heinz Kühne (1914–?) was for no good reason denied his job when he returned from military service, and the Korean scholar Han Hung-Su (1909–1953?) was employed only for the "duration of the war" (Schirmer 2013, 281).[155] Röck's successor Robert Bleichsteiner and Dominik Josef Wölfel, now back from his enforced retirement, were only a few years away from retirement, and new personnel was not hired before 1946.

Becker-Donner and Hefel were also the founding editors of the museum's journal *Archiv für Völkerkunde*, which was supposed to make a contribution to the "development of the great fraternization of humanity without regard to race and ethnic origin" (Bleichsteiner 1946, VI). The first volume, published in 1946, included only four contributions, including Hans Becker's last anthropological publication, "*Die Schmuckplatten der Calchaqui*" (The Ornamental Plates of the Calchaqui). Together with the three other authors (Josef Haekel, Martin Gusinde, Annemarie Hefel), Becker, who was tipped as the future director of the museum (Gotschim-Jauk 1990, 275), stood for a new beginning of Austrian anthropology, an honor he certainly owed to his wife, but also to the fact that his essay was readily available. With a few exceptions, it cites only literature published before 1931, and Becker had already offered it to Walter Krickeberg in 1943.[156]

The article was Becker's return to the beginning of his interest in the study of indigenous American cultures. It focused on the ornamental plate discovered by Juan Carlos Dávalos in 1923, which, together with sixteen other similar objects, he now submitted to a stylistic analysis and iconographic interpretation. As in his dissertation, the closing remarks express his concern about the likely disappearance of the old traditions in the wake of the "mental results of the newly constructed roads for cars in these valleys, still totally cordoned off at the time of my visit" (Becker 1946c, 180). Because Argentina had been largely isolated from Austria for the past several years, Becker was unaware of the publication by Dávalos (1937) on his researches in the 1920s, made in the company of Becker.

Even if Becker liked to refer to himself as an "ethnologist" ever since receiving his PhD, his ethnological legacy is small.[157] Of lasting value are primarily the ethnographic data from the Chaco published in his dissertation. His Calchaquí essay and his article on corn may also be regarded as scholarly works, although in view of the present state of our knowledge the latter has hardly any relevance anymore, even in the history of research on this subject. The remaining publications, whether in the *Zeitschrift für Geopolitik* or elsewhere, belong to the genre of feuilleton, to which he had devoted himself already prior to his training as an anthropologist. His unpublished fragment "*Weltkrieg der Dummheit*" (World War of Stupidity) is equally committed to this tradition, but represents a notable example of the diffusion of anthropological knowledge beyond the boundaries of the discipline. In addressing the general public rather than his fellow anthropologists, Becker stresses the importance of a "view from the outside," deplores the absence of anthropological insights in the "assessment of the European humanity," criticizes Sigmund Freud's abuse of dated anthropological theories in *Totem and Taboo*, and explains "culture" and "nationality" (in the present sense of ethnic identity) as historical processes (even if underpinned with the rather loose usage of terms taken from the culture-historical school, such as "Kulturschicht" and "Kulturkreis") (Becker MS, 7–8, 11–12).

After little more than a year, Becker's frustrations in his job for the development of tourism had become nearly unbearable, and he was looking for a new challenge. Raoul Bumballa, who had served as undersecretary of the interior in the provisional government of Austria, and Edmund Weber (1900–1949), formerly director of the "Official News Office" of the Corporative State and detained with Becker in Dachau, intervened with Chancellor Leopold Figl and Foreign Minister Karl Gruber to have their friend appointed to a position in the diplomatic service in South America. Since suitable persons with a good knowledge of Spanish were hard to find, Gruber took up the proposal and on 15 March 1947 assigned Becker to the embassy in Rio de Janeiro, the only Austrian diplomatic outpost in South America at that time. Here the fifty-two-year-old newcomer was supposed to breathe some diplomatic air and prepare himself for a more elevated position, perhaps in the new Austrian embassy in Buenos Aires (Gotschim-Jauk 1990, 276–79).

His new boss in Rio, Anton Retschek (1885–1950), would have preferred a young career diplomat as his assistant and was not at all pleased by the appointment of Becker, whose life was made very difficult by the "abysmal difference of character" between the two men. On 20 September 1947 Becker was sent to Buenos Aires, but only as a proxy until the arrival of the new envoy, and was finally appointed on 5 April 1948 as *chargé d'affaires* of the newly opened embassy in Santiago de Chile. The persisting insecurity about his final assignment and his appointment only as chargé d'affaires, rather than as ambassador, gave him cause for concern and were seen as impeding the effectiveness of his activities, yet he was able to convince the Foreign Office of his expert knowledge and skills (Gotschim-Jauk 1990, 279–87, 290).

Thanks to his previously acquired intimate knowledge of Latin American usage, he quickly took roots in Santiago. In the company of his wife and two daughters he was finally able to devote himself to an interesting and congenial activity and to look forward to the "truly peaceful existence in South America" his friend Hermann Schefter had bid him upon his appointment.[158]

On 18 December 1948, however, the Polish emigrant Leo Sikorsky, whose wife was employed as Becker's housekeeper, entered Becker's office. He requested verbally as well as in writing a retribution for alleged wrongs committed against him and the removal of his wife from the house of the chargé d'affaires. When Becker declined the request and attempted to escape, Sikorsky killed him with two pistol shots and then shot himself (Gotschim-Jauk 1990, 288).

The background of Becker's assassination has never been properly elucidated. Blackmail, jealousy, and political motives have been offered in explanation, but they are all devoid of evidence. Becker, who had earlier written about the astounding frequency of apparently pointless killings in Paraguay (Becker 1932b), had now become a victim of one himself.

POSTHUMOUS REPUTATION

Becker's assassination was received in Austria with dismay. Newspapers reported about the event without reference to Becker's former activities, whether as anthropologist or artist, in the Patriotic Front or in the resistance. In the conservative daily *Das Kleine Volksblatt* his old colleague Fritz Bock invited to attend the requiem for the deceased in St. Stephen's cathedral all those "who, like Becker, love their native country and wish for its freedom" (Gotschim-Jauk 1990, 289). Only the initiated could understand the meaning of these words.

No professional anthropological journal published an obituary, if only because in the absence of an institutional affiliation of Becker nobody felt obligated to do so. The response to his publications was likewise muted, not only because all of his writings had been published in German and were thus increasingly inaccessible to international research. The time of publication of his dissertation in the *Zeitschrift für Ethnologie* was responsible for the lack of its consideration in Alfred Métraux's synthesis of the ethnography of the Chaco—definitive for a long time to come—in the *Handbook of South American Indians*, in which other German research is cited copiously (Métraux 1948).[159] Readers of the Vienna museum's journal *Archiv für Völkerkunde* found Becker mentioned in Martin Gusinde's historical summary of ethnographic research in South America (Gusinde 1946, 69, 77–78); others had to wait for Timothy O'Leary's *Ethnographic Bibliography of South America*, where, however, his publication did not receive the coveted asterisk for "significant works" (O'Leary 1963, 229). Čestimir Loukotka (1968, 57) referred to him in connection with linguistic data, despite their near-absence in Becker's writings. The recent ethnographic literature appears to have forgotten Hans Becker. Branislava Súsnik (1920–1996), the native Slovenian anthropologist and reader of German literature who, in the decades after World War II, became the unquestioned authority in this field, does not cite him in any of her works, including those dealing specifically with the Lengua (Súsnik 1977, 1979–85; Súsnik and Chase-Sardi 1994).

Upon her return from Chile, his Africanist widow had to change her regional focus to the Americas, because the position of an Africanist at the museum was already occupied by her friend Annemarie Hefel. Her first publication in the new field dealt with the museum's archaeological collection from the Diaguita and Calchaquí, the very region of Argentina where Hans Becker had first become interested in the archaeology and folklore of South America. This article lists Becker's unrelated dissertation in the bibliography, but does not cite it in the text (Becker-Donner 1950–52). She kept faith with him until the end. In one of her last publications, accompanying an exhibition on the ethnography of South America, her husband's dissertation at least appears in the bibliography (Becker-Donner 1973).

"Some things are taking a rather long time in Austria," Becker (1946a, 39) wrote toward the end of his account of Austria's struggle for freedom, "even the appreciation of the dead."

NOTES

Abbreviations of Archival Repositories

- AWW Archiv des Weltmuseums Wien [Archive of the Weltmuseum Wien, Vienna]
- DAW Diözesanarchiv Wien [Archive of the Diocese of Vienna]
- DÖW Dokumentationsarchiv des österreichischen Widerstands [Documentation archive of Austrian resistance, Vienna]
- ÖNB Österreichische Nationalbibliothek [Austrian National Library, Vienna]

PACL   Privatarchiv Christoph Lechner [Private archive Christoph Lechner, Vienna]
PAFL   Privatarchiv Franka Lechner [Private archive Franka Lechner, Vienna]
UAW   Universitätsarchiv Wien [Archive of the University of Vienna].

1. A PhD dissertation submitted to the University of Vienna (Gotschim-Jauk 1990) offers a useful summary of Becker's life, but devotes little space to his activities as an anthropologist, partly because of its author's lack of expertise in this field. Except in cases where different conclusions are drawn from the sources, general data on Becker are here cited after this dissertation, even when the underlying archival sources were independently consulted (Archive of the University of Vienna, Documentation Center of Austrian Resistance, private archive of Franka Lechner).
2. An abbreviated German version of this essay will be published in a volume dealing with Austrian anthropology during the period of national socialism (Feest in press), which regrettably will not contribute to a better understanding of this complex chapter in the history of anthropology by those unable to read German.
3. Special thanks are due to Franka Lechner, one of Hans Becker's daughters, for her readiness to give me access to documents in her possession and to place them in the context of family history, as well as my colleague Barbara Plankensteiner and her husband Christoph Lechner (Hans Becker's grandson) for additional material assembled by them.
4. Family tree of Moritz Alois Theodor Becker, PAFL.
5. See also PAFL, k.k. Staats-Gymnasium Pola, final report card for Hans Sidonius Becker, 5 July 1913.
6. Becker (MS, 13, 19–21). This text, written in pencil, is the beginning of an unfinished attempt to interpret the developments leading to World War II in front of the backdrop of personal experiences.
7. Certificates of colloquia and attendance for Hans Becker, University of Vienna, winter term 1913/14, summer term 1914, PAFL.
8. Deutschösterreichisches Staatsamt für Heerwesen, Certificate for Hans Becker, 1 March 1919, DÖW, 12032/1a.
9. K.k. Staatsprüfungskommission, state exam certificate for Hans Becker, 14 October 1919; Dekan der Fakultät für Rechts-und Staatswissenschaften, Universität Wien, certificate for Hans Becker, 25 October 1919, both in PAFL.

10. Technische Hochschule in Wien, legitimation card for Hans Becker, 18 November 1927, PACL.
11. Bundeskommissariat für den Heimatdienst [Federal Commissariat for Homeland Service], official instruction, 16 July 1934, DÖW, 12032/1b.
12. Anonymous 1938; Kommandatur des Staatlichen Konzentrationslagers Mauthausen, certificate of release for Hans Becker, 19 December 1940, PAFL.
13. Devisenzentrale to Hans Becker, 20 May 1920; Devisenzentrale, employment reference letter for Hans Becker, 7 October 1920; Gefex, employment reference letter for Hans Becker, 1 February 1921; Treuga, employment reference letter for Hans Becker, 22 October 1922, all in DÖW, 12032/1b.
14. Dely to Becker, 23 October 1922; Verband Österreichischer Banken und Bankiers, employment reference letter for Hans Becker, 23 October 1922, both in DÖW, 12032/1b.
15. Schefter to Becker, 21 October 1948, PAFL.
16. See, e.g., Anonymous 1921: "Never before in my life I have seen the plutocracy assembled in such exponential form as in the open-air theater in front of the church."
17. Hans Becker, résumé, undated [ca. 1941], DÖW, 12032/8.
18. Becker to Fiebrig, 22 October 1941, DÖW, 12032/8.
19. At the request of Alma Mahler-Werfel, Becker interceded with the mayor of Vienna, Theodor Körner, on behalf of a grave of honor at the central cemetery of Vienna for Alma's recently deceased third husband, the poet Franz Werfel (Mahler-Werfel to Becker, 18 March 1946; Becker to Mahler-Werfel, 17 May 1946; Becker to Körner, 17 May 1946, all in DÖW, 12032/7).
20. Frank (2007, 77, 253). Similarly divergent views are found in the reports of Viennese journals, and even in the same journal: "The achievements of this young lady . . . were greeted with rapturous applause" (*Deutsches Volksblatt* 32 [11386]: 8 [18 September 1920]). "Among the many dance artists demanding their art to be rated as such, Annie Lieser is not. While she distinguishes herself by the exquisite taste of her costumes, the same cannot be said of her dancing. She is lacking in technique and spirit, and one may well ask why she refers to her movements as dance" (*Deutsches Volksblatt* 33 [11756]: 9 [2 October 1921]).
21. Lieser (Becker) to Korngold, 4 February 1927, ÖNB, Handschrift 939–3/2.

22. Becker's résumé attached to his application for admission to his PhD oral exams (and appearing in abbreviated form in his dissertation) erroneously gives the year of his emigration as 1921 and that of his return to 1928 (UAW, Phil.Fak., doctoral record 15.567); these dates were published by Gusinde (1946, 77). A little later Becker even refers to his sojourn in South America as having lasted "nearly eight years" instead of close to five (Becker MS, 4).
23. The headline has been taken from the table of contents of Becker (MS). The corresponding chapter was unfortunately never written.
24. On Ludwig and his later relationship with Becker, see Urbanek (2011, 14–15, 18) and the account given below.
25. Ludwig, certificate about Becker's assignment, 1922–1928, 10 October 1946, later redated to 10 May 1946, DÖW, 12032/4. This is the only source for the duration and legal basis of Becker's position as correspondent of the Federal Press Service. The certificate was obviously issued in connection with the allowance of previous work for the government on the occasion of Becker's appointment at the Department of Commerce on 1 October 1946 and was based on an "official recollection" by Ludwig. This also explains why Becker's return to Europe was certified to have been on 1 March 1928, although he had actually returned in October 1927. Since Becker had started to work for the Spritzer company on 1 March, the certificate provided evidence for an unbroken chain of employment and insurance.
26. Ludwig to General Consulate in Buenos Aires, 23 October 1922, DÖW, 12032/1a.
27. Passport for Hans Becker, 28 August 1922, DÖW, 12032/1aPolizeidirektion Wien.
28. Becker (1941a: V; 1946c, 164, 173, 178); , Hans Becker, untitled and undated lecture manuscript [probably 1942], PAFL.
29. Hans Becker, résumé, undated [c. 1941], DÖW, 12032/8.
30. Hans Becker, résumé, undated [c. 1941], DÖW, 12032/8.
31. The role of the Catholic missionaries in this "biased abbreviation" is not discussed by Becker.
32. Designations in square brackets are the currently common self-designations (with variations) in Paraguay or linguistic designations. In the case of the Lengua, Becker (1941, 365, 367) notes the self-designations *Einzelt* or *Enzelt* ("human beings"), but opts against their use, because they are identical with those used by other Mascoy groups and therefore impractical for the designation of specific "tribes."

33. Gusinde to Becker, 11 and 18 November 1944, DÖW, 12032/6.
34. Hans Becker, undated watercolor (Feest in press), PAFL.
35. Hans Becker, undated notes on the ethnography of the Lengua and their neighbors, PAFL.
36. Becker to Fiebrig, 22 August 1941 and 26 October 1942; Fiebrig to Becker, 25 August 1942, DÖW, 12032/7.
37. This subtitle was only added in 1941 (see note 102 below).
38. Lieser to Korngold, 24 November 1926, ÖNB, Handschrift 934–41/7.
39. Lieser (Becker) to Korngold, 4 February 1927, ÖNB, Handschrift 934–41/7; Landgericht Wien, annulment of marriage Hans von Becker/Anna Becker, 31 May 1941, DÖW, 12032/1a.
40. Lieser (Becker) to Korngold, 8 July and 14 September 1927, ÖNB, Handschriften 934–41/3 and 5.
41. Compañía Internacional de Productos to Becker, 20 August 1927, DÖW, 12032/1a.
42. Lieser (Becker) to Korngold, 8 July and 14 September 1927, ÖNB, Handschriften 934–41/3 and 5.
43. A very similar assessment is found in an article published in 1934, where he identifies the death of Viktor Adler (1852–1918), who was succeeded as chairman of the Social Democratic Party by Otto Bauer (1881–1938), as the possible reason for the different tone after the party had reached "positions of power in Vienna and Austria" (Becker 1934c). Friedrich Austerlitz (1862–1931) had been editor-in-chief of the *Arbeiter-Zeitung* since 1895.
44. Freiheitsplatz (today, Rooseveltplatz).
45. Arnold Spritzer (1882–?) escaped from persecution by the Nazis as a Jew by emigrating in 1938 (Jüdisches Museum Hohenems 2014).
46. Magistrat der Bundeshauptstadt Wien, certificate of driving test for Hans Becker, 24 February 1928, PAFL.
47. AG für Bauwesen, employment reference letter for Hans Becker, 4 May 1929, DÖW, 12032/1a.
48. *Reichspost* 34 (321): 11 [24 November 1927]; *Neuigkeits-Welt-Blatt* 54 (270): 5 [26 November 1927].
49. *Reichspost* 37 (342): 7 [12 December 1930].
50. Zentralverband Bildender Künstler Österreichs, share certificate 1087 for Hans Becker, 5 April 1929, PAFL. On 25 May 1938, when Becker was already in a concentration camp, the organization reminded him of his outstanding dues for 1937 (PAFL).

51. Hans Becker, résumé, undated [ca. 1941], DÖW, 12032/8. Such lectures cannot presently be verified.
52. Baťa's enthusiasm for aviation suggests Becker may have been introduced to Baťa by Hermann Schefter, himself a Moravian industrialist and founder of the German Aviation Association of Czechoslovakia (Engelmann 2015).
53. Bundespolizei Wien, certificate of good conduct and visa for Argentina, 28 May 1929, PAFL; T. & A. Baťa, employment reference letter for Hans Becker, 2 November 1929, DÖW, 12032/1a.
54. *Reichspost* 36 (315) [29 November 1929].
55. *Neues Wiener Tagblatt* 64 (15): 11 [16 January 1930]; *Wiener Zeitung* 227 (13): 7 [17 January 1930].
56. Bundeskommissariat für den Heimatdienst, official instruction, 16 July 1934, , , and Vaterländische Front, official instruction, 29 December 1934, all in DÖW, 12032/1b. The Geographical Society in Vienna even made Becker a PhD when announcing his lecture (invitation, 20 November 1934, Geographische Gesellschaft, PAFL).
57. Gewerbeförderungsinstitut/Hochschule für Welthandel in Wien, Report card for Hans Becker (advertising law), 14 February 1930; Hochschule für Welthandel in Wien, registration sheet for Hans Becker, summer term 1930; Gewerbeförderungsdienst des Bundesministeriums für Handel und Verkehr, report card for Hans Becker (advertising training course), 2 July 1930, all in PAFL. Becker passed the exams with an A. During this period of time, Becker also wrote a series of short book reviews relating to business and economic matters for an unidentified periodical (undated clippings and manuscripts, [c. 1930–32], PAFL).
58. Becker appears to have been the only Austrian anthropologist among the freemasons. A list of the members of the Vienna lodges prior to 1938 (Kodek 2009) does not include anyone—except for Schefter—known to have played a significant role in Becker's personal or professional life. Robert Bleichsteiner joined the lodge "Humanitas renata," of which Becker was a member in 1945/6, in 1946. The same is true for Hermann Michel, another member of the resistance group at the Museum of Natural History (Kodek 2014, 25, 160). For Bleichsteiner and Michel, see below.
59. Bisanz (1975, 29) gives 1932–35 as the years of Becker's membership; Becker states that he was a member from 1928 to 1938 (résumé, undated [ca. 1946], PAFL).
60. Collector's file, Alexander Langer, AWW.

61. *Wiener Salonblatt*, 61 (23): 9 [9 November 1930].
62. "Ethnography" had been taught at the University of Vienna since the late 1880s and an *"Institut für Anthropologie und Ethnographie"* [Department of (Physical) Anthropology and Ethnography] was established in 1919 (Feest 1995, 124–27).
63. Registration forms of Hans Becker, winter term 1931/2 to summer term 1934, UAW, Phil.Fak.
64. Doctoral record 15.567; Hans Becker, résumé, July 1941, UAW, Phil.Fak.
65. Hans Becker, Kultur der Chaco Indianer, incomplete and undated manuscript [probably 1934], PAFL.
66. Alfred Rinnerthaler, personal communication, 2015. Until early 1935 Schmidt was chairman of the Vienna Circle of Friends (see *Mitteilungen des Katholischen Universitätsvereins Salzburg* 1934/35 [6]: 9).
67. On Bernatzik and his later involvement with national socialism, see the account of his daughter Doris Byer (1999), herself an anthropologist.
68. Registration forms of Hugo Bernatzik, winter term 1931/2 and summer term 1932; registration forms of Emmy Bernatzik, winter term 1932/3 and summer term 1934, UAW, Phil.Fak.
69. Haekel (1956, 1); *Arbeiter-Zeitung* 44 (320): 10 [20 November 1931] and 44 (322): 19 [22 November 1931]; *Radio Wien* 8 (7): 16 [13 November 1931].
70. Becker should also have been interested in the public lecture on 25 August 1928 by another Swedish anthropologist, Gustaf Bolinder (1888–1957), who had done fieldwork in Colombia (*Reichspost* 35[56]: 9 [25 February 1928]; "Indianer ohne Romantik," *Das kleine Blatt* 2 [118]: 8–9 [28 April 1928]), although this occurred prior to Becker's academic interest in anthropology.
71. Angelika Heinrich, personal communication, 2015.
72. *Mitteilungen der Anthropologischen Gesellschaft in Wien* 63 (1933), Sitzungsberichte: [14]. Compare Horwitz 1920.
73. *Mitteilungen der Anthropologischen Gesellschaft in Wien* 67 (1937), Sitzungsberichte: [30].
74. Obermeier (2012, 241–52); Fiebrig to Becker, 13 March and 25 August 1941, DÖW, 12032/7.
75. Lifezis to Becker, 2 November 1948, PAFL.
76. *Wiener Zeitung* (246), Amtsblatt: 720 [22 October 1932].
77. *Jedermann* to Becker, 16 November 1932, PAFL.
78. Also broadcast by the Vienna radio station RAVAG on 25 December 1934, *Radio Wien*, 15 [10]: 53 [1934].
79. Hans Becker, affidavit, 8 November 1948, PAFL.

80. *Arbeiter-Zeitung* 46 (94): 3 [5 April 1933].
81. It is not without a certain irony that Becker's former employer Karpeles had tried to prove the absolute incompatibility of the Fascist state with the papal encyclical *Quadragesimo anno* of 1931, whereas in a booklet of the Homeland Service edited by his new boss Kruckenhauser, the same encyclical was declared to be the ideological foundation of the Corporative State (Karpeles 1933; Schmitz 1933).
82. Versicherungsanstalt der Presse, registration of Hans Sidonius Becker, 21 July 1933, PAFL.
83. Vaterländische Front, Order 6, 29 December 1933, and official instruction, 1 January 1934, Bundeskommissariat für den Heimatdienst, official instruction, 16 July 1934; Versicherungsanstalt der Presse to Becker, 10 August 1934,all in DÖW, 12032/1a,
84. For an early overview of the Austrian resistance against national socialism, see Engel-Jánosi (1934), who extensively cites Becker (1946a) as a source. Engel-Jánosi correctly points to the "anti-Prussian" sentiments prevailing in Austria since 1866 as a significant factor in the anti-Nazi stance of many Austrians. This is certainly also true for Becker.
85. After the occupation of Austria by Hitler the Masonic lodges were liquidated in 1938. In 1945 Becker at first rejoined the collective lodge "Humanitas renata" and in 1946 his old lodge "Zukunft" (Patka 2010, 116).
86. In the registers of the responsible parish St. Paul (Wien-Döbling) there is no record of this marriage, either on the date later claimed by Becker, or at any other time between 1932 and 1936 (Matricula online).
87. *Österreichische Film-Zeitung* 1936 (46): 1 [13 November 1936]. Becker's deletion from the trade register occurred in May 1938 (*Neues Wiener Tagblatt* 72 [147]: 5 [29 May 1938]).
88. *Österreichische Film-Zeitung* 1937 (28): 3 [9 July 1937].
89. *Variety* 127 (8): 12 [1937]; Almanac 1937; Burke (2012, 68–69, 92, 111–54).
90. Pfarramt St. Paul, Wien-Döbling, certificate of baptism for Johann Nikolaus Becker, 24 September 1936, PAFL.
91. Lieser (Becker) to Kornblum, 30 March 1937, ÖNB, Handschrift 934–41/6.
92. Angestelltenversicherung für Handel, Verkehr und öffentlichen Dienst, notice of cancellation of insurance for Hans Becker, 18 May 1938, PAFL.
93. The most extensive account of Becker's experiences in the Dachau and Mauthausen concentration camps is found in his testimony of May 1945 before an American commission to investigate war crimes (Rath-

kolb 1985, 29–34). The circumstances and details of Becker's detention in Dachau are summarized in Gotschim-Jauk (1990, 111–34).

94. Consulate General for Paraguay in London, memorandum relating to entry permit in Paraguay for Hans Becker, 2 February 1939, PAFL.
95. On Becker's detention in Mauthausen see Gotschim-Jauk (1990: 135–139); see also Becker's own account in Rathkolb (1985, 32–34).
96. Hans Becker, affidavit, 10 October 1948, DÖW, 12032/5.
97. In the winter term 1929/30 she also took Chinese for Beginners, taught by Becker's "uncle" Arthur Rosthorn (Universität Wien, enrollment book of Violetta Jelinek-Donner, 1928–33, PAFL).
98. Enrollment record of Hans Becker, 1931–1933, UAW, Phil.Fak..; Universität Wien, enrollment book of Violetta Jelinek-Donner, 1928–1933, PAFL.
99. Plankensteiner (2011a,. 19) assumes Becker may have used his political influence already in the course of her preparations for her first trip to Liberia.
100. Landgericht Wien, annulment of marriage Hans von Becker/Anna Becker, 31 May 1941, DÖW, 12032/1a.
101. Donner to Becker, 12 February 1941, PAFL.
102. Becker to Mahler-Werfel, 17 May 1946, DÖW, 12032/7, ; Franka Lechner, personal communication, 2015.
103. Donner to Becker, 10 January 1941, PAFL.
104. Becker to Fiebrig, 22 August 1941, DÖW, 12032/7; ; Universität Wien, report card for Philosophy, for Hans Becker, 21 May 1941, PAFL.
105. A manuscript version of the dissertation (PACL) appears to represent this state. It has some corrections by Becker as well as additions in Donner's hand—nearly all of them relating to details of Lengua ethnography, thus identifying the additions as dictations by Becker. The title of the dissertation was changed, in Donner's hand, from "Die Maskoistämme des Gran Chaco und ihre Nachbarn" [The Mascoy Tribes of the Gran Chaco and Their Neighbors] to "Lengua und Kaiotuguí. Indianerstudien im Chaco Boreal."
106. The references to Krickeberg were possibly added only in 1941, particularly since the bibliography also includes Krickeberg 1939, which is not cited in the dissertation itself. Krickeberg was an anthropologist with strong affinities to the German culture-historical school of anthropology, but also a Nazi sympathizer and former colleague of Hermann Baumann at the museum in Berlin.
107. Donner to Becker, 12 February 1941, PAFL.
108. Becker to Fiebrig, 22 August 1941, DÖW, 12032/7.

109. The preface is dated June 1941 and the résumé July 1941 (Becker 1941a, 3, V).
110. Doctoral record 15.567, UAW, Phil. Fak..
111. In a more extensive résumé attached to his application for admission to the final exams, the delay of the submission of the dissertation five years after the absolutorium is merely explained by "work orders for various organizations of the former federal state" (doctoral record 15.567, UAW, Phil. Fak.).
112. There is no evidence for the assertion that Baldus's books had been burned by the Nazis (Becker 1972, 1308). They were apparently also not included on the blacklist of prohibited literature (see Fischer 1990a, 191–92).
113. Doctoral record 15.567, Hermann Baumann, report on Becker's dissertation, 30 June 1941, UAW, Phil. Fak.; Becker (1941b, 358).
114. Becker to Fiebrig, 22 August 1941, DÖW, 12032/7.
115. Doctoral record 15.567, UAW, Phil. Fak..
116. Becker to Fiebrig, 22 August 1941, DÖW, 12032/7.
117. Christian to Becker, 28 April 1942, PAFL.
118. Becker to Krickeberg, 21 March 1942; Krickeberg to Becker, 28 March and 25 July 1942, DÖW, 12032/8.
119. Nevermann to Becker, 5 October 1942; Becker to Nevermann, [mid-October 1942], DÖW, 12032/8.
120. Württembergischer Verein für Handelsgeographie to Becker, 13 August, 26 August, 4 September, 11 September 1942; Becker to Württembergischer Verein für Handelsgeographie, 6 September 1942, DÖW, 12032/8.
121. Andreas Reischek (1845–1902) was an Austrian amateur ornithologist who had done fieldwork in New Zealand between 1887 and 1889, assembled a huge ethnographic collection now in Vienna, and has become most notorious for having robbed a Maori grave (e.g., King 1981, Kolig 1985).
122. Although Wölfel had supported the Corporative State in a less prominent way than Becker, his academic career was essentially blocked by Viktor Christian and Oswald Menghin, who had no problem with Becker.
123. Klaus Vowinkel to Becker, 9 September 1941, DÖW, 12032/6.
124. Vowinkel to Becker, 25 January 1944; Becker to Vowinkel, 29 January 1944, DÖW, 12032/6.
125. *Zeitschrift für Geopolitik* to Becker, 29 March 1943; Vowinkel to Becker, 12 April and 5 May 1944, DÖW, 12032/6.

126. Vowinkel to Becker, 31 May and 30 November 1943; Becker to Schwarz, 22 May 1943, DÖW, 12032/6.
127. Becker to Krickeberg, 21 March 1942, DÖW, 12032/8.
128. Strobl (*Kunst dem Volk*) to Becker, 4 January 1943, and certification of "Dr. Hans Becker having worked for us as a freelancer," 16 March 1943, DÖW, 12032/7.
129. The Ernst Reinhardt Verlag was shut down by the national socialists in 1944 (Wikipedia 2015b).
130. Ernst Reinhardt Verlag to Becker, 4 August and 16 November 1943, DÖW, 12032/8.
131. Schöningh Verlag to Becker, 23 September and 12 December 1944, DÖW, 12032/8.
132. Oswald Arnold Verlag, Verlagsvertrag mit Hans Becker, 17 March 1944, 12032/6.
133. Kühn to Becker, 25 April 1944; Becker to Kühn, 2 May 1944, DÖW, 12032/6.
134. Becker to Kühn, 26 May 1944, DÖW, 12032/6.
135. Kühn to Becker, 25 April 1944; Becker to Kühn, 26 May 1944, DÖW, 12032/6.
136. Reichskammer der bildenden Künste to Becker, 27 April 1942; Gotschim-Jauk (1990, 148), DÖW, 12032/8.
137. Thäte to Becker, 7 January and 20 April 1943; Becker to Thäte, 18 April 1943, DÖW, 12032/8.
138. Catalog of pictures, 1942: one watercolor, 62 by 120 cm; collector's file H. Becker, Post XIII/1943: two watercolors, 45 by 80 cm and 45 by 95 cm, AWW.
139. Becker to Fiebrig, 26 October 1942, DÖW, 12032/6.
140. His painting "Procession (Crucifixion)," recently dated without good reason in the 1930s (Husslein-Arco 2014, 293), is more likely to stem from Becker's period as a church painter, 1942–44.
141. Finanzkammer der Erzdiözese Wien (Alois Penall) to Pfarramt Breitensee, 26 March, 2 June, 29 June, and 16 December 1943; Becker to Finanzkammer der Erzdiözese Wien, 7 August 1944, DAW, Bauamt 73/2, Breitensee bei Marchegg, 1941–1969, S/IV-172–1942.
142. Finanzkammer der Erzdiözese Wien (Alois Penall) to Pfarramt Alberndorf, 20 July 1943; Finanzkammer der Erzdiözese Wien to Becker, 23 July 1943; Alois Penall, File memos, 3 August, 6 September, and 27 October 1943; Becker to Finanzkammer der Erzdiözese Wien, 12 January 1944; Parish chronicle Alberndorf, vol. 2 (1929–1986), 46–

47 (microfilm), DAW, Bauamt 63/3, Alberndorf 1943–1970, S/IV-1085–1943.
143. Unfortunately, neither the paintings in Breitensee nor those in Alberndorf have been preserved (Christoph Lechner, personal communication, 2016).
144. Finanzkammer der Erzdiözese Wien (Alois Penall) to Pfarramt St. Hubertus, 8 January 1944; receipts of payments to Becker, DAW, Bauamt, St. Hubertus 1940–1969, S/III-275–1941.
145. It is unknown whether Becker completed the pictures prior to his arrest on 28 February 1945, after his return to Vienna on 4 June, or at all. The last payment recorded in the files of the archdiocese is dated 18 May. At that time 1,900 reichsmark of the contractual total were still due.
146. Hans Becker, affidavit, 10 October 1948, DÖW, 12032/5.
147. Kattus to Becker, 3 September, 1 October 1942, and 18 March 1945; Becker to Kattus, 19 October 1942, DÖW, 12032/7.
148. Hans Becker, fee note to Heinz Patzas, bookbinder, 18 March 1942, for "implementation of a plant engineering plan of your business," DÖW, 12032/8.
149. Becker (1946a, 13); Hans Becker, affidavit, 10 October 1948, DÖW, 12032/5.
150. Linimayr (1994, 169–72); W. Schmidt (1949, 248–53); Hermann Michel, report about salvage operations [after 1945], DÖW, 12032/3, .
151. Linimayr (1994, 171–73); Hans Becker, report about resistance activities of Hermann Michel [after 1945], 2, DÖW, 12032/3, .
152. By coincidence Draws-Tychsen was relocated from Sachsenhausen to Mauthausen on 16 February 1945 (Fischer 2004, 140), but was moved to a work assignment in Amstetten prior to Becker's arrival (Hellmuth Draws-Tychsen, Das nationalsozialistische Konzentrationslager und die europäische Jugend, excerpts from a lecture given on 27 October 1945 at the Österreichische Kulturvereinigung in Vienna, PACL). This typescript, found among Becker's papers, indicates that the two men met again in Vienna after the end of the war.
153. Staatsamt für Industrie, Gewerbe, Handel und Verkehr to Becker, 21 September 1945; Präsidium des Bundesministeriums für Handel und Wiederaufbau to Becker, 5 February 1946; Stelle für den Wiederaufbau der Österreichischen Fremdenverkehrswirtschaft to Becker, 1 October 1946; Bundesminister für Handel und Wiederaufbau to Becker, 7 December 1946, PAFL; Gotschim-Jauk (1990, 270–73; see also Becker 1946b).
154. Becker to Fiebrig, 15 June 1946, DÖW, 12032/6.

155. Heinz Kühne, personal communication, 1978.
156. Becker to Krickeberg, 5 April 1943, DÖW, 12032/7.
157. Becker (MS, 20). According to Fischer (2004, 144–45), the self-designation "*Ethnologe*" (instead of "*Völkerkundler*"), also used by Draws-Tychsen, was rather unusual at that time. However, the German flagship of the discipline had been the *Zeitschrift für Ethnologie* since 1869.
158. Schefter to Becker, 4 March 1947, PAFL.
159. The preface of this volume is dated October 1944.

REFERENCES

Agstner, Rudolf. 2015. *Handbuch des Österreichischen Auswärtigen Dienstes* 1: 1918–1938. Wien: LIT.

Alarcón y Cañedo, José, and Riccardo Pittini. 1924. *El Chaco paraguayo y sus tribus: apuntes etnográficos y leyendas; la misión Salesiana*. Torino: Soc. Ed. Internacional.

Almanac. 1937. *International Motion Picture Almanac 1937–38*. New York: William Hastings.

Anonymous. 1887. "Hofrath Ritter v. Becker†." *Die Presse* 40 (230): 2. Wien 1887.

———. 1921. "Die Jedermann-Festspiele." *Tagblatt* (Linz) 1921(180): 6 [21 August 1921].

———. 1927. "Kolonisationsland Paraguay." *Neuigkeits-Welt-Blatt* 54 (270): 5 [26 November 1927].

———. 1931. "World's Workers." *Seamen's Journal* 45 (7): 220.

———. 1938. ". . . doch sie leben alle noch." *Das schwarze Korps* 10: 16.

———. 2003. "Mährens Rückkehr nach Europa." *Neue Zürcher Zeitung*, 13 November 2003.

———. [c. 1986]. *50 Jahre St. Hubertus + St. Christophorus*. N.p.

Arthaber, Gustav von. 1935. "Auszug aus dem Jahresberichte." *Mitteilungen der Geographischen Gesellschaft in Wien* 78: 314–317.

Baldus, Herbert. 1931a. *Indianerstudien im nordöstlichen Chaco*. Leipzig: C. L. Hirschfeld.

———. 1931b. *Madame Lynch*. Berlin: Büchergilde Gutenberg.

———. 1954. *Bibliografia crítica da etnologia Brasileira* vol. 1. São Paulo: Servicio de Comemorações Culturais.

Baldus-Hasselpflug, U. 1933. *Im Herzen Südamerikas*. Berlin: Büchergilde Gutenberg.

Becher, Hans. 1970. "Herbert Baldus." *Zeitschrift für Ethnologie* 95: 157–63.

———. 1972. "Herbert Baldus, 1899–1970." *American Anthropologist* n.s. 74 (5): 1307–12.

Becker, Hans S. 1925. Bilder aus Paraguay. Paraguari, im Januar 1925. *Argentinisches Tageblatt*. (Clipping in PAFL.)

———. 1926a. "Rainer Maria Rilke†." *Deutsche Blätter* 1 (3): 45–46.

———. 1926b. "Historische Streiflichter zur Flaggenfrage." *Deutsche Blätter* 1 (3): 47–49.

———. 1926c. "Skizzen aus dem Innern Südamerikas." *Deutsche Blätter* 1 (3): 57–59.

———. 1928a. "Unter den Indianern des Chaco." *Neues Wiener Tagblatt* 62 (11): 3–5 [11 January 1928].

———. 1928b. "Der Kampf um den Chaco. Der Konflikt zwischen Paraguay und Bolivien." *Die Stunde* 6 (1735): 6 [22 December 1928].

———. 1929. "Zwischen Wasser und Durst. Reise in Bolivien." *Die Bühne* (Vienna) 219: 44, 51–52.

———. 1930a. "Luxus und 'Lujo.'" *Neues Wiener Tagblatt* 64 (51): 23 [21 February 1930].

———. 1930b. "Angelito." *Neues Wiener Tagblatt* 64 [29 October 1930].

———. 1931. "Ackerbauminister will auswandern." *Neuigkeits-Welt-Blatt* 58 (47): 1, 7 [26 February 1931].

———. 1932a. "[Review of] Herbert Baldus, Indianerstudien im nordöstlichen Chaco, 1931." *Anthropos* 27 (3–4): 679–81.

———. 1932b. "Menschen im Gran Chaco." *Neuigkeits-Welt-Blatt* 59 (247): 9–10 [23 October 1932].

———. 1932c. "Der Streit um den Gran Chaco." *Jedermann* 1 (10): 3 [10 December 1932].

———. 1932d. "Weihnachten im Sommer." *Jedermann* 1 (12): 4 [24 December 1932].

———. 1933a. "Tanz durch Jahrhunderte. Zur Ausstellung 'Der Tanz' im Hagenbund." *Jedermann* 2 (8): 5 [19 February 1933].

———. 1933b. "Der nördliche Chaco." *Radio-Wien* 12 (14): 8 [29 December 1933].

———. 1934a. "In den Urwäldern und Sümpfen des Gran Chaco." *Radiowoche* 11 (1) [1 January 1934].

———. 1934b. "Indianer Südamerikas [Book reviews]." *Neues Wiener Tagblatt* 68 [20 December 1934].

———. 1934c. "Arbeiterschaft und Presse." *Arbeitsfriede* (= Österreichische Volksschriften 4): 40–42.

———. 1941a. "Lengua und Kaiotuguí. Indianerstudien im Chaco Boreal." PhD diss., University of Vienna.

———. 1941b [1943]. "Lengua und Kaiotuguí. Indianerstudien im Chaco Boreal. Erster Teil." *Zeitschrift für Ethnologie* 73: 358–415.

———. 1942a [1944]. "Lengua und Kaiotuguí. Indianerstudien im Chaco Boreal. Zweiter Teil." *Zeitschrift für Ethnologie* 74: 70–111.

———. 1942b. "Spanisch-Südamerikas gewachsene Vielfalt." *Zeitschrift für Geopolitik* 19 (9): 404–412.

———. 1943. "Der karibische Bereich." *Zeitschrift für Geopolitik* 20 (4–5).

———. 1944a. "Der Großraum Brasilien." *Zeitschrift für Geopolitik* 21 (2): 59–64.

———. 1944b. "Zur Frage der geschichtsbildenden Elemente." *Zeitschrift für Geopolitik* 21 (3): 113–15.

———. 1944c. "Der Ursprung des Mais und seine Bedeutung für Amerikas Kulturen." *Zeitschrift für Geopolitik* 21 (4): 151–57.

———. 1944d. "Die Malerfamilie Marko." *Kunst dem Volk* 6 (11–12): 36–41.

———. 1946a. *Österreichs Freiheitskampf: Die Widerstandsbewegung in ihrer historischen Bedeutung*. Wien: Verlag der Freien Union der Ö.V.P.

———. 1946b. "Um den Wiederaufbau des Fremdenverkehrs in Österreich." *Österreichische Monatshefte* 5 (February 1946): 190–92.

———. 1946c. "Die Schmuckplatten der Calchaqui." *Archiv für Völkerkunde* 1: 164–88.

———. 1947. *Reform oder Neubau? Zur Verwaltungsreform*. Wien: Verlag der Freien Union der Ö.V.P.

———. Ms. "Weltkrieg der Dummheit." Undated manuscript [ca. 1945]. PAFL.

Becker-Donner, Etta. 1950–52. "Die nordwestargentinischen Sammlungen des Wiener Museums für Völkerkunde." *Archiv für Völkerkunde* 5: 1–103, 7: 229–362.

———. 1973. *Indianer in Südamerika*. Museum für Völkerkunde: Wien.

Berlichingen, Adolf. 1884. *Gabriel Garcia Moreno, Präsident der Republik Ecuador: Ein Leben im Dienst des Königtums Jesu Christi*. Einsiedeln: Benziger.

Bermann, Richard Anton. 1932a. "Der Lugende Elch." *Jedermann* 1 (3): 8–9.

———. 1932b. "Ein moderner Indianer." *Jedermann* 1 (9): 8–9.

Bernatzik, Hugo Adolf. 1933. "Mädchenraub am oberen Nil." *Jedermann* 2, no. 9 (1933): 8–9.

Bisanz, Hans. 1975. *Der Hagenbund*. Wien: Museen der Stadt Wien.

Blaschitz, Edith. 1992. "Auswanderer, Emigranten, Exilanten—die österreichische Kolonie in Buenos Aires. Von den Anfängen bis zum Ende des

Zweiten Weltkrieges, unter besonderer Berücksichtigung der Jahre 1918–1945." Master's thesis, University of Vienna.

Bleichsteiner, Robert. 1946. Vorwort. *Archiv für Völkerkunde* 1: 5–6.

Burke, William Hastings. 2012. *Hermanns Bruder: Wer war Albert Göring?* Berlin: Aufbau. [Originally published as *Thirty-Four*. 2009. Richmond upon Thames: Wolfgeist.]

Byer, Doris. 1999. *Der Fall Hugo A. Bernatzik*. Wien: Böhlau.

Chesterton, Bridget-Maria. 2013. *The Grandchildren of Solano López: Frontier and Nation in Paraguay, 1904–1936*. Albuquerque NM: University of New Mexico Press.

Dávalos, Juan Carlos. 1925. *Los casos del zorro: Fábulas campesinas de Salta. Ilustraciones de Juan S. v. Becker*. Buenos Aires and Cordoba: El Ateneo, P. García.

———. 1928. *Los gauchos*. Buenos Aires: La Facultad Roldan.

———. 1937. *Los valles de Cachi y Molinos: Andanzas, narraciones de viajes, tradiciones, costumbres, arqueología, etc*. Buenos Aires: Editorial La Facultad.

Dempf, Alois. 1954. *Sacrum Imperium: Geschichts-und Staatsphilosophie des Mittelalters und der politischen Renaissance*. Darmstadt: Wissenschaftliche Buchgemeinschaft.

Engel-Jánosi, Friedrich. 1953. "Remarks on the Austrian Resistance, 1938–1945." *Journal of Central European Affairs* 13 (2): 105–22.

Engelmann, M. 2015. "Seidenfabrik Hermann Schefter Hohenstadt und Mährisch Trübau." Accessed 28 November 2015. http://mengelmann64.magix.net/public/Schefter.htm.

Feest, Christian. 1978. "Kurzer Abriß der Geschichte der Wiener völkerkundlichen Sammlungen vor 1928." *Archiv für Völkerkunde* 32: 3–7.

———. 1980. "Das Museum für Völkerkunde." In *Das Museum für Völkerkunde*. 13–34. Salzburg: Residenz-Verlag.

———. 1995. "The Origins of Professional Anthropology in Vienna." In *Kulturwissenschaft im Vielvölkerstaat/L'Anthropologie et l'état pluriculturel*, edited by Britta Rupp-Eisenreich and Justin Stagl, 113–31. Wien: Böhlau.

———. 2014. "Painted Jaguar Hides of the Bororo da Campanha." *Tribus* 63: 84–117.

———. In press. "Hans Becker. Ethnologie und Widerstand." In *Geschichte der Wiener Völkerkunde in der NS-Zeit*, edited by Andre Gingrich and Peter Rohrbacher.

Fischer, Hans. 1990a. *Völkerkunde und Nationalsozialismus: Aspekte der Anpassung. Affinität und Behauptung einer wissenschaftlichen Disziplin*. Hamburger Beiträge zur Wissenschaftsgeschichte 7. Berlin: Reimer.

———. 1990b. "An den Rändern der Wissenschaft. Über Hellmuth Draws-Tychsen." In *Transpazifica: Festschrift für T. S. Barthel*, edited by Bruno Illius and Matthias Laubscher, vol. 2, 339–62. Frankfurt/Main: Peter Lang.

———. 2004. *Randfiguren der Ethnologie: Gelehrte, Amateure, Schwindler und Phantasten*. Berlin: Reimer.

Frank, Nicole. 2007. "Mich zu fixieren ist unmöglich." Schreibstrategien von Joseph Roth. PhD diss, University of Freiburg. https://doc.rero.ch/record/28466/files/FrankN.pdf.

Fried, Jakob. 1947. *Nationalsozialismus und katholische Kirche in Österreich*. Wien: Dom-Verlag.

Geisenhainer, Katja. 2005. *Marianne Schmidl (1890–1942): Das unvollendete Leben und Werk einer Ethnologin*. Veröffentlichungen des Instituts für Ethnologie der Universität Leipzig, Reihe: Fachgeschichte 3. Leipzig: Leipziger Universitätsverlag.

Gohm, Julia, and Andre Gingrich. 2014. "Rochaden der Völkerkunde. Hauptakteure und Verlauf eines Berufungsverfahrens nach dem 'Anschluss.'" In *Geisteswissenschaften im Nationalsozialismus: Das Beispiel der Universität Wien*, edited by Mitchell G. Ash, Wolfgang Niess, and Ramon Pils, 167–97. Göttingen: V&R Unipress.

Gotschim-Jauk, Elisabeth. 1990. "Hans Becker. Ein Beitrag zu seiner Biographie unter besonderer Berücksichtigung seiner Opposition zum Nationalsozialismus." PhD diss., University of Vienna.

Grubb, W. Barbrooke. 1911. *An Unknown People in an Unknown Land: An Account of the Life and Customs of the Lengua Indians of the Paraguayan Chaco*. London: Seeley.

Gusinde, Martin, S.V.D. 1946. "Beitrag zur Forschungsgeschichte der Naturvölker Südamerikas." *Archiv für Völkerkunde* 1: 1–94.

Gütl, Clemens. 2015. "Das Institut für Ägyptologie und Afrikanistik im Schnittfeld von Wissenschaft und Politik 1923–1953." In *Reflexive Innensichten aus der Universität: Disziplinengeschichten zwischen Wissenschaft, Gesellschaft und Politik*, edited by Karl Anton Fröschl, Gerd B. Müller, Thomas Olechowski, and Brigitta Schmid-Lauber, 501–512. Göttingen: V&R Unipress.

Haekel, Josef, ed. 1956. *Die Wiener Schule der Völkerkunde: Festschrift anläßlich des 25-jährigen Bestandes des Institutes für Völkerkunde der Universität Wien*. Horn: Berger.

Horwitz, Hugo Th. 1920. "Die Entwicklung der Drehbewegung." *Jahrbuch des Vereins der Ingenieure* 10: 179–95.

Husslein-Arco, Agnes. 2014. *Hagenbund: A European Network of Modernism, 1900 to 1938*. Wien: Österreichische Galerie.

Jüdisches Museum Hohenems. ed. 2014. "Arnold, Ing. Spritzer." Hohenems Genealogie. Jüdische Familiengeschichte in Vorarlberg und Tirol. Last update: 9 April 2014. http://www.hohenemsgenealogie.at/gen/getperson.php?personid=i3971&tree=Hohenems.

Karpeles, Benno. 1933. *Klassenkampf, Faschismus und Ständeparlament: Ein Beitrag zur Diskussion der berufsständischen Neuordnung*. Wien: Typographische Anstalt.

King, Michael. 1981. *The Collector: A Biography of Andreas Reischek*. Auckland: Hodder & Stoughton.

Kleintzel, Brigitta and Ilse Korotin, eds. 2002. *Wissenschaftlerinnen in und aus Österreich: Leben—Werk—Wirken*. Wien: Böhlau.

Klamper, Elisabeth. 2014. "Art in the Service of Power: The Cultural Policy of Austrofascism 1934–1938 and the Dissolution of the Hagenbund." In *Hagenbund: A European Network of Modernism, 1900 to 1938*, edited by Agnes Husslein-Arco, 349–55. Wien: Österreichische Galerie.

Kodek, Günter K. 2009. *Unsere Bausteine sind die Menschen: Die Mitglieder der Wiener Freimaurer-Logen 1869–1938*. Wien: Löcker.

———. 2014. *Die Kette der Herzen bleibt geschlossen: Mitglieder der österreichischen Freimaurer-Logen 1945 bis 1985*. Wien: Löcker.

Kolig, Erich. 1985. "Collector or Thief: Andreas Reischek in New Zealand and the Problem of Scientific Ethics in the 19th Century." *Archiv für Völkerkunde* 39: 127–46.

Kraft, Friedrich. 2009. "Aus dem Leben eines Hochstaplers. Biographie des Fleißer-Verlobten Hellmut Draws-Tychsen." In *Schriftenreihe der Fleißer-Gesellschaft* 7.

Kriechbaumer, Robert. 2005. *Österreich! und Front Heil!: Aus den Akten des Generalsekretariats der Vaterländischen Front*. Wien: Böhlau.

Kühn, Richard. 1934. *Elise von Lützow und Lützows Wilde Jagd*. Dresden: Reißner.

———. 1935. *Greta Garbo: Der Weg einer Frau und Künstlerin*. Dresden: Reißner.

———. 1942. *Richard Kühn: Hofdamen-Briefe um Habsburg und Wittelsbach (1835–1865)*. Berlin: O. Arnold.

Laicus, Phillip (Phillip Wasserburg). 1880. *Kreuz und Kelle*. Einsiedeln: Benziger.

Langer, Alejandro. 1935. "Ensayo de cultivo de plantas forrajeras para ganado vacuno de la Sección Agrícola Experimental del Jardín Botánico (1925–28)." *Revista del Jardín Botánico* (Asunción) 4: 81–114.

Lehmann. 1921/2. *Lehmanns Allgemeiner Wohnungsanzeiger . . . für die Bundeshauptstadt Wien.* 63. Jahrgang. 2 vols. Wien: Österreichische Anzeigen-Gesellschaft.

———. 1930. *Wiener Adressbuch: Lehmanns Wohnungsanzeiger 1930.* 71. Jahrgang. 2 vols. Wien: Österreichische Anzeigen-Gesellschaft.

———. 1932. *Wiener Adressbuch: Lehmanns Wohnungsanzeiger 1932.* 73. Jahrgang. 2 vols. Wien: Österreichische Anzeigen-Gesellschaft.

———. 1939. *Wiener Adressbuch: Lehmanns Wohnungsanzeiger für das Jahr 1939.* 80. Jahrgang. 2 vols. Wien: August Scherl Nachfolger.

Liener, Stefanie Maria. 2010. "Wanda Hanke (1893–1958): Eine österreichische Ethnologin in Südamerika." Master's thesis, University of Vienna.

Linimayr, Peter. 1994. *Wiener Völkerkunde im Nationalsozialismus.* Frankfurt/Main: Peter Lang.

Loukotka, Čestimir. 1968. *Classification of South American Indian Languages.* Reference Series 7. Los Angeles: Latin American Center, University of California, Los Angeles.

Matricula Online. 2016. "Österreich, Erzdiözese Wien, Wien Stadt, 19. Döbling, 02–18 Trauungsbuch 1932–1935, 1936–1938." Accessed 3 January 2016. http://www.data.matricula.info/php/main.php#3.

Métraux, Alfred. 1948. "Ethnography of the Chaco." In *Handbook of South American Indians,* vol. 1: *The Marginal Tribes,* edited by Julian H. Steward, 197–370. Bulletin of the Bureau of American Ethnology, 143/1. Washington DC: Government Printing Office,.

Obermeier, Franz. 2012. "Der Hamburger Karl Fiebrig, Gründer des Botanischen Gartens Asunción, und die Guarani-Forschung." *Auskunft* 32 (2): 241–52.

O'Leary, Timothy J. 1963. *Ethnographic Bibliography of South America.* New Haven CT: Human Relation Area Files.

Olechowski, Thomas, Tamara Ehs, and Kamila Staudigl-Ciechowicz. 2014. *Die Wiener Rechts-und Staatswissenschaftliche Fakultät 1918–1938.* Göttingen: V&R Unipress.

Patka, Marcus G. 2010. *Österreichische Freimaurer im Nationalsozialismus: Treue und Verrat.* Wien: Böhlau.

Pessler, Franz. 1949. "Hans Becker und seine Arbeit." *Der Freiheitskämpfer* 2: 9–10.

Plankensteiner, Barbara. 2011a. "Eine Dame im Urwald." In *Abenteuer Wissenschaft: Etta Becker-Donner in Afrika und Lateinamerika*, edited by Barbara Plankensteiner, Gerard van Bussel, and Claudia Augustat, 9–23. Wien: Museum für Völkerkunde.

———. 2011b. "Etta Donners Liberia-Forschung." In *Abenteuer Wissenschaft: Etta Becker-Donner in Afrika und Lateinamerika*, edited by Barbara Plankensteiner, Gerard van Bussel, and Claudia Augustat, 25–49. Wien: Museum für Völkerkunde.

Prutsch, Ursula. 2012. "Das Projekt Thaler—Dreizehnlinden." Accessed 5 December 2015. http://www.lateinamerika-studien.at/content/geschichtepolitik/brasilien/brasilien-27.html.

Rathkolb, Oliver, ed. 1985. *Gesellschaft und Politik am Beginn der Zweiten Republik: Vertrauliche Berichte der US-Militäradministration aus Österreich 1945 in englischer Originalsprache*. Wien: Böhlau.

Ratzlaff, Gerhard, ed. 2011. "Lexikon der Mennoniten in Paraguay." Last update: 4 August 2011. http://www.menonitica.org/lexikon/.

Regel, Fritz. 1914. *Argentinien*. Angewandte Geographie. IV. Serie, 10. Heft. Frankfurt/Main: Heinrich Keller.

Rhode, Ulrich, S. J. 2014. Vorlesung "Das kirchliche Eherecht." Accessed 5 January 2016. http://www.kirchenrecht-online.de/lehrv/ehe/e-skriptum.pdf.

Rinnerthaler, Alfred. 1988. "Der Universitätsverein und der Traum von einer katholischen Universität in Salzburg." *Jahrbuch der Universität Salzburg* 1983–85: 46–75.

Roth, Joseph. 1994. *Unter dem Bülowbogen: Prosa zur Zeit*. Edited by Rainer-Joachim Siegel. Köln: Kiepenheuer & Witsch.

Sandgruber, Roman. 2013. *Traumzeit für Millionäre: Die 929 reichsten Wienerinnen und Wiener im Jahr 1910*. Wien: Styria.

Schebesta, Paul, S.V.D. 1932a. *Bambuti, die Zwerge vom Kongo*. Leipzig: Brockhaus.

———. 1932b. "Die Zwerge vom Kongo." *Jedermann* 1 (9): 5.

———. 1932c. "Congorilla." *Jedermann* 1 (13): 5.

Schedlmayer, Christina. 2010. "Die Zeitschrift 'Kunst dem Volk': Populärwissenschaftliche Kunstliteratur im Nationalsozialismus und ihre Parallelen in der akademischen Kunstgeschichtsschreibung." PhD diss., University of Vienna.

Schefter, Hermann Heinrich. 1927. *Yankees und Indianer*. Wien-Berlin-Leipzig: Spiegel Verlag.

Schirmer, Andreas. 2013. "Ein Pionier aus Korea: Der fast vergessene Han Hung-Su–Archäologe, Völkerkundler, Märchenerzähler, Kulturmittler." *Archiv für Völkerkunde* 61–62: 261–318.

Schmidt, Hans. 1921. *Meine Jagd nach dem Glück in Argentinien und Paraguay*. Leipzig: A. Voigtländer.

Schmidt, Wilhelm, S.V.D. 1949. *Rassen und Völker in Vorgeschichte und Geschichte des Abendlandes, 3: Gegenwart und Zukunft des Abendlandes*. Luzern: Josef Stocker.

Schmitz, Hans. 1933. *Die berufsständische Ordnung nach der "Quadragesimo anno."* Schriftenreihe des österreichischen Heimatdienstes 3, edited by Pankraz Kruckenhauser. Wien: Österreichischer Heimatdienst.

Schnitzler, Arthur. 1933. *Tagebuch 1920–1922*. Wien: Verlag der Österreichischen Akademie der Wissenschaften.

Šebestová, Irena. 2008. *Die Fremde in der Fremde: Zur künstlerischen Identität im Schaffen von Erica Pedretti*. Frankfurt: Peter Lang.

Sprengel, Rainer. 1996. *Kritik der Geopolitik: Ein deutscher Diskurs, 1914–1944*. Berlin: Akademie-Verlag.

Suchy, Irene. 2008. "Lilly Lieser—eine Übersehene. Eine Co-Produzentin der Schönberg'schen Musikgeschichte." *Österreichische Musikzeitschrift* 10: 6–16.

Súsnik, Branislava. 1977. *Lengua-Masko: su habla, su prensa, su vivencia*. Asunción: Museo Etnográfico "Andrés Barbero."

———. 1979–1985. *Los aborigines del Paraguay*. 6 vols. Asunción: Museo Etnográfico "Andrés Barbero."

Súsnik, Branislava and Miguel Chase-Sardi. 1996. *Los indios del Paraguay*. Madrid: Ed. MAPFRE.

Tálos, Emmerich. 2013. *Das austrofaschistische Herrschaftssystem: Österreich 1933–1938*. 2nd ed. Wien: LIT.

Urbanek, Gerhard. 2011. "Realitätsverweigerung oder Panikreaktion?: 'Vaterländische' Kommunikationspolitik in Österreich zwischen Juliabkommen 1936, Berchtesgadener Protokoll und 'Anschluss' 1938." Master's thesis, University of Vienna.

Venus, Theodor, and Alexandra-Eileen Wenck. 2004. *Die Entziehung jüdischen Vermögens im Rahmen der Aktion Gildemeester: Eine empirische Studie über Organisation, Form und Wandel von "Arisierung" und jüdische Auswanderung in Österreich 1938–1941*. Wien-München: Oldenbourg.

Wahrhaft, Franz (Benno Karpeles). 1917. *Die neue Partei*. Wien: Moritz Perles.
Wells, H. G. 1922. *A Short History of the World*. London: Cassell.
Wikipedia. 2014. "Der Friede." Last update: 16 February 2014. https://de.wikipedia.org/wiki/Der_Friede.
——— . 2015a. "Adelsaufhebungsgesetz." Last update: 20 May 2015. https://de.wikipedia.org/wiki/Adelsaufhebungsgesetz.
——— . 2015b. "Ernst Reinhardt Verlag." Last update: 9 November 2015. https://de.wikipedia.org/wiki/Ernst_Reinhardt_Verlag.

NANCY J. PAREZO AND CATHERINE A. NICHOLS

3

Is It Anthropology?

Exhibiting Latin American Cultures at the 1892 Madrid International Expositions

Spain's *Exposición Histórico-Americana* and the *Exposición Histórico-Europe* (October 30, 1892 to January 31, 1893) were held jointly in Madrid as a government-sponsored international undertaking commemorating the four hundredth anniversary of Europe's first sighting of American lands. Though hosted by Spain, foreign governments organized displays and appointed commissioners to contribute to the international effort. The exhibitions were designed to do more than perfunctorily celebrate Columbus's "discovery" by displaying all known portraits of the explorer, which of course the organizers did; in addition, they acknowledged the subsequent Spanish exploratory and imperialistic voyages by presenting the accumulation of extracted cultural and natural resources. These were the material spoils of empire, displayed for the world to admire. The expositions were also intended to justify Spanish colonialism, particularly in light of their colonies' political independence. Intellectually, Europe still wished to play the role of a parent educating "a daughter, courageous and untamed, but vigorous and beautiful" (Luce 1895, 9). Oversight and guidance was needed for the former colonies' full participation in the modern world at the turn of the twentieth century. The expositions would help Spain (and the rest of Europe) assess the political development and sophistication of former colonies. It was anticipated that the new nations in the Americas—though independent—had yet to mature and reach equal status. They still needed guidance in economic, political, and cultural realms.

The organizers of the exposition also added a second layer to their celebration. In contemporary terminology, they endeavored to make the joint expositions a locale for transnational and cross-cultural comparison, using European-based anthropological interpretive frameworks and anthropology's basic nineteenth-century methodological technique: the comparison of similar social units on a worldwide basis, arranged by universalized classificatory criteria. In short, intellectual colonialism over the New World would continue, at least when trying to interpret indigenous cultures and their histories. Not only is this a key theoretical point that we must empirically interrogate when conducting research into the history of science; this intellectual hegemony is an important sociopolitical feature of nineteenth-century anthropology. Although colonizing nations asserted political control of indigenous lands, they also sought to retain intellectual control over the interpretation of ethnological and archaeological data in postcolonial nations. Importantly, this quest for anthropological control occurred at a time when the United States was transforming itself from a postcolonial nation into a colonizing nation—with the accompanying conceit that American anthropology understood what empirical information was needed to fruitfully advance the world's understanding of humanity's origins and its cultural, economic, social and technological progress as a species.

European nations and their anthropologists felt they had the proper intellectual paradigms to control knowledge, and, in the case of the Madrid expositions, each proposed to advance their nationalist framework thereby ensuring that the expositions were intellectually sophisticated and educationally useful. The combined Madrid expositions were to constitute a venue of anthropological debate and synthesis where practitioners would ask:

What do we really know about the indigenous cultures of the Americas?
How similar were they to contemporaneous cultures in Europe?
How similar were they to each other?
Were all American civilizations encountered at contact the same? If not, in what ways did they differ?

The display of art and technological artifacts were the means through which organizers addressed these questions. Contextual information about the objects themselves and their cultures of origin were relatively scarce in the exhibits, requiring viewers to draw their own conclusions based on an aesthetic response to style and design. The organizers hoped that this conceptual design would allow viewers "to realize the influence which the one [continent] may have exercised upon the other [continent]" (Luce 1895, 8). The underlying idea in the cross-cultural comparison was to contrast the degree of civilization (in the unilinear evolutionary sense) between the two continents. The evidence should support the contention that Europe was more advanced, but this was not a foregone conclusion.

The questions were designed to be answered by the visitors themselves as they walked through the two expositions. Each exposition would contain half of the necessary information. The *Exposición Histórico-Europe* would display distinct European societies, concentrating on cultures of the Iberian Peninsula at the time when indigenous Americans were first encountered (Luce 1985 citing Madrid Commission 1892,7). The *Exposición Histórico-Americana* would focus on American cultures at the time of contact but, due to historical circumstance, how contact was defined required chronological flexibility, as the time of contact varied by place over a 250-year period (Catalogo 1892). Organizers anticipated that contributing nations could answer the question: "What were your nation's identifiable societies like in 1400 and 1500?" (the periods defined as pre-Columbian and proto-Columbian, respectively). If this was not possible, exhibitors were asked to show visitors what indigenous societies were like when they were first encountered by Europeans during a period labeled "the Columbian Epoch" (Luce 1895, 8). It was hoped that this could be accomplished by extending the time frame to 1650. This time depth was needed in order to include those peoples living in the interiors of the American continents, but it created a chronological issue that muddied the idealized controlled comparison.

The Madrid organizers explicitly instructed participating nations to erect anthropological exhibits as components of the singular exposition-wide display. Exhibitors were *not* to erect displays of isolated cabinets of curiosities or treasures owned by a collector or individual museum, in order to awe visitors with their national wealth and cultural heritage. Instead, national commissioners were to combine their government-sponsored and private submissions into seamless units that identified and visualized the indigenous peoples within their territories. The unit of display was indigenous cultures, not individual and institutional collections of the exhibitor nation as these existed in 1892. This request essentially required exhibitors to turn highly diverse collections, obtained for different purposes, into an integrated anthropological collection based on contemporary national ownership while excluding the historical and political circumstances that led to each collection's development. Though museum and collecting practices pioneered in the European Enlightenment spread hand-in-hand with colonialism, by the late nineteenth century scientific and museum institutions had a particular national character, which manifested through styles of display (Kohlstedt 1987). Regardless of national or regional style, exhibitors were to show what they knew about the ancestors of the indigenous peoples in their geographical territories, using the interpretive framework of modern science as conceptualized in Europe, particularly Spain.

As a result of these directions there were many displays that foundational European, American, and Latin American anthropologists could use to study European and American indigenous cultures. As anthropologist Walter Hough noted in his exposition report in the *American Anthropologist*, "It will be a long time before a similar opportunity is afforded to compare the ethnological and archaeological products from so many American sources." The displays from twenty-one American and six European nations that had collected indigenous materials constituted "the greatest collection of Americana ever under one roof" (1893, 271). Expectations for an opportunity to make cultural comparisons were high.

Did the Madrid exhibits achieve the goal of presenting objects in an anthropological manner? Was it the exposition as a whole, the two distinctive exhibits (Europe versus the Americas), or each nation's individual displays that best embodied the anthropological perspective? Or did displays contain items that an anthropological authority could transform into anthropological data? This latter possibility required anthropologists to assess how well different countries met exposition organizers' basic request that displays be organized to reflect distinctive contact civilizations. Once each nation's display was in place, the exposition organizers intentionally gave visitors no help in understanding how objects contributed to an anthropological understanding of cultural difference. By touring the expositions, the idea was for a viewer as an observant individual to recognize meaningful patterns among objects and from there develop their own conclusions. But how could anyone tell when a beautiful piece of gold jewelry constituted anthropological information? What should the curious student see and pay particular attention to, without being overwhelmed by a glut of material scarcely labeled with contextual information? How reliable was an individual display as a whole, with respect to scientific methods of specimen collection? Which individual pieces were important for answering anthropological questions? In short, was there an anthropological perspective being presented and how could nonprofessional viewers recognize and understand it? Aside from being the stated goal of the Madrid exposition, these questions constituted important considerations— with contemporary political and status implications— for the exhibition of countries. The scientific community would decide which of the postcolonial American nations were doing contemporary anthropology, and, by extension, were advanced enough to be participants in modern scientific endeavors. More was at stake in this exercise for the new American nations than for European nations; the reputation and status as modern nations were implied in the results.

Anthropology at the time of the 1892 expositions was in its formative disciplinary stage. In the United States and England, the central idea of anthropological thought in the late nineteenth century was unilinear evolution, in which there existed "one dominant line of evolution" that "all societies progress through at different rates" (Barnard 2000, 29). Comparisons as to the particular evolutionary stage could be determined through various criteria including subsistence strategies, kinship patterns, and material culture, especially technological artifacts. This comparative perspective was usually termed ethnology by the practitioners of the day. Ethnology, in turn, was a distinct topic and methodological subset of anthropology as the science of man. Like his colleagues, Otis T. Mason—curator of ethnology for the U.S. National Museum and a proponent of evolutionary theories—employed a deductive approach to the arrangement and categorization of material culture, cultures, and languages when he practiced ethnology. In one of his public lectures, he presented a classification system that described the different "grades of culture" which range from "lower savage" to "civilized," following Lewis Henry Morgan's scheme. Within each grade, there were a variety of categories based on human behavior and cultural traits, including race, food, clothing, habitations, industries, and social structure, etc., the most important of which was technology and material culture. For "Middle Savage," which characterized "Australian [Aborigines]," clothing was limited to "capes of skin or coarse matting," while habitations were "temporary huts and wind-breaks." Using this classificatory scheme, groups of people could be both defined and limited in terms of their progress and potential based on their "grade of culture" (Mason 1882, 16–17). Because the majority of American anthropologists at the time were based in museums, knowledge of the source of objects was critically important in order to perform anthropological work.

Modified from today's four-field approach, anthropology united work in ethnology, racial typology, and linguistics, with archaeology viewed at that time primarily as a dimension or a methodological focus to add time depth to evolutionary studies (Darnell 2003, 25). But the theoretical paradigm allowed technology from the past and the present to be used without distinction; if properly classified, any single item would represent universal categories of development and progress. The assessment of the Madrid exposition's anthropological nature questioned whether the arrangements of each nation's exhibits within the two exhibitions allowed anthropologists and lay visitors to comprehend the major anthropological theory of the day—unilinear evolution—through comparisons of material culture removed from their original contexts of production and use. In order for artifacts to be anthropological, the exhibits would need to communicate information about the location where artifacts were found and who made them. Some context was thus needed.

The question then became who would decide if each nation's exhibits contained information and objects of value to anthropology and, by extension, whether a nation had the capabilities to conduct anthropology. The obvious answer would have been Spain and its anthropologists. The exposition corporation, however, was not prepared to undertake this intellectual assessment and the award list reflects a range of considerations, not only how well exhibitors met the organizers' goals for a retrospective sweep of contact cultures. Nor did the anthropologists in Spain's national museum undertake the intellectual exercise; they were too busy ensuring that the exhibits were simply finished.

Two official members of the United States' delegation and one unofficial member decided to pursue this intellectual challenge for the English-speaking world. Each would evaluate the extent to which the expositions contributed to anthropology's scope and questions. They undertook this early form of peer-review to help the anthropological community separate anthropologically valuable artifacts and collections from unusable, decontextualized ethnic curiosities and antiquarian relics. The first reviewer was one of two commissioners sent by the U.S. government, Dr. Daniel G. Brinton (1837–1899), a physician who was a professor of linguistics and archaeology at the University of Pennsylvania (Chamberlain 1899; Darnell 1988). One of the most prolific and prominent scholars of the late nineteenth century, Brinton studied all of the Americas but concentrated on Mexico and Latin America. He was a generalist and synthesizer, remembered especially for his analysis and classification of indigenous languages, his work in religion and indigenous literature and mythology (what is today called oral literature), and the development of the concept of race using a neo-Lamarckian framework that emphasized evolution (Baker 2000, 395). Brinton served as president of the American Philosophical Society, the American Folklore Society, and the American Association for the Advancement of Science; he was also a member of several European learned associations. A man with encyclopedic knowledge and boundless intellectual curiosity, Brinton was critical in the development of American anthropology, particularly concerning the identification of its important intellectual questions, and the application of methodological rigor in the search for cultural universals (Baker

2000). In both medicine and anthropology, he was committed to the standardization of terminology to increase professionalism (Darnell 1988, 7; see also Darnell 1976). Brinton's opinions carried weight with other scholars; he was a peer reviewer who insisted upon high-quality scholarship. While Brinton contributed to the overall intellectualism of the U.S. commission, he did not produce any exhibits. This reflected his regular scholarly activities. According to Lee Baker (2000, 397), "Brinton's method for research included critiquing and synthesizing other peoples' writings on a given subject, then drawing conclusions from all the work he read." Brinton's main publication on Madrid, "Report upon the Collections Exhibited at the Columbian Historical Exposition" (1895), was a critique of the anthropological scholarship presented at both expositions. It was a descriptive report with an introduction but no conclusion. Brinton used the information he had gleaned from the exposition in several papers. Theoretical issues stemming from his assessment of whether the expositions were anthropological was highlighted in his papers at the International Congress of Anthropology held in Chicago in 1893, particularly with respect to the place of the concept of nation in anthropology and an attempt to encourage consensus and standardization in linguistic terminology (Brinton 1894a, 1894b).

The second evaluator was Dr. Water Hough (1859–1936), a young ethnologist, archaeologist, museologist, and what today would be called a materiality and technology expert, who spent his entire career as a government scientist. A future president of the American Anthropological Association, at the time of the Madrid celebration Hough was an aide to Otis T. Mason at the Smithsonian Institution's U.S. National Museum. Hough had not yet conducted institutionally-sponsored fieldwork but spent his time cataloguing and analyzing artifacts (constructing a natural history style catalogue) and building exhibits under Mason's direction. Following the Madrid exhibition, Hough would be promoted to assistant curator of ethnology (1896–1910), then, after Mason's death, to curator, and later head curator in 1923 (Judd 1936). Thus Hough's evaluation of the anthropological nature of the Madrid exhibits was influenced by the sensibilities of a young scholar immersed in cultural materials and a concern for museological sophistication—

that is, effective exhibit techniques. His own efforts at constructing exhibits for the Madrid exposition were rewarded by the Spanish government; the Queen Regent made Hough a knight of the Royal Order of Ysabel la Católica. Hough published his assessment shortly after the exposition in a widely-read report in the *American Anthropologist* entitled "The Columbian Historical Exposition in Madrid" (Hough 1893).

Brinton and Hough brought two domains of professional expertise to their independent reviews. Their opinions varied due to age, intellectual interests, and experience. However, they had a common concern for anthropology's intellectual and practical development. Both men were excellent scholars for their time period. They valued accurate descriptions of the languages, cultures, and technologies of contemporary indigenous communities, the systematic unearthing of archaeological materials, and the classification of any data into formal typologies that could be used to help scholars understand human cultural development and the distribution of cultural traits around the world. Neither liked speculation or sloppy work. Throughout their careers, they helped establish anthropological standards of information, deciding which objects and sets of objects could be used in the work of classification to bring order to a culturally complex world. In short, they were referees, asking of each artifact in each national display, "Can object X be anthropological data?"

In this paper we look at how Brinton and Hough evaluated Latin American countries' displays and decided whether constituent exhibits constituted presentations of decontextualized curios or anthropological specimens containing scientific information. We assess the ways in which Brinton and Hough decided how useful the displayed objects were for anthropological research and what anthropologists could learn from them. Brinton, especially, was interested in anthropological objects as potential "ethnographic parallels" (Brinton 1895, 248), raw evidence that proved there were human universals. This notion required that comparable objects be contextualized by geography and culture. Identification was evidenced by proper linguistic classification and cultural affiliation of the artifact's maker and users. Hough—and, to a lesser degree, Brinton—discussed whether the exhibitor used good display techniques enabling visitors to learn in an effective manner. They viewed each display with the following questions in mind:

> Were the materials arranged so that the student of anthropology could use them to address contemporary issues?
> How were the artifacts obtained and could the collector be trusted (i.e., did he or she use modern anthropological methods and techniques)?
> Were artifacts effectively labeled?
> Were there outstanding pieces that American scholars must see in order to understand cultural diversity in Latin and South America or universal cultural development?

The latter concern focused on either outstanding pieces that captured viewers' attention (well-placed and pedestaled to provide visual focus in a sea of objects) or artifacts that Brinton and Hough had never seen. Rarity and newness, as well as an artifact's ability to serve as a type specimen for taxonomic classification of societies and their affiliations with other societies, was the most important consideration for selection of a noteworthy object.

Brinton's and Hough's evaluation was a challenging intellectual exercise that required them to ignore actual display intent. For example, the displays containing objects collected after a country's independence were conceptualized as the nation's cultural patrimony and controlled in large part by the settler majority. These objects were not contextualized as belonging to—intellectually or physically—the distinctive indigenous groups that had a right to an independent existence. Brinton and Hough tried to ignore these features, although they were judging each country on the time and effort they spent constructing their anthropological displays. The extensiveness and overall character of these national displays indicated the level of federal support for each country's participation in "modern" anthropology. As we will demonstrate, Brinton and Hough concluded that the most scientific and well-designed display demonstrated that a country was intellectually advanced. They identified which Spanish-speaking scholars should be considered members of an American-based anthropological network. Membership meant their work supported and enhanced North American and European scholarship.

ASSESSING THE COMBINED EXPOSITIONS

The grand universal cultural comparison never materialized for the two expositions, so the organizers' reliance on space and placement to signal units of cultural comparison turned out not to be a museological problem. There were no formal labels or introductory texts that informed visitors of each exposition's scope or the overall intellectual goals. Nor did each country's commissioners write labels describing the scope, origins, and purpose of their exhibits. Placement was the primary means by which visitors were introduced to the central division of Europe versus the Americas. The two expositions were intended to be situated on separate floors of a single permanent building, *El Palacio de la Biblioteca y Museos Nacionales*. The Americas were located on the ground floor and Europe on the upper floor—a spatial hierarchical distinction designed to visually reinforce the cultural and political status of formative versus advanced national units, rather than to enable people to question its efficacy through rapid comparisons of a Castilian pot and a Mayan pot. Since the location of the comparable ceramic pieces in the exhibit reflected the geographical location of the nation and its supposed placement in a binary of social progress, visitors had to remember what they had seen several thousand objects previously if they wanted to make a direct evolutionary comparison. It was an impossible exercise, even for trained scholars.

The spatial organization assumed that every viewer would recognize one implicit comparison taken as a foregone conclusion: civilized (technologically and socially complex) Europe versus more simplistic and, by definition, unsophisticated American indigenous cultures. To Brinton the overall exhibit was bisected into the cultures of "the European invaders" (as he called them) and the cultures of the indigenous peoples whose societies fell after European conquest and were subjugated to subsequent colonial control. In actuality Europe was a misnomer, for England and France chose not to participate in the exposition. The countries that erected exhibits were Portugal, Germany, Denmark, Sweden, and Norway. The exposition halls primarily focused on Spain's colonial conquests in Central and South America, Mexico, and the Caribbean. In the Madrid exposition's basic equation, Spain equaled Europe. The United States was the only nation that did not conform to the mother country–colony comparative format, even though, after Spain, it sent the largest display complex. The extant comparison actually reflected how Spanish civilization and its components compared to American civilizations in their former colonies.

The intended geographically-based dichotomy situated on separate floors was lost, because the American exhibits invaded the European exhibition space. Since European countries declined to participate, there were a series of empty rooms on the upper floor. Vacant spaces were not tolerated in exposition exhibits, especially during a period when displaying as much as possible in tight spaces was the norm. Unoccupied areas would have silently communicated the sentiment that expending diplomatic dollars to participate in the exposition was not worthwhile, undermining the host country's international status; unfilled exhibition areas were social and political failures. Spain's organizers solved this problem by having the *Exposición Histórico-Americana* take over two-thirds of the space on the second floor. There were no empty areas, but the hemispheric binary comparison was no longer spatially self-evident.

In addition there was little material displayed that illustrated European cultures in 1500. Most entries—especially those coming from national museums—focused on the indigenous ethnographic and archaeological materials that had been amassed through exploration and later scientific expeditions. For example, Norway exhibited a Viking ship that was dated to about 900 AD, while Denmark exhibited Icelandic objects such as medieval manuscripts and architectural pieces that dated to the Middle Ages (Brinton 1895, 74). There were no displays of household ceramics, tools, or weapons used in daily life, or ritual paraphernalia by nationality, region, or ethnicity that would provide a temporally controlled comparison for the American material. As a result, neither Brinton nor Hough discussed the European exhibitions, except to report on anthropological collecting expeditions or exceptional items, like codices.

The Latin and South American displays had been plotted to move the visitor geographically from Mexico to Argentina, through the Caribbean and Central America. In actuality, the amount of space each nation needed determined its placement. Columbia was sandwiched in a room on the second floor between Mexico and Sweden; Ecuador was between Nicaragua and Guatemala on the other side of the building. Meanwhile Santo Domingo, Cuba, and Argentina were located on the ground floor. Thus, the geographical flow was lost, and the potential for the entire exposition to serve as a showcase for understanding environment and culture as a geographical exercise went unrealized.

The lack of common items also undermined an exposition-to-exposition comparison. Each nation sent whatever it chose. The exposition commission issued no guidelines about classification schemas except that the artifacts had to be indigenous: made and used by the peoples who came in contact with Europeans. Each exhibit was then to be arranged by nation. As Brinton notes, this undermined the intended comparisons by indigenous cultures, for

> in some instances, numerous specimens from various localities which had come into the possession of some museum were displayed together. This fact required that the study of any one culture in the American continent should be conducted by visiting several departments of the museum. Indeed, a certain number of objects distinctively American were exhibited on the upper floor, which was theoretically reserved for European displays exclusively. This was the case with some of those rare and valuable manuscripts [codices], the composition of native American scribes, which have been preserved by accident to our own times. (1895, 23)

Current ownership of artifacts was thus the underlying organizational principle. Practical considerations of the amount of space required for each nation's entry was the deciding factor for placement.

To Brinton this organizational placement was not anthropological or informative, because it forced any curious visitor interested in learning about a specific group of people to search through unsystematized displays in all sections of both exposition complexes. This was not a scientific display technique because it hindered visitors from uncovering patterns. It also required visitors to possess a good deal of prior knowledge and fantastic memories. Brinton concluded that the entire combined exposition framework was nonsystematic; it did not have a top-down, specialist-produced, uniform system of classification placement that could reinforce a knowledge-organizing framework. The combined expositions were not a good teaching tool for anthropological scholarship as a scientific approach to understanding human beings. The organizers' goal for an integrated picture of European and American cultures at the time of contact was not fulfilled. From an anthropological standpoint, the commission's principle of organizing the exhibits by nation, as distinct geopolitical entities, created a false picture. For example, in the Mexican national display, the Aztecs and Maya became components of a nonanthropological classificatory unit, based on a European political concept—the modern nation-state, with colonized population components—rather than two very distinct geopolitical societal complexes that could each be conceptualized as early civilizations using an evolutionary scale. An anthropological organizational scheme would have been satisfied by grouping collections by culture and linguistic group, not by postcolonial ownership of indigenous artifacts. This was probably beyond the scope of the organizers and each set of national exhibitors. Having a genuine anthropological framework would have required that the Mayan materials from Mexico and Guatemala be combined with similar materials from Spain's national museum and Edward Seler's collection, which was found in the German displays. For Brinton, the Madrid expositions represented a lost opportunity for American anthropology.

Hough disagreed with Brinton's overall assessment that the organizer's lack of actualization of their initial goal meant the displays were a complete failure. Assessing more diplomatically and at a more detailed level, Hough said that the combined expositions as a whole had an "admirable historical and scientific motive." Then he switched to basic museological considerations and artifactual highlights—something that did not interest Brinton as a practitioner who was not embedded in museum curation or material culture studies. Overall Madrid was exceptional "in the taste displayed in the presentation of the valuable material" (1893, 271). Hough's work on previous expositions led him to realize that the organizer's overall goal was impossible and, as a result, he never took it seriously or felt it was worthy of comment, unlike Brinton. There had never been a chance of a seamless, unified anthropological exhibition. The anthropological perspective would only be evident on three different levels—that of the national display, the individual collection, and the individual artifact.

ASSESSING NATIONAL DISPLAYS

Turning to the level of the national display, Brinton noted that the internal arrangement of each nation's exhibits was variable. The anthropological value of each display depended on the amount and type of information sent by collectors, institutions, and commissioners, as well as the types of objects procured. Some nations produced synthetic and thematic exhibits based on major collections while others consisted of several minor (that is, small in number and scientifically unimportant or uninformative) collections that were the property of different individuals and institutions. In most cases these were not integrated. For political and social reasons, collections were kept separate, so the focus became the current owner of the materials. In almost all cases the information accompanying the artifacts included the owner's name, reflecting the importance of his contemporary socioeconomic position, a labeling emphasis similar to the prominent placement of the names of wealthy sponsors on museum and art gallery labels (and even building wings) today. To Brinton this was an educational disservice, demonstrating that the displays were not anthropological exhibitions, but showcases that reinforced the social hierarchy of settler colonialism. The individual exhibits and the desire to emphasize owners and exhibitors "interfered with the systematic display, such as would be desirable for scientific purposes" (Brinton 1895, 24).

Since Brinton and Hough would be publishing assessments for the scientific community, their next task was to decide which national exhibits were anthropological. Since Brinton was more specific in this assessment, we have summarized his conclusions in table 1. Hough simply did not mention nonanthropologically useful displays or objects; Brinton explained why he had made his evaluation. Hough did not emphasize his methodological choice before diving into a selective description of each display he considered worthy of anthropological mention; Brinton's assessment was based on the overall orientation and systematic treatment of materials as scientific specimens or as haphazard curiosities and treasures. Hough's assessment varied with each nation. He did not use a common diagnostic and defining criterion.

According to Hough, only Mexico, the United States, and Spain had major anthropological collections (based on the number of artifacts, artifact quality, and their presentation density), while twenty-one countries sent smaller archaeological and ethnological collections. Hough dismissed most of these (Cuba, Santo Domingo, Bolivia, Argentine Republic, Brazil, Chile, Honduras, El Salvador, and Paraguay) without further description, because the indigenous objects were used "only for decoration or in an unsystematic way" (1893, 271). As such they were not anthropological collections, but simply groupings of collectible antiquities and historic relics. Hough made sure, however, to mention Latin American countries whose small collections were placed in special displays that used the anthropological concept of culture and demonstrated technological development, or the interactions among technology-culture-environment, but which contained nothing of exceptional interest. Hough gave greater attention to larger representative or developmental collections that showed regional variability and offered informative comparisons for the scholar, or contained a truly unique item. Two examples were Ecuador (eleven cases of "lustrous, dark and usually inundating pottery," interesting because of their "curious forms" that resemble Chinese and Korean ceramics) and Costa Rica (forty cases in two halls, with seventy-two pounds of wrought-gold objects and stone carvings that provided "an enlarged idea of the progress of the sculptor's art").

In contrast to these brief mentions, Hough devoted an entire paragraph to collections containing unique artifacts. For example, he found the Guatemalan exhibit of pottery and caved stone figurines especially beautiful: "an oval dish of polished quartz of bluish tint," "an exquisitely carved bead of jade," and "a curious globular pottery whistle or flute" (1893, 273–74). These brief descriptions indicate what Hough found aesthetically important and anthropological, evidenced by his characterization of objects as suited for comparison or demonstrating progress, in each national exhibit, even if the entire display was nonanthropological in intent. He recognized "museum quality" art. As an

Table 1: Brinton's assessments of national exhibit's anthropological value

National exhibit or individual collections	Collection source or donor	Research results clearly catalogued and displayed objects identified	Peoples and cultures identified if possible	Exhibit thematic
THE AMERICAS				
Mexico	Plancarte and Leon excavations in Michoacán	Yes	Yes	Yes
	Plancarte other objects	No	No	No
Guatemala	Government through national museum	Unclear	Rarely	Unclear
	Juaquin de Minondo collection	Yes	Yes	Unclear
	Julio de Arellano collection	No	No	Unclear
Nicaragua	Government	Yes	Yes	Yes
	Julio Gavinet collection	Yes	Yes	Yes
Honduras	No mention			
El Salvador	No mention			
Costa Rica	Government and national museum	Yes	Partly	Yes
	Troyo family collection	Unclear	Unclear	Unclear
	Julio de Arellano Yrazu collections	Yes	Yes	Yes
	1891 Guyabo cemetery collection	Yes	Yes	Yes
Cuba (colony)	No collections shown			
Dominican Republic	No information	No	No	No

Columbia	Restrepo collection	Yes	Yes	Yes
Ecuador	Government collection	No	No	No
	August Cousin collection	No	No	No
	Minister Flores ethnographic collection	No	Yes	No
Peru	None given	No	No	No
Bolivia	None given	No	No	No
Uruguay	Juan Zorrilla de San Martin research collection	Yes	Yes	Yes
Paraguay	No mention			
Chile	No mention			
Brazil	No mention			
Argentina Republic	La Plata museum and F. B. Moreno illustrations of best pieces; no artifacts	Yes	Some	No

EUROPE

Spain				
National Museum of Archaeology	Museum curators	No	No	No
Portugal	Government	No	No	No
Empire of Germany	National Ethnographic museum and Edward Seles	Yes	Yes	Yes
	Hermann Stüber collection from Vera Cruz and Peru	Yes	Yes	Yes
Denmark	Greenland Inuit collection	Unclear	Yes	Yes

National exhibit or individual collections	Collection source or donor	Research results clearly catalogued and displayed objects identified	Peoples and cultures identified if possible	Exhibit thematic
EUROPE				
Norway and Sweden	Gustave Storm, Baron Nordenskiöld, Charles Bovallius; arranged by research trip	Yes	Yes	Yes
UNITED STATES				
	Arranged by US Commission (described in another report)	Yes	Yes	Yes

assistant in the U.S. National Museum, Hough understood the political reality of government-funded exhibits and acknowledged that displays contained cultural spoils, the results of colonialism and conquest, and the use of indigenous materials for the creation of nationalism. In this case, indigenous materials were deployed as evidence of shared historical memories, specifically of exploration, settlement, and colonialism—a critical element in the creation of nations (Smith 2005). They also invoked ideas of homeland and territory, because these objects were collected from a place in the national territory. Similar to maps and other technologies of geographic visualization, artifacts acted as a physical means of making perceivable the connections between object, place, and collector (Duclos 1998).

The element of temporal control enters here. Brinton and Hough made a distinction based on whether an exhibit focused only on archaeological materials or included ethnographic materials in their assessment of anthropological value. The exposition organizer's intended plan theoretically controlled for time but offered essentially an ahistorical frame (in the sense of salvage ethnography and a concept of cultures as enduring, isolated, social units). This meant that, theoretically, the expositions were two synchronic anthropological units—what European and American societies and cultures were like right before contact. Such an approach would illuminate holes in anthropological knowledge as well as illustrate what was known in 1892.

Brinton decided to focus only on the materials that were relevant to the anthropological exercise at hand: what cultures were like in 1500. To this end he never mentions ethnographic collections and whether they had any anthropological value. From reading his report one would never know of the extensive ethnographic materials from Mexico that were displayed. Hough used a longer historical lens, allowing him to assess whether his own exhibits for the U.S. commission had anthropological value even though they did not meet the exposition requirements for comparative material. Brinton basically ignored them, for they were all too late in time. Instead they were, to him, examples of a post-contact world. He would talk about them elsewhere but not as part of his controlled review.

While Hough essentially ignored time, Brinton was very cognizant of the problems temporal issues caused for fulfilling the expositions' goals: any culture that was displayed and used for an Europe-America comparison that stemmed from a time period after ca. 1600 was probably already influenced by the presence of Europeans and was therefore no longer a discrete unit of analysis. They were "contaminated" through cross-cultural interaction, and therefore could not be seen as the independent, isolated units required for a valid comparison. Organizers chose to ignore non-face-to-face impacts like the spread of disease or material culture acquired through established trade relationships, though these facts had extraordinarily impactful consequences on cultural knowledge transmission and social organization (Wolf 1982). The goal was to provide snapshots of indigenous societies before the imposition of colonial authority, not to see how Native peoples had fared in the so-called post-Columbian periods or whether they "needed" settler colonialism to culturally and technologically advance. Organizers asked exhibiting countries to simply identify and describe indigenous societies as they existed when the two worlds met and began to interact intensively, *without* explicit reference to the continuing impact of colonialism or imperialism. We can think of this as a classificatory exercise, an attempt to document who lived where, and how identified groups related to each other linguistically and materially—a common natural history method for assessing historical origins. It constituted, as Barbara Mundy and Dana Leibsohn (1996, 327) have insightfully noted, an attempt to authoritatively reproduce precontact and contact-era American societies using a Spanish-centric lens, and a desire "to render the colonial era peripheral, to see it as one sees a frame which sets off, but does not interrupt, a view of the more precious picture it encloses, the pre-Columbian past." In short, organizers did not want visitors to see, let alone reflect on, the historical effects of Spanish colonialism and imperialism. They offered "pure" nineteenth-century ethnological-archaeological units of discrete societies that viewers could compare as distinct entities existing within the established binary framework of the Old and New Worlds. In addition, there was in the background an implicit theoretical orientation of unidirectional cultural evolutionary advancement and notions of social progress and modern sophistication. The Old World affected the New World because a complex society always pulls a simple society toward complexity upon contact and intensive interaction.

If scientifically controlled information was not available for the indigenous American societies, exhibitors could use a proxy: what indigenous peoples were like during the early colonial period (combining archaeology and history but not ethnography). But some participating countries did not have either set of anthropological materials, so they substituted contemporary ethnographic objects—that is, anything that was indigenous (exotic or aesthetically pleasing), but not contaminated by European technology or materials. From the standpoint of each national collection in its entirety, the displayed pieces thus included individual treasures and settler-made assemblages, as well as unsystematic and systematic professionally obtained collections. The resulting displays, seen as a series of discrete units, thus reflected the range of nineteenth century collecting activity by individuals and institutions, including intensive ethnographic and archaeological fieldwork using methods that were both acceptable for the time and that were outdated. Therefore when Brinton and Hough decided which displays were anthropological, they had a wealth of collecting and representational techniques from which to choose. Their critiques thus included an assessment of which types of collections were anthropological because of how they were made.

EVALUATING SECTIONS OF NATIONAL DISPLAYS

The next analysis was conducted at the level of the individual institutions or collectors displayed within national exhibits as distinctive units. It was in this realm that Hough devoted most of his emphasis, thus enabling him to focus on specific items of anthropological and artistic value. Mexico's exhibit was enormous—over fifty cases—and, according to Hough, "magnificent" and awe-inspiring (1893, 273). Other reviewers had a different experience as they walked through the Mexican displays. Charles Read (1893) of the British Museum found the thousands of pieces of pottery and stone overwhelming, eclectic, and dazzling, but an educational moment lost due to the lack of identifying labels in portions of the display. The Porfirio Diaz government, which sent over twenty thousand artifacts, lavished numerous resources on its national display to ensure that it was a memorable, clear symbol of Mexico as a mature nation with a glorious non-European past (identified with and centered on the Mayan and Aztec empires) and a promising future (Mundey and Leibsohn 1996, 331). In their anthropological reviews Hough and Brinton completely ignored this ideological and political intent, even though it affected what objects were chosen for display. For example, Mexico showed almost none from its colonial period, which made the use of its displays for historical research questionable. Even though the displays were loosely chronological beginning with the precontact past, their purposeful ignorance of the vice-regency, combined with a temporal jump to the present, sought to demonstrate that European-derived civilization had successfully melded with the indigenous. This implied that Mexico's organizers were not focused on culture histories or the comparisons requested by the exposition's organizing committee. Nevertheless, the painstakingly made copies of rare and delicate codices (the originals were too valuable to display) were shown for their usefulness in understanding indigenous precontact knowledge and worldview according to Brinton, enabling European scholars to see materials they would have no other opportunity to study.

Hough felt Mexico's overall exhibit was important because it was jointly arranged by two professionals: Francisco del Paso y Troncoso, director of the National Museum of Mexico, and American archaeologist Thomas McGuire, a lithic expert who gave the presentation a research orientation: How were tools made and what skills did Native artisans need to produce such high quality? Del Paso y Troncoso and McGuire also provided the exhibit with a classificatory scheme and rules for sorting excavated objects into meaningful temporal and geographic units. Del Paso y Troncoso was a linguist who spoke Nahuatl, and an ethnologist and archaeologist who worked in Vera Cruz and had conducted numerous scientific excavations. He was in the process of producing an archaeological history of Mexico's distant past, and his display included massive amounts of evidence for his manuscript.

The ambitious exhibit was housed in five rooms next to the main entrance, whereas most other countries' contributions fit into a single room. The "magnificent collection of antiquities, chiefly pottery and stone," filled over fifty cases (Hough 1893, 272). Hough was impressed with the display technique, in which the most important case was placed in the middle of the room and contained "the gems of the collection": obsidian masks, vases, labrets, mirrors, tiles, a carved notch femur (probably a musical instrument), copper rings, and jade objects. From a technological and artistic standpoint, Hough considered a series of high-polished obsidian rings of hour-glass shape worked to a thickness of one-sixth of an inch "very remarkable specimens of lapidary work" that would "tax Mr. McGuire's skill and ingenuity in stone-working" (1893, 273). To Hough, who was interested in the anthropological question of the technological development of culture, the Mexican exhibits provided numerous specimens for those interested in how stone was turned into exquisite art.

Equally important as the artifacts were the casts of famous antiquities, copies of codices, and pictures, models, and photographs of ancient ruins, including the "grand model of the Temple mayor of Cempoala" (Vera Cruz), which was an exhibitionary focal point. Brinton noted that the national display also included a large number of manuscripts (including native-produced maps, lienzos, codices, and eight native calendars) and a vast quantity of objects used by a number of native tribes. Unlike Hough, Brinton mentions that a special exhibit case was produced by Zelia Nuttall, the recognized expert on calendrical systems who showed how she made her elaborate mathematical computations (analysis data sheets) and the extreme accuracy of Nahuatl astronomers and priests that she contended was superior to calculations produced by European scholars at the time.

Brinton decided that the extensive Mexican exhibits were important, not only for the government displays that demonstrated intellectual control over the archaeological materials, but also due to the research of Señor Francisco Plancarte (1856–1920). Plancarte was a professor at the College of San Joaquin, Tacuba, Mexico, and Archbishop of Navarrete, who had excavated extensively in Michoacán, producing a personal collection reflecting the region's history. The exhibit constituted an illustrated publication (2,803 specimens obtained in 1889), which he had used to generate his conclusions about the makers and their precontact technological and artistic development (Plancarte 1893). Plancarte's exhibit met all of Brinton's quality criteria and was an especially good dissemination tool—the ideal educational exhibit. It supplied consistent evidence of a hereto unrecognized and as yet unnamed ancient people living near Jacona in Michoacán, and it advanced anthropological knowledge.

Next in importance was the extensive work of Dr. Nicolas Leon, who carried out archaeology among the Tarasco of Michoacán, represented by 1,325 objects from an unnamed single site west of Jacona. Brinton found the painted clay objects the most interesting items because of their great variety of forms and decoration. This offered a good platform for comparisons within a culture. Brinton also noted the metates and pestles, miniature toys, stone and clay processing tools, spindle whorls, ornaments, musical instruments, weapons, clay flower pots, and religious figurines. The object type that impressed Brinton the most, however, was the unusual clay smoking pipe with its elaborate ornamentation, which he compared to Mississippian examples, implying new areas of study (such as trade networks) that would not become common for many years. Another object he singled out for special attention was a twisted wire copper needle, "the only one which could be obtained on the American continent in objects made from metal" (Brinton 1895,

26). Singularity and rarity made it an anthropological treasure—a new type specimen for Hough. For Brinton, these highlighted pieces were also indicators that Morgan and Tylor's evolutionary schemes would need to be revised. The exhibit and its diagnostic artifacts were fundamentally important for the advancement of anthropology.

While Brinton was impressed with the Jacona materials, he was less captivated with the artifacts derived from other sources and localities that Plancarte exhibited. Many were shown without having been fully analyzed: "Of many of these we are in considerable uncertainty as to their relationship." In Brinton's estimation, the display was not anthropological, though it included materials from at least twelve ethnographic groups throughout Mexico. Brinton felt the material unnecessary and duplicative of the Jacona material, showing only what Plancarte had collected without having transformed them into anthropological data through systematic analysis. Brinton also found the scholarship sloppy: "There is not in all instances a sufficiently clear indication as to where the objects individually were obtained." As a result, Brinton concluded that Plancarte's desire to display Otomis artifacts, "characterized by a marked deficiency of skill, showing that they had little knowledge of the arts," reflected only a partial reading of the literature. He had not read "several excellent authorities" who had recently debated this contention (1895, 26). Even though the exhibited objects had been collected by an established scholar, the fact that they were lacking provenance information and contextualization within anthropological scholarship caused Brinton to criticize the decision to include them in the exhibit.

In contrast to this detailed collection-level analysis—and notation as to whether the exhibitor was a scholar—was Hough's simple mention that there were fourteen cases devoted to the historic Zapotec and the Mexican exhibit, as a whole, included materials from twenty-three ancient civilizations. We can assume that space limitations in Hough's publication led to a less detailed analysis, a situation that occurred in almost all assessments written for national periodicals when compared to Brinton's assessment (see table 2).

Both reviewers felt Guatemala was the second national display with anthropological importance. The display consisted of manuscripts and several object collections: the main one erected by the national

Table 2: Important or especially interesting objects in exhibits

Nation	Brinton	Hough
Mexico: Plancarte collection	Circular rough stone with rough outline of a human head found together near Jacona with obsidian lance	No mention
Mexico: Leon collection	Copper wire needles with eyes ("only example of twisted wire found on the American continent")	No mention
Mexico: government collection arranged by Troncoso	Codices (Porfirio Diaz and Baranda), painted records (Lienzos), Mapa de Mizquiahuala	No mention
Mexico: government collection of Troncoso, Vera Cruz	Wooden reproductions of (1) Cempoallan temple, sacred edifice and enclosure at time of Cortez visit and (2) Temple of Tajin near Papantla, Vera Cruz; small clay heads, yokes, double terra cotta cups	Grand model of Temple Mayor of Cempoala (Vera Cruz), obsidian masks, carved notched femur, obsidian rings
Mexico: Pedro Baranda collection from Campeche	Clay idols and stone objects	No mention
Guatemala	Manuscripts: (1) Isagoge Apologético General de las Indians" and "Historia de la Proincia de san Vicente Ferier de Guatemala y Chiapa" and (2) Columbus's autograph letters	No mention
Guatemala	Stone idols number 1, 6, 7, and clay idols 74, 100, 177 mostly from Quiché	No mention

Guatemala	Clay vases, cups, and jars, numbers 94, 106, 126	Globular pottery whistle or flute, pottery trumpet
Guatemala	Stone in government collection: 12, 14, 32, 33, 36–38, 46, 66–69, 76–80, 87	Finely carved stone images, oval dish of polished quartz-bluish tint, jade bead
Guatemala	Most important piece no. 23 from Quiché capital city due to glyphs	3 rare vases with Quiche glyphs
Nicaragua	Pulp pounder (no. 1162)	Nothing memorable
Costa Rica	Catalogue essay by de Peralta and 38 miniature gold figurines, sacrificial stone metate (ethnographic)	Paintings of excavations, Alfaro gold objects and jade carvings, ornamented metate, sacrificial stone
Cuba	Wooden box that held Columbus's bones (1796)	Nothing memorable
Columbia	Any of the gold pieces (totality, not individual pieces)	Any of the gold or copper pieces
Ecuador	Mortar with large ears, resonating stone, Jivaro shrunken head trophy	Lustrous dark pottery in unique forms
Peru	No mention	Red and black pottery in human and animal forms (totality), 4 with nose eaten away
Chili	No mention	Nothing memorable
Argentine Republic	No mention	Nothing memorable
Paraguay	No mention	Nothing memorable
Bolivia	Two stone idols, Aymara male and female complete dress ensembles	No mention
Brazil	No mention	Nothing memorable
Uruguay	Two axes with figurative designs	Two axes with figurative designs

Nation	Brinton	Hough
Spain: National Arch Museum	Codex Troano, Chibcha sacrificial stone, stone no. 345, Ecuador polished obsidian mirror, Incan seated figure sculpture	Peruvian coat, Troano and Cortesian codices, case of fraud specimens of stone idols
Portugal	No mention	Two rare Sandwich Island feather cloaks
Austria: William Hein	No mention	No mention
Germany: Edward Seler	No mention	Santa Lucia Cozumahualpa sculpture cast from Guatemala, two Mexican feather shields
Sweden: collections of Nordenskijöld and Bovallius	No mention	No mention

Note: Nothing memorable means that Hough noted that there were small collections of archaeological or ethnological materials in the nation's display but nothing worth mentioning further. No mention indicates that neither Hough nor Brinton noted that there were any indigenous-made artifacts on display.

government, a second by Joaquin de Minondo, and a third by Julio de Arellano. Whereas Brinton had concentrated on the objects in the Mexican displays, starting with the largest and most important collections, he gives no indication of the size and artifact density for the Guatemalan exhibits. Instead he mentions the importance of several Spanish-authored manuscripts and questions theories mentioned in the catalogue. For Brinton the catalogue was as important as the artifacts themselves. Combined, they formed the unit of study for the interested student. This is consistent with Brinton's emphasis on identification and classification.

Hough tells his readers that most of the Guatemalan exhibit consisted of pottery, but he provides no further information, implying that none of it was especially remarkable. Instead he lists artifacts that struck him as aesthetically interesting: finely carved stone images, a polished quartz oval dish, and an "exquisitely carved" jade bead (Hough 189, 273). In addition to beautiful objects and technically superb artistry, Hough notes two unusual artifacts: "a curious globular pottery whistle or flute somewhat like an ocarina, with four holes, giving five tones, running from C to F sharp, and a pottery trumpet, with four pipes blown from one mouthpiece" (1893, 273). These noteworthy pieces reflected Hough's as well as Brinton's research interests. Hough comments that Brinton had said three rare and beautiful vases ornamented with Quiché Maya hieroglyphs were the only ones ever discovered. Hough also takes the Guatemalan exhibitors to task for sloppy scholarship, noting that a misidentified Egyptian scarab and bronze *shubti* were in the exhibit. It is the only time either author notes blatant misclassification and ignorance.

Brinton wanted to give his readers an impression "of the general character of the antiquities" of Guatemala, because he could find no anthropological theme in the exhibit. He never says from which of the three collections objects come but approaches the combined exhibits by object classification and discusses theories for the object type's use. A specific type of artifact captured Brinton's attention: skillfully worked stone or clay idols in human form, in numerous positions. He lists those that he found most intriguing, although he never gives a reason for his choices. Clearly aesthetics was one criterion, as was good workmanship. Another was distinctive form and shape, especially for figurative work. His listings of important pieces seem more like type specimens than treasures—what the serious student who wants a general overview of Guatemalan antiquities should see. Brinton's requirement that the exhibit provide object identification by geography (regional and site) and culture is, in this case, less of a factor in his review and is mentioned only rarely, indicating that this information was unavailable to the visitor.

Rather than an exhibit of anthropological assertions to stimulate scholarly debate, the Guatemala exhibit struck Brinton as a forum highlighting the types of research that needed to be undertaken by professionals, due to the richness of the area. He notes that people should begin by making comparisons to the Yucatan region and also by studying the peoples and their cultures; this would provide more information about regional diversity among the Mayan groups and allow researchers to see whether the Nahuatl had influence in the region as a whole or in subregions. The ultimate goal of the proposed study would be to look at civilizations' interactions and how they influence hinterlands.

Brinton was more pleased with the small exhibit from Nicaragua, for two reasons. First, one of its component collections belonged to private collector Julio Gavinet and included 426 labeled artifacts. Second, the government made the effort to write 775 labels for their exhibit. Both collections, he noted, had been "obtained with great care from comparatively recent excavations, usually clearly localized, and presented." This produced "a satisfactory picture of the former industry of the indigenes there resident at the time of the Conquest" (Brinton 1895, 35). Since the artifacts were so well contextualized, especially an extensive series of black and red pottery vessels, Brinton could summarize the nation-states' cultural diversity at the time of contact and discuss connections with other Mesoamerican cultures and their proposed interactions.

Hough simply states that Nicaragua presented a small collection of pottery, flaked lithics, and polished stone tools, and a few pieces of jade and gold work. He essentially felt the display had no special anthropological importance. Brinton mentions the same types of constituent objects: pottery, funerary urns, human figurines, stone tools (including those made of obsidian), and colored stone jewelry. Only one object, a pulp-pounder, was singled out for special reference, in part because its function was being debated in the pages of *Science*. Brinton noted that Gavinet's collection contained objects that would be most suitable for developing typologies. Obviously, Gavinet was an individual who would enhance the anthropological record. Brinton was especially enamored with the polished stone bead necklaces, the elaborate polychromic designs and symmetry of the pottery, and the molded clay musical instruments. Unlike Hough, Brinton obviously felt that the Nicaragua display had anthropological value.

Brinton and Hough agreed about the value of the Costa Rican exhibits. Both noted that Costa Rica sent a rich collection, "admirably arranged" by Envoy Manuel M. de Peralta Anastasio Alfaro, director of the National Museum. These were placed in forty cases. Since De

Peralta had supervised many of the excavations from which the artifacts were obtained, and because of his careful citing of place ("strict localization," Brinton 1895, 38), Brinton considered the total collection a useful tool for anthropological study. Indeed, from Brinton's standpoint the most valuable part of the country's exhibit was De Peralta's catalogue summary of the region's peoples and history in precontact and post-contact periods. Brinton found this essay so compelling that he reprinted a multipage English translation in his report (1895, 40–43) remarking that it "condenses so much information not easily accessible into such clear outlines" (1895, 39). He also noted its value in an article in *Science* (Brinton 1893). The collection was encyclopedic in scope, and categorized cultures by geography, social connections, and language, emphasizing Costa Rica as a world where peoples had met and interacted. As such it helped the anthropologist study culture contact and migration as well as cultural development and the effects of European contact.

The Costa Rican exhibit (rather than the catalogue) consisted of distinct individual collections, the most important of which from the standpoint of anthropology was that of Bishop Thiel, a noted linguist. Brinton and Hough both considered the most important objects were eighteen small gold figurative images. The total amount of gold was 282 grams, Hough noted, giving a measure that is no longer considered critical today—the amount of raw material shown in a display, and an intimation of a collection's monetary value. Brinton believed these items were of the greatest interest to visitors—much like the focal points used today to draw individuals to a display as a whole and capture their interest and therefore attention. Hough found the case of jade carvings interesting, but Brinton does not note it. Hough notes that the pottery was similar to that of Nicaragua, drawing comparisons for his readers. The stone carvings of volcanic rock were particularly good (Hough 1893, 273–74). Of greater interest to antiquarians were the stone vases, of which Brinton describes the three he feels were most important: one with three symbolic animals united together, a second with an owl holding a man in its beak, and a third showing a creation symbol of man being placed on the earth. Also noteworthy for both scholars were six "curious" stone seats for priests. Brinton presents a long typology of other stone tools, pottery vessels, figurines, and flutes, as well as some miscellaneous ethnographic items, noting key dimensions of study and identification—size and form—for many. Hough informs his readers that they will have an opportunity to see this collection in Chicago at the next world's fair. He recommends that anthropologists seek this out, for the collection will "give an enlarged idea of the progress of the sculptor's art in ancient Costa Rica" (Hough 1893, 274).

On the basis of aesthetics and intellectual value, Brinton decided the best exhibition technique was that of the Republic of Columbia. Prior to the exhibition, less than 100 objects from some regions had found their way to museums and other venues of scientific analysis. The focal point was 452 gold objects—which, Hough informed readers, constituted 72 pounds—and 383 copper objects, noteworthy for their aesthetic beauty, supplemented by a few ethnographic artifacts. Brinton was pleased that the collection was divided into regions without separating the materials from different donors. The integration into a geographical format allowed the curious student to observe cultural variation and everyone to see what the Spanish invaders had destroyed. Columbia's display of gold was impressive to many. As Thomas Wilson, Curator of Prehistoric Archaeology for the U.S. National Museum, wrote, "When I saw this magnificent and glittering display of prehistoric gold ornaments from this little country [Columbia], I decided I could never put mine on display" (Wilson 1893, 911). Wilson did not want to risk embarrassment on behalf of his nation by exhibiting a meager selection of comparable material. Never before seen in public, new artifacts and unpublished drawings and paintings of artifacts not brought to Madrid were ready to be analyzed by an anthropologist looking for larger patterns and the "degree of culture" achieved by the nation. The 155 specimens of Chibcha worked gold in a "tasteful arrangement attracted the attention of all visitors" with its "judicious arrangement" (Brinton 1895, 44). Visitors with "antiquarian taste" admired the novelty and perfection of the designs of the 69 human figures, 6 masks, 23 animal figurines, 19 instruments, and 38 bone ornaments. These were accompanied by 24 copper animal and human form figurines, 38 pottery vessels, and 20 stone tools. Brinton was especially enthusiastic that 1012 artifacts from a hitherto unrecognized culture—the Quimbaya—were presented. He learned something new and saw opportunities for further research on a highly artistic culture which controlled symmetry and proportion to perfection.

Both Brinton and Hough noted that the excellent exhibit was the work of Ernest Restrepo, a well-known archaeologist. Brinton also admired the fact that Restrepo published three summary publications that provided the discipline with a "fairly complete" description of the great variety of native peoples living at the time of European contact. Brinton further states that Restrepo's publications were "most creditable to the extent of his scholarship and the energy with which he has pursued investigations in the library as well as in the field" (1895, 44–45). Brinton found the maps especially valuable because of Restrepo's attention to detail. This made the variability by culture, controlled through time, useful for scholars interested in cultural evolution as well as in cultures constantly at war. For Brinton, Restrepo presented the opportunity to study cultures which remained isolated and culturally distinct rather than those that borrowed from or traded with each other. Brinton found this cultural pattern evident both before and after contact. He concluded this was evidence of cultural stagnation.

Hough felt that Argentina's displays did not warrant special mention, an assessment that modern historian Ashley Kerr (2017, 63) would see as dismissive, a missed opportunity which reflected the fact that Latin and South American countries did not represent its peoples in ways that supported nineteenth-century anthropological concepts of racial superiority and inferiority. As Kerr eloquently demonstrates, this was not for lack of trying on the part of Argentinian scholars who wanted to have their own exposition in Argentina and hence did not send any of their artifacts. Brinton was also disappointed but noted that Argentina had been home to a good deal of research during the 1880s that combined geology and archaeology and led to many conclusions about early human occupations. The Argentinian display concentrated on this work in the La Plata region, in an integrated exhibit constructed by Francisco B. Moreno, the director of Argentina's national museum. Moreno's display combined geology and archaeological specimens, but the best pieces from these research endeavors were not brought to Spain. Instead a series of watercolors depicting representative artifacts provided a means for scholarly comparisons. Brinton thought these were aesthetically pleasing and very educational. He does not describe any individual artifacts but instead mentions research questions for future students. For Hough, the lack of real artifacts made the exhibit second-rate, a debate that continues in the museum world today.

Ecuador contributed an exhibit of 1,327 artifacts comprised of several private collections and one from the government. These were not integrated and did not tell a coherent story of cultural history or interaction; therefore neither Hough nor Brinton thought they were of any value to anthropology in their present state. Hough did note that the ten cases of dark indurated pottery were interesting because of their curious forms. There were no explanations available due to the lack of archaeological control, but the materials were intriguing. Uruguay's contribution was the opposite: a small but well-displayed anthropological collection. Hough lists the types of objects that were shown; Brinton goes into more depth. The entire display was the work of one distinguished scientist, Juan Zorrilla de San Martin. This material had potential as anthropological data, but only if the excavator kept good notes about where objects were found. What San Martin displayed was essentially everything he had recovered from his excavations at village sites (*paraderos*). From Brinton's descriptions we can see that the displayed artifacts constituted surface collections and items uncovered through shallow digging. Unfortunately, San Martin provided no indication whether these were from a single site or multiple sites in one region. As a result, Brinton was leery of concluding that San Martin had any temporal control over the materials. Due to the inclusion of European manufactured beads, Brinton decided it was post-contact. Brinton felt the collection illustrated that the native peoples continued to make abundant stone tools even after they had begun trading with Europeans. And there were many stone tools shown; while Brinton does not give a total number of artifacts, he does state that more than nine thousand projectile points were mentioned in the catalogue! While Brinton does not say anything about the exhibition technique, the Uruguay display must have been densely packed.

For the sake of completeness Brinton included mention of several other countries which sent historic items but no archaeological material to illustrate the industries and cultures of indigenous inhabitants, while Hough did not even mention these displays. Cuba, which concentrated on natural resources that could be used for economic development, provided no indication that native peoples had ever lived on the island. Bolivia had a very small collection, primarily ethnographic, that did little to help visitors and scholars learn about the precontact and early-contact indigenous history of the region. Similarly, the Dominican Republic sent mainly historic settler materials supplemented by a few decorative pieces of indigenous manufacture: small idols, stone projective points, pottery figurines and utensils, and stone collars. Brinton considered the lack of anthropological perspective a lost opportunity to educate. He noted in particular that no one had evidently read his 1871 publication on the demographic origins and the linguistic affiliation of the native peoples. This poor scholarship meant that the Dominican Republic had no scholars who could undertake modern anthropology.

Brinton was clearly disappointed in these small, nonintegrated displays, but what really frustrated him was Peru's contribution. Peru, he says, was "small and unsatisfactory" (Brinton 1895, 51), especially when one considers the "unusual riches which that country offers in articles of American antiquity." There was no theme, no research-based initiative, just the odds and ends of ordinary forms. Nothing spectacular stood out to capture the viewer's attention and those who viewed it learned nothing. There was no attempt to integrate the materials from several private collections; neither did Brinton feel the need to name any of the donors, because none was contributing to knowledge. Brinton gives the impression that he had had high expectations for Peru and was disappointed at their lost opportunity to educate others about the exposition's central theme. Hough, on the other hand, did not express disappointment but noted that the red and blackware pottery bottles were interesting, especially four specimens illustrating human noses that had been eaten away—evidence of what Spanish physicians had diagnosed as lupus, an autoimmune disorder. As he did throughout his article, Hough concentrated on what was shown, not on what he wished had been shown.

CONCLUSION

Both Brinton and Hough concluded that, either singly or combined, the two expositions had not met the organizer's goal—a comparison of American and European cultures "when the new world was discovered and colonized" (Luce 1895 citing Madrid Commission 1892, 7). It had been a highly commendable goal but unattainable given the methodological problems of variable time for initial contact among American cultures, the dearth of comparable European archaeological materials, and the lack of control over national display methods and their placement. Equally important was the lack of understanding of what constituted real anthropological scholarship by all exhibitors. Most simply interpreted the exposition commissioners' goals as a request that they use indigenous-made materials in their displays. This resulted in the antiquarianism and amateurism of numerous displays that were based on collecting for personal reasons, without the work of transforming objects into scientifically useful specimens. As a result of exhibitors not following directions, Brinton and Hough concluded, Madrid as a whole did not display anthropological knowledge, but there were niches of anthropological conversion, and glimmers that certain postcolonial nations were modernizing and capable of conducting "scientific" research—if they followed the American model.

Brinton and Hough both noted that individuals in previously colonized nations were capable of conducting state-of-the-art anthropology that could be seen as either American or European in intent, modernity, and sophistication, and that a few nations were ready to come into the fold as progressive scientists. From a nationalist standpoint, Hough and Brinton claimed the Madrid Exposition and its components for Americanist anthropology. They decided which countries had individuals whose contemporary anthropological research met quality standards in methods of data collection, data analysis, interpretation, presentation, and basic standards of scholarship, using both exhibit and catalogue formats. Equally important was whether these scientific activities were supported by national governments. This meant that Mexico (which had received significant assistance from an American archaeologist-museologist), Costa Rica, Nicaragua, Columbia, and Uruguay were ready to be considered modern centers of Americanist anthropology. Their premier scientists should be recognized and their works read by all American anthropologists interested in the region. There was also hope for Guatemala, but the rest of Central and South America were still not ready to engage in modern science. In a sense, their collecting of indigenous materials was mere antiquarianism or a display of imperial spoils of conquest and colonial settlement.

For Brinton, these individuals provided scientific information to help with his personal intellectual goal of mapping, recording, and classifying peoples in time and space. Hough found even more material of use. His focus on material objects rather than the classifying of cultures meant he had greater latitude to find new items (single objects and collections) to extend his knowledge of material culture and technology. These materials were contextualized sufficiently enough to be used in studies where evolutionary developmental rank was more important than specific cultures. Like peer review today, Hough's and Brinton's critiques contain indications that the scholarship under review helped them with their own research projects. Their reports constitute an acknowledgement that exposition exhibits could be read and critiqued like publications. The problem, of course, was that exhibits were ephemeral, and future scholars could not return to them as scholarly resources. What remained were summaries such as those Brinton and Hough had written, catalogues published by the exposition organizers, and the objects themselves, which were returned to their owners and, in a sense, scattered. There is no adequate photographic record of any display case.

Brinton and Hough found nothing in the displays that made them question their theoretical frameworks, the superiority of Americanist anthropology, their assumptions of the utility of unilinear evolution, or their notions of progress and the superiority of American racialized civilization—an assessment that extended to Spain as an imperialistic and colonizing entity. Brinton noted that the displays "show[ed] the progress of the arts and sciences in the century following 1492 and in a general manner the genius of that civilization which was introduced into the New World in that period" (1895, 23). Hough seems less concerned with this theory and more interested in taking intellectually orphaned objects and transforming them into potential anthropological data that could be used for technological development studies. To a lesser degree their use could extend to fulfill the central goals of nineteenth-century anthropology: to find and acknowledge, name, date, classify, and catalogue the different peoples of the world. Assuming his readership understood the importance of properly documented and scientifically arranged artifacts, Hough basically reported on the most useful materials. Size, measured in the tonnage of artifacts sent or the number of floor cases erected, was an important marker of importance, for it indicated how common the item was in the source culture. It also became a proxy for how much space the exposition organizers allotted, how much effort the postcolonial nation had taken, (i.e., how important a country felt anthropology was), and how much anthropological research was occurring in a particular area. This assessment of significance was based on floor space or density of artifacts, object authenticity, and an object's potential usefulness for understanding technology, cultural advancement, and artistic ability, rather than on quality of display. It also indicated that one type of artifact (pottery, gold jewelry, or stone tools) was not uniformly displayed across exhibits as indications of their transformation into anthropological specimens. The general category "well-made object," as a proxy for distinct ways of life that could then be compared, was dominant and the central unit of analysis for Hough. The second unit of analysis was the collection of an individual who recognized and used anthropological discourse and categories. National display was superfluous except as an organizing frame for discussing exhibits; arrangement by postcolonial nation did not make an exhibit anthropological.

Brinton's report was concerned with what a comparative anthropologist rather than an interested layperson could learn from the displays. He thus rarely comments on the effectiveness of the displays as educational tools. Brinton assessed exhibits with anthropological potential, focusing on potential networks of scholars and institutions, as is evident from the fact that he mentioned all contributions, regardless of whether anthropological interpretation centered the display. His assessment of whether each exhibit embodied an anthropological perspective for archaeological exhibits became the standard criteria for exhibits and book reviews. It was the background work—how the material was collected and then analyzed—that constituted the anthropological perspective or anthropological potential of displayed indigenous objects. What was more important than the display technique was whether the materials shown were obtained from excavations or fieldwork by a recognized individual who understood and used modern anthropological methods of data recovery, especially the documentation of object location within a site context, and recorded geographically location information for the objects in a site or region. Equally important was evidence of anthropological transformation through post-excavation or collection categorization and classification. Only then did museology enter Brinton's assessment, and his primary criterion was whether the exhibit was constructed with care—that is, whether the research results were clear. This meant that the catalogue descriptions and the hierarchical classification scheme were as important as the objects themselves. Brinton saw published catalogues as sets of artifact labels that should include "minute descriptions where the various objects were found, and also assign them to their probable original makers" (1895, 24). Whether an exhibit was anthropological was more than simply supplying indigenous-made objects; uniqueness and rarity of artifacts were not enough to make an exhibit anthropological. It was the process of scholarly work, systematically applied, that transformed objects into data-carrying specimens and made exhibits anthropological. The science was in the analysis, not the objects themselves. This is an important consideration and conclusion that will impact anthropology as much as its conceptions of sociocultural progress and assumptions about technological evolution.

Brinton and Hough were pioneers of anthropological science in the United States. Their theoretical and methodological approaches were in line with European anthropologists. Establishing intellectual control over indigenous societies of the Americas, particularly those in the territories claimed by the United States, were priorities. Expanding government funds for science beginning around the mid-nineteenth century meant there was more institutional support for natural-history-style science: systematic collecting, centralized accumulation, and publication of detailed analyses. The United States was building the infrastructure for leading Americanist anthropology. At the time, most professionals were employed by museums. Hough and Brinton's reviews placed positive valuations on each nation's ability to display scientifically contextualized collections and disseminate the work of local scholars. Based on participation in the expositions, the United States and Mexico were the leaders. The ability of other nations to produce exhibits of material of *anthropological* interest remained to be seen. Building the infrastructure for anthropological science would continue to unfold over time, dependent on each postcolonial nation's capacity for development. Peer review was necessary to establish benchmarks for what constituted anthropological scholarship on the American continents.

REFERENCES

Baker, Lee D. 2000. "Daniel G. Brinton's Success on the Road to Obscurity, 1890–99." *Cultural Anthropology* 15 (3): 394–423.

Barnard, Alan. 2000. *History and Theory in Anthropology*. Cambridge: Cambridge University Press.

Brinton, Daniel G. 1871. "The Arawack Languages of Guiana in its Linguistic and Ethnological Relations." *Transactions of the American Philosophical Society* 14 (3): 427–44.

———. 1893. "Current Notes on Anthropology—No. 24." *Science* 22 (562): 256–57.

———. 1894a. "The 'Nation' as an Element in Anthropology." In *Memoirs of the International Congress of Anthropology*, edited by C. Staniland Wake, 19–36. Chicago: Schulte.

———. 1894b. "The Present Status of American Linguistics." In *Memoirs of the International Congress of Anthropology*, edited by C. Staniland Wake, 335–38. Chicago: Schulte.

———. 1895. "Report upon the Collections Exhibited at the Columbian Historical Exposition." From the Report of the Madrid Commission, 1892. Washington: Government Printing Office.

———. 1896. "The Aims of Anthropology." *Journal of American Folklore* 8 (30): 247–49.

Chamberlain, Alexander F. 1899. "In Memoriam: Daniel Garrison Brinton." *Journal of American Folklore* 12 (46): 215–25.

Crane, Agnes. 1893. "Discovery of Mexican Feather-Work in Madrid." *Science* 32 (518): 11.

Darnell, Regna. 1976. "Daniel Brinton and the Professionalization of American Anthropology." In *American Anthropology: The Early Years*, edited by John V. Murra, 69–85. Proceedings of the American Ethnological Society, 1974. St. Paul MN: West.

———. 1988. *Daniel Garrison Brinton: The "Fearless Critic" of Philadelphia*. Philadelphia: University of Pennsylvania Publications in Anthropology No. 3.

———. 2003. "Daniel Garrison Brinton and the View from Philadelphia." In *Philadelphia and the Development of Americanist Archaeology*, edited by Don Fowler and David Wilcox, 21–35. Tuscaloosa: University of Alabama Press.

Duclos, Rebecca. 1999. "The Cartographies of Collecting." In *Museums and the Future of Collecting*, edited by Simon Knell, 48–62. Aldershot, England: Ashgate.

Exposición Histórico-Americana. 1892. *Catálogo de los Objectos que Presenta La nación Español a la Exposición Histórico-Americana de Madrid*. 2 vols. Madrid: Sucesores de Rivadeneyra.

Hough, Walter. 1893. "The Columbian Historical Exposition in Madrid." *American Anthropologist* 6 (1): 271–77.

———. 1895. "The Ancient Central and South American Pottery in the Columbian Historical Exposition at Madrid in 1892." Report of the U.S. Madrid Commission, 1892, 339–65.

Judd, Neil M. 1936. "Walter Hough: An Appreciation." *American Anthropologist* 38 (3): 471–81.

Kerr, Ashley. 2017. "From Savagery to Sovereignty: Identity, Politics and International Expositions of Argentine Anthropology (1878–1892)." *Isis* 108 (1): 62–81.

Kohlstedt, Sally G. 1987. "International Exchange and National Style: A View of Natural History Museums in the United States, 1850–1900." In *Scientific Colonialism: A Cross-Cultural Comparison*, edited by Nathan Reingold and Marc Rothenberg, 167–90. Washington DC: Smithsonian Institution Press.

Luce, Stephen B. 1895. *History of the Participation of the United States in the Columbian Historical Exposition at Madrid. Report of the United States Commission to the Columbian Historical Exposition at Madrid 1892–93.* 7–17. Washington: Government Printing Office.

Mason, Otis T. 1882. "What is Anthropology? A Lecture Delivered in the National Museum." Washington DC. March 18, 1882. Judd & Detweiler.

Mundy, Barbara and Dana Leibsohn. 1996. "Of Copies, Casts and Codices: Mexico on Display in 1892." RES: *Anthropology and Aesthetics* 29–30: 326–43.

Nuttall, Zelia. 1896. "Ancient Mexican Feather Work at the Columbian Historical Exposition at Madrid, 1892." *Science* n.s. 3 (59): 243.

Peralta, M. de. 1893. *Etnographia de la República de Costa Rica*. Madrid: Exposición Histórico-Americana.

Plancarte, Francisco. 1893 "Archeologic Explorations in Michoacán, Mexico." *American Anthropologist* 6 (1): 79–84.

Read, Charles H. 1893. *Report on the Historical Exhibition at Madrid on the Occasion of the Fourth Centenary of Columbus in 1892*. London: William Clowes & Sons for the British Museum.

Smith, Anthony. 2005. "Ethno-Symbolism and the Study of Nationalism." In *Nations and Nationalism: A Reader,* edited by Philip Spencer and Howard Wollman, 23–31. New Brunswick NJ: Rutgers University Press.

Wilson, Thomas. 1893. "Archaeology and Ethnology." *American Naturalist* 27 (322): 907–12.

Wolf, Eric. 1982. *Europe and the People without History*. Berkeley: University of California Press.

JOHN LEAVITT

4

Worcester, Massachusetts, 1909

Language, Culture, and the Boas-Freud Intersection

During the first part of September in 1909, the then all-graduate Clark University in Worcester, Massachusetts, and its president, the psychologist G. Stanley Hall, commemorated twenty years of the university and his presidency with a celebration that included four conferences: one on psychology, pedagogy, and school hygiene; another on child welfare; another on science and mathematics; and a conference on China and the Far East (Evans and Koelsch 1985; Rosenzweig 1992). Among the speakers at the psychology conference were Sigmund Freud, C. G. Jung, and the psychologist William Stern (who had all come over from Europe on the same boat, under Clark's auspices); Edward Titchener, often considered the founder of experimental psychology in the United States; Adolf Meyer, one of the most influential psychiatrists of the first half of the twentieth century; and Franz Boas, then professor of anthropology at Columbia University in New York. Among the attendees were William James and the anarchist Emma Goldman. Most of the psychology lectures were published the following year in Hall's *American Journal of Psychology*. The circumstances and the content of the lectures reveal a moment of contact, or failure of contact, or of unacknowledged contact, among some of modernity's major theories of the unconscious and its relationship to language and culture.[1]

ROADS TO WORCESTER

In 1909, Freud was the head of what still looked rather like a cult of psychoanalysis, which received little respect from either most psychologists or most psychiatrists. Unusually among academic psychologists, President Hall, on the other hand, had been an admirer of Freud's for some time and was eager to have Freud present his ideas in an American context. For Freud, this was a chance to legitimate the movement internationally. He traveled from Vienna to Bremen, where he met up with his collaborators C. G. Jung and Sandor Ferenczi (Jung was also an invitee to the Clark conference, and Ferenczi seems to have come along to offer support) and, from there, all sailed for America.

Freud's personal diary for this trip has been preserved.[2] On the boat, Freud was disturbed by the presence of the psychologist William Stern, who had written a hostile review of Freud's great work *The Interpretation of Dreams* (Stern 1901), calling it unscientific—the worst epithet that could be directed against Freud. Stern had also been invited to Clark: he was a theorist of personality, a specialist on the psychology of legal testimony and memory, the inventor of what we now call the Intelligence Quotient, and, along with his wife Clara, one of the first serious students of child language—their joint book, *Die Kindersprache*, had been published in 1907. In his diary Freud calls Stern an *Ekel*, someone or something that provokes disgust, and a "shabby Jew" (Rosenzweig 1992, 57). Clearly, something about Stern and his self-presentation rubbed Freud the wrong way. Besides Freud himself, most of his most important followers were Jewish, and he was very concerned that his scientific movement not be treated as a kind of Jewish club. This is one of the reasons he seized on the Swiss Protestant Jung as his apparent successor.[3]

Boas, for his part, just came up from New York, but this trip was a continuation of a long history with Hall and with Clark University. In 1887, after his initial Northwest Coast fieldwork, Boas had decided to give up on his increasingly bleak job prospects in Germany—largely due to his own Jewish background—and stay in the United States as assistant editor of the journal *Science*. The following year, Hall, whom Boas had met by chance on a train, invited him to the newly-founded Clark University and made him head of the new anthropology department. But Hall had made promises to a lot of people when founding the university. Unable to fulfill many of these, largely due to the stubbornness of the millionnaire Maecenas of the university—Jonas Gilman Clark himself—Hall dissembled, which only enraged many of his faculty. In 1892, after a period of demands from the faculty and prevarication, then refusal, from Clark, a number of faculty members, including Boas, resigned.[4] The 1909 conference, with honorary doctorates awarded to the speakers, may be seen as Hall's attempt to mend fences; a large percentage of the North American speakers were in fact former Clark professors who had left in protest.[5]

CROSSING PATHS

The first day of lectures was Monday, September 6. It included the first of Stern's three talks on legal testimony, forgetting, and the nature of personality. The next day, Boas was supposed to have the "prime time" slot at 11 a.m., but at the last minute he was asked to give it up for Freud, which Boas was apparently happy to do. As the Boston *Evening Standard* reports,

> Dr. Franz Boas, now of Columbia University, formerly of Clark, who had generously yielded his place on the morning program, was enthusiastic over the sacrifice, and though Dr. Boas's friends consoled themselves that he was worth waiting for, they were glad of an early introduction to the Viennese, who seemed fairly entitled to the honor of an epoch-making discovery.

So Freud spoke on Tuesday morning, Boas that afternoon.[6] While the European invitees each gave several lectures, the North Americans had been asked to give only one each. Boas's talk, "Psychological Problems in Anthropology," was published the following year in the *American Journal of Psychology* (1910). In it, he reprises his critique of evolutionistic models of human stages based on similarities of institutions, arguing that, since what to us look like similar institutions often have very different psychological and social motivations, a real anthropological psychology should compare these motivations, not their mere results. The talk represents what George Stocking (1974, 220, cited in Kenny 2015, 178) calls "a much more sophisticated view of the cultural determination of behavior" than that in his earlier work.

Stern, Freud, and Jung spoke in German, which does not seem to have discomfited anyone. Freud's lecture was the first of five. Each morning he would go for a walk with Ferenczi to work out what the day's topic should be; he then delivered his lecture without notes, as was his custom. Freud started with the case of Anna O, as treated by his colleague Josef Breuer, the founding case of the *Studies in Hysteria* and, indeed, of psychoanalysis; he then presented the history of the development of his and Breuer's therapeutic model, from hypnosis to the "talking cure" to free association. The second of Freud's lectures was on repression and the unconscious, the third on dreams and the psychopathology of everyday life, the fourth on sexuality, and the fifth on transference and issues of modern life. Freud thought his fourth topic might be dicey for what he took to be the puritanical American public, and he wanted to have the convincing evidence from dreams in place before taking it on.

After appearing in an English translation in Hall's journal (Freud 1910a), the lectures were published in German (1910b); they are now part of the Standard Edition under the title *Five Lectures on Psychoanalysis* (1910 [1957]) and are still considered one of the best short introductions to the field. My own citations here will be from the initial translation published in the *American Journal* (1910a).

On Friday, September 10, William James came to Worcester from Boston, heard both Jung and Freud speak, and spent the afternoon walking with Freud (Simon 1967). That evening, Freud, Jung, Boas, and others were presented with honorary degrees. Along with Freud and Jung, James ended up passing the night at Hall's house, where he spent much of the evening talking with Jung and encouraging his interest in spiritualism and the occult. Both of these were anathema to Freud, and their increasing centrality in Jung's work would be one of the factors leading to Jung's complete break with Freud and psychoanalysis.

On that Friday afternoon, a now-iconic group photo was taken of most of the participants in the psychology conference [figure 1]. We note first the utter and complete absence of women, even though at least one is mentioned in the newspaper report as taking part in the conference. There are two Japanese visitors and one African American, the neuropathologist Solomon Carter Fuller, one of the early researchers on Alzheimer's disease, who stands in back on the far right.

Hall—the convener—stands squarely in the middle of the front row, with Freud, looking very dapper with hat and walking stick, to his immediate left. The (apparently enormous) Jung towers over both Freud on one side and the diminutive Dr. Meyer on the other; also behind Freud are his acolytes Ernest Jones, Ferenczi, and A. A. Brill. On Hall's right is Leo Burgerstein, a specialist in school psychology, then Stern and Titchener, in what looks like a place of honor for the academic psychologists, flanking honored guest William James. At the end (or beginning) of the line stands Boas, looking straight at the camera. His crooked half-smile may be faintly ironic, or it may be the effect of his dueling scars. The cultural critic Lewis Mumford would later write about Boas's "gaping forehead," his "distorted mouth," and "the bulging eyes that seemed to focus on one like a magnifying glass" (1970, 80). Certainly, here, Boas looks like his own man. We note, too, that his outfit is virtually identical to that of Stern, whom Freud had mocked as a shabby Jew, except that Stern's coat is double-breasted and his bowtie is straight.[7] While this may be unwarranted speculation, one wonders to what extent Freud's apparent deafness or resistance to Boas's message—this will be discussed below—was in part a reaction to Boas's presentation of self.

THE CONTENTS: THE UNCONSCIOUS AND LANGUAGE

In September 1909, Freud was fifty-three, Boas fifty-one. Both had arrived at the stage of systematizing and institutionalizing what each felt were the great and in fact world-changing discoveries of their earlier years. Freud's was the discovery of coherent unconscious mental processes that could be glimpsed through gaps in conscience functioning: in dreams, mistakes, and neurotic symptoms. Freud's mission was to extend the scope of subjectivity to encompass more and more of this repressed material, and coming to America was a way of gaining legitimacy for this mission. As he put it in his autobiography:

> In Europe I felt as though I were despised; but over there I found myself received by the foremost men as an equal. As I stepped onto the platform at Worcester to deliver my *Five Lectures upon Psychoanalysis* it seemed like the realization of some incredible day-dream: psychoanalysis was no longer a product of delusion, it had become a valuable part of reality. (Freud 1925 [1963], 99)

Fig. 2. Psychology Conference Group, Clark University, September 1909. *First row, left to right*: Franz Boas, E. B. Titchener, William James, William Stern, Leo Burgerstein, G. Stanley Hall, Sigmund Freud, Carl S. Jung, Adolf Meyer, H. S. Jennings. *Second row*: C. E. Seashore, Joseph Jastrow, J. McK. Cattell, E. F. Buchner, E. Katzenellenbogen, Ernest Jones, A. A. Brill, Wm. H. Burnham, A. F. Chamberlain. *Third row*: Albert Schinz, J. A. Magni, B. T. Baldwin, F. Lyman Wells, G. M. Forbes, E.A. Kirkpatrick, Sandor Ferenczi, E. C. Sanford, J. P. Porter, Sakyo Kanda, Hikoso Kakise. *Fourth row*: G. E. Dawson, S. P. Hayes, E. B. Holt, C. S. Berry, G. M. Whipple, Frank Drew, J. W. A. Young, I. N. Wilson, K. J. Karlson, H. H. Goddard, H. I . Klopp, S.C. Fuller. Photograph credit: Wellcome Collection, photo number v0027600.

The foundation of Boas's thinking was the automatism of much of thought and behavior and the nonconsciousness of most of language structure, and a large part of a person's beliefs and feelings. His discovery was that of the adequacy of all languages, the legitimacy of all cultures, and a new definition of civilization: the greater and greater spread of identification of the self to encompass, eventually, all of humankind. Rather than lumping together diverse societies and languages as "primitive" because they lacked particular elements possessed by the modern West, Boas and his students were in the process of investigating their diversity and their specificities. This was particularly the case for societies without writing, and so deemed "prehistoric." In an address to the joint meeting of the American Anthropological Association and the American Philological Association in 1905, Boas had argued that the world's oral literatures deserved the kind of respect and philological attention that his audience devoted to Greek and Latin texts (1906). Instead of the three-layered world of savage, barbarian, and civilized peoples envisioned by most evolutionistic anthropologists of the late nineteenth century, Boas was proposing an alternative universe of a multitude of languages comparable to Greek and Latin, literatures comparable to classical ones, and civilizations comparable to those of Greece and Rome.

At Clark, both Freud and Boas spoke of unconscious mental processes, and, for both, language and languages played a central role in their conceptualization.

Freud began his lectures recounting his colleague Josef Breuer's work with a patient they called Anna O.[8] One of the main features of what Breuer and Freud called her hysteria was her proneness to states of dissociation, which the psychologist Pierre Janet had called *double conscience*, manifested by linguistic changes: in these states she would apparently forget German and speak only in another language, particularly in English. In one situation, "she could not express herself in any language, until finally she thought of the words of an English nursery song, and thereafter she could think and speak only in this language" (Freud 1910a, 186).

Anna O.'s mastery of English in these states was hard for her doctors to explain. Breuer first induced her to speak under hypnosis: "Symptoms of the disease would disappear when in hypnosis the patient could be made to remember the situation and the associative connections under which they first appeared, provided free vent was given to the emotions which they aroused." It was Anna O who called this method "the talking cure"—and she called it that in English (1910a, 184).

The model of the mind offered by Freud is that of the city of London, with its layers and layers of historical associations and monuments to the past. The neurotic patient is analogized to someone who spends his or her time weeping in front of a monument to a tragedy that happened five hundred years ago, without knowing why. (Later, Freud would substitute Rome, with its layers of history, for London.) Note that here the concern is with the meaning of the monuments as carried in their inscriptions: the monuments bear a verbal message.

In the second lecture, Freud describes how he abandoned hypnosis as a method, having found that free association in the normal state was as effective in connecting to lost memories which, when verbalized with the appropriate emotion, led to the disappearance of symptoms. He argues that the unconscious is made up of repressed memories that manifest themselves in dreams and slips of the tongue and, if powerful enough, in neurotic symptoms. The way to defuse these is to bring them to consciousness, which means verbalizing them. This is the real sense of the "talking cure": that making something conscious means giving it a linguistic form. In his paper on the unconscious published some years later, Freud would call this—the only way to know the unconscious—a process of "transformation or translation (*Umsetzung oder Übersetzung*) into something conscious" (1915 [1957], 161). In the same paper he would go so far as to equate consciousness or potential consciousness with access to "word-presentations" (*Wortvorstellungen*) connected to "thing-presentations" (*Sachvorstellungen*), while the unconscious—that is, that which is barred from conscious awareness—is made up of "thing-presentations" alone (1915 [1957], 201–202; for an elaboration of this dichotomy, see Laplanche and Leclaire 1961 [1972]).

The lecture on dreams was the first time Freud called them the *via regia* (the royal road) to an understanding of the unconscious (cf. Leavitt 2010). But dreams can only be known through their retelling, in language. Dream ideation is the result of processes of disguising an original unacceptable message, processes that are typical of the unconscious. And while most of the dream contents are attributable to the circumstances of the dreamer, some, primarily those of a sexual tenor, stand out as apparently far more widespread and archaic.

[Dream] symbolism in part varies with the individual, but in part is of a typical nature, and seems to be identical with the symbolism which we suppose to lie behind our myths and legends. It is not impossible that these latter creations of the people (*Schöpfungen der Völker*) may find their explanation from the study of dreams. (1910a, 203)

Already in *The Interpretation of Dreams* Freud had quoted Havelock Ellis to call dreams "an archaic world of vast emotions and imperfect thought" (1900 [1953], 591)—meaning, presumably, that they derive from the early stages of personal development, but by no means avoiding the implication of cavemen and savages.

Freud was trained in medicine and otherwise shared his milieu's general presumption of the superior rationality of the modern European adult male over all other kinds of humans. Freud always seems to have been sympathetic to an analogy between levels of mental functioning in the individual and the level of the psychological development of the human race, so that exploration of the "depths" of the modern adult unconscious could give access to the "archaic" modes of the small child and of our primitive ancestors. The work of two major scholars, work that Freud knew very well indeed, would have encouraged this view. One was the "psychology of peoples" (*Völkerpsychologie*) of the great experimental psychologist Wilhelm Wundt (1832–1920), which saw epochs of human history as universally characterized by distinctive modes of thought, from the primitive to the civilized (e.g., Wundt 1913 [1916]; on schools of *Völkerpsychologie*, see Klautke 2013). The other was the British neurologist John Hughlings Jackson (1835–1911), who maintained that the modern human brain contains different structures associated with different functions. Those involving rational functions were the most recent to develop; when they failed in some way, primitive impulses deriving from more archaic strata would emerge (cf. Jackson 1884; Kenny 2015, 177). Both of these theories drew heavily on the evolutionist anthropology of Herbert Spencer, E. B. Tylor, John

Lubbock, and J. G. Frazer, which equated the social institutions and, in the cases of Spencer and Lubbock, the mentality of early man with those of children, peasants, and contemporary colonized peoples, all of whom they regarded as "primitive." For all of these theorists, similar phenomena must have similar causes, and ontogeny and history recapitulate phylogeny.

This is precisely the approach that by 1909 Boas had been denying and debunking for over twenty years. For Boas, there was simply no reason to assume, much less to maintain as a methodological principle, that all phenomena that to us seemed similar had the same meaning for those who practiced them, and so the same origin. On the contrary, the evidence suggested overwhelmingly that apparently similar institutions could arise from different motives and reflect different assumptions about the world. Behind this was the foundational claim, borne out by Boas's own field research, that people in different societies had different central concerns. This fact, long evident for historical societies—it was precisely what historians and philologists studied—was in fact true for all societies, including those that had been colonized and partially destroyed and that Spencer et al. were labeling primitive.

Although he was trained in physics, Boas's central interest had been the relationship between the world as science analyzed it and the world as lived by human subjects. This concern drew him from physics to psychology, then, as he became convinced that these questions were collective as much as individual, to geography, and finally to anthropology and linguistics. Among his inspirations was the work of the brothers Wilhelm and Alexander von Humboldt in the early nineteenth century and the non-Wundtian, Humboldt-inspired *Völkerpsychologie* developed from midcentury by the philosopher Moritz Lazarus and the linguist Heymann Steinthal (Kalmar 1987; Trautmann-Waller 2004). This older tradition relied much less on simple evolutionist models and sought, rather, to characterize languages and cultures as distinctive wholes before moving to grand comparisons. Boas became familiar with this tradition when working with the field ethnologist Adolph Bastian at the Royal Ethnological Museum in Berlin in the mid-1880s. From it he drew the idea of a cultural and linguistic unconscious and of the individual as guided, without knowing it, by grammatical and cultural rules.

For Boas, as he shows in his Clark lecture, the unconscious is not an archaic layer held down by conscious rationality, but rather that which has become so automatic, so habitual, as not to require conscious attention. This kind of automatism characterizes all human societies, at whatever "level of development." The great example here is languages.

> I believe this subject can be made clear most easily by a comparison with a similar phenomenon in languages.... The automatic and rapid use of language has brought it about that the infinitely large number of ideas have been reduced by classification to a lesser number, which by constant use have established firm associations, and which can be used automatically.

More than this, however, such automatized collective systems differ from each other. They are historical products, not emanations of universal stages.

> It seems important to emphasize the fact that the groups of ideas expressed by specific words show very material differences in different languages, and do not conform by any means to the same principles of classification. (1910, 376)

Here he gives the example of multiple words in English for different forms of water—lake, stream, glass of water—which speakers of English conceptualize as different "things" even though they know they are all forms of water. In the *Handbook of American Indian Languages* and the *Mind of Primitive Man*, both published in 1911, this would be followed by the now-famous example of Eskimo words for snow (Leavitt 2011, 126).

Boas's central argument here is that language itself provides a model for the indubitable existence of unconscious mental processes.

> The behavior of primitive man makes it perfectly clear that all these linguistic classes have never risen into consciousness, and that consequently their origin must be sought not in rational, but in entirely unconscious processes of the mind. They must be due to a grouping of sense impressions and of concepts which is not in any sense of the term voluntary, but which develops from entirely different psychological causes. It is a characteristic of linguistic classifications

that they never rise into consciousness, while other classifications, although the same unconscious origin prevails, often do rise into consciousness. (1910, 377)

There is an interesting shift in this passage. First Boas asserts that it is the behavior of primitive man that reveals the presence of unconscious linguistic categories; then, two sentences later, their unconsciousness is now a characteristic of linguistic classifications in general. Such classifications never rise into consciousness for anybody, primitive or civilized—except, perhaps, for the trained linguist or, in an idea that Sapir and Whorf would carry forward from Humboldt, the person who knows a number of very different languages and can contrast them.

Boas continues to talk about irrational taboos that characterize modern civilized life. His overall claim is that the anthropological comparison of social practices—as well, of course, as the comparison of languages—reveals the enormous role played by unconscious mental processes.

We can certainly read this as an endorsement of this central tenet of Freudianism, and Boas indeed remained sympathetic to the fundamentals of psychoanalysis. Freud is mentioned only once in the 1911 edition of *The Mind of Primitive Man* (1911, 121), as part of a discussion of atavism, but it is a fully approving mention. Boas is replying to those who argue for the biological foundation of racial primitivity on the basis of stories of people born into "savage" societies who become civilized, then one day go "savage" again. Boas cites Freud's insistence on the continuing effect of early childhood experience as confirmation of his own theory of the power of habit. His reference is to Freud's Clark lectures.

AFTER WORCESTER

When Boas gave his lecture at Clark, his doctrine seems to have been fully formed. Two years later he would publish his two major single works, the *Handbook of American Indian Languages* and *The Mind of Primitive Man*, both of which reproduce entire sections from the Clark talk. For Boas, the best model for the unconscious would continue to be language, which of necessity must be massively habitual and automatic and so largely outside the purview of conscious awareness. Since languages and cultures are both diverse, the unconscious systemic aspect of thinking will also differ depending on the social situation in which one comes into being. This kind of unconscious mental process—unconscious not because it has been repressed but simply because of the complexity that makes it impossible to be the object of conscious awareness—overlaps with what Freud called the preconscious (*Vorbewusste*).

Many of Boas's most important students were friendly with psychoanalysis (Benedict, Mead, Lowie, Sapir), and his first Columbia PhD, A. L. Kroeber, trained and practiced as a psychoanalyst himself (Burnham 2012). The Boasian school as a whole would come to adopt various modes of psychoanalytic thinking in the development of the "Culture and Personality" school (Bock 1988).

At the time of the Clark lectures, Freud had launched psychoanalysis as an international movement (albeit a primarily European, Germanophone, and largely Jewish one), with its associations, congresses, regular journals, and established doctrines and practices. Yet many of what we now think of as key Freudian ideas—especially those about evolution and myth, which are the ones that still most upset anthropologists—had not yet been formulated and do not appear in the Clark lectures. The next few years would see some major expansions of psychoanalytic doctrine: starting immediately after their American journey, both Freud and Jung would seek, respectively, to apply psychoanalysis and Jung's depth psychology—hitherto clinical tools and theories bearing on individuals and their personal histories—to questions of myth, religion, and social organization. The shift is manifested in the founding of a new journal, *Imago*, the mission of which was to offer psychoanalytic insights into broad cultural and historical questions.

Soon after their American voyage, both Freud and Jung worked on elaborating the difference between what Freud called "two principles of mental functioning": a development of the primary and secondary processes, characteristic, respectively, of conscious and unconscious thought, that he had distinguished in *The Interpretation of Dreams*. Freud's paper "Two Principles of Mental Functioning" (1911 [1958]), which he published in 1911, maintains that there are two kinds of thinking—one associated with dreams and slips of the tongue, small children, and primitive people; the other with rationality, a characteristic of healthy modern civilized adults.

Jung published his version of the theory of the two principles in 1912, as the first chapter of his *Psychology of the Unconscious* (1912 [1916]). In it, he distinguishes two kinds of thinking— modern, rational thinking, closely bound up with language; and an archaic, nonrational form expressed in symbols and which was to be found in dreams, in mythology, and in the thinking of lower, primitive races. The passage from primitive to rational thinking was understood as another case of ontogeny recapitulating phylogeny (27).

It is remarkable that these texts, coming so soon after both authors heard Boas at the Clark conference (in fact, the basic ideas for both were expressed in letters in 1910), would so completely ignore Boas's central argument, an argument that seemed to have demonstrated the inadequacy of the gross equivalence of "primitive" people with early humans, children, neurotics, and dream-mentation that remained central to both of their arguments.[9]

Freud intensified his evolutionism with the 1912–13 publication of *Totem and Taboo*, originally under the title "Some Points of Agreement between the Mental Lives of Savages [*Wilden*] and Neurotics," which would become the subtitle upon its appearance in book form. Here, in 1912, after presumably hearing Boas, Freud adopts and restates the fundamental tenets of Spencerian evolutionism:

> There are men still living who, as we believe, stand very near to primitive man, far nearer than we do, and whom we therefore regard as his direct heirs and representatives. Such is our view of those whom we describe as savages, or half-savages (*sogennanten Wilden oder halbwilden Völker*), and their mental life must have a particular interest for us if we are right in seeing in it a well-preserved picture of an early stage of our own development. (1912-13 [1955], 1)

Boas, of course, had showed again and again—and yet again in the Clark lecture—that "those whom we describe as" *Wilden* did not constitute a single uniform category, but a vast variety of civilizations and languages. Yet Freud's project of comparing neurotics and *Wilden* apparently required the existence of *Wilden* as such. Moreover, Freud says that his inspiration for this comparison came from Wundt and Jung. Boas and his mentor Bastian are cited only for bits of ethnographic data. Boas is mentioned as one of a number of "eminent American ethnologists" who derive totems from an ancestral guardian spirit (119)—an attribution many were making to Boas and which Boas himself would deny was his general position (1916).

In his discussion of animism, Freud says that "I will merely refer to the standard works of Herbert Spencer, J. G. Frazer, Andrew Lang, E. B. Tylor, and Wilhelm Wundt, from which all that I have to say about magic and animism is derived" (1912-13 [1955], 75n1). The ethnography he draws on is primarily that of Australian aboriginal peoples, held by many evolutionists to be the most primitive of living humans and so the best available source of data on all aspects of early human life.

> I shall take as the basis of this comparison the tribes which have been described by anthropologists as the most backward and miserable of savages, the aborigines of Australia, the youngest continent, in whose fauna, too, we can still observe much that is archaic and that has perished elsewhere. (1)

Already, in 1912, we might call this an archaic position, even an atavism. Boas would attack it in the revised 1938 edition of *The Mind of Primitive Man*:

> Particularly Freud's comparison of primitive culture and the psychoanalytic interpretations of European behavior seem to lack a scientific background. They appear to me as fancies in which neither the aspect of primitive life nor that of civilized life is sustained by tangible evidence. (176)

And even Kroeber, who was about to begin training in psychoanalysis, concluded his discussion of the English translation of *Totem and Taboo* with the following:

> One remark may be extended to psychologists of the unconscious who propose to follow in Freud's footsteps: there really is a great deal of ethnology not at all represented by the authors whom Freud discusses. To students of this side of the science the line of work initi-

ated by Tylor and developed and most notably represented among the living by Frazer, is not so much ethnology as an attempt to psychologize with ethnological data... If psychoanalysts wish to establish serious contacts with historical ethnology, they must first learn to know that such an ethnology exists. (1920, 55)

Totem and Taboo, and its many successors, would drive a wedge between anthropology and psychoanalysis—and it was undertaken immediately after Freud and Jung received warnings, in person, from Boas, that this kind of unjustified overgeneralization was no longer acceptable.

FAILURE TO CONNECT? OR TOUCH AND REBOUND?

After the encounter in Worcester, then, Freud continued in precisely the direction Boas had warned against. In his turn to collective psychology and the history of the human mind, he proposed rethinking human nature based on the asserted duality of, on the one hand, a primitive mode of thought characterizing early humans, contemporary savages, small children, the dreaming mind, and the mentally ill, expressed in mysterious symbols or disguised messages; versus, on the other hand, a civilized mode of thought characterizing healthy urbanized modern Euro-American adults and expressed in verbal language. To maintain this equivalence, which was denounced by Boas and increasingly denied by twentieth-century anthropologists, Freud somehow looked away from the anthropological literature then being produced and instead limited his sources to earlier and more and more discredited evolutionistic materials, a brew of Spencer, Lubbock, Tylor, Frazer, and Wundt.

Did Freud symptomatically fail to hear Boas, since his direction was already set? Is it a case of simple lack of intersection, of ships that pass in the night? This certainly seems to be the consensus view: that Freud had always been fascinated by ancient civilizations and myths and waited until psychoanalysis was on a firm footing to begin his major explorations of this material (Kenny 2015, 173–74). As one historian puts it,

> In terms of the history of psychoanalysis, [Boas'] paper could hardly have been more timely, or as the case may be, untimely, coming shortly before Freud and Jung embarked upon their colonization

of anthropological material. . . . [I]t is not going too far to say that had they heeded [Boas'] recommendations for the negotiation of the interdisciplinary relation of anthropology and psychology, the fate and reception of their work in anthropology would have been totally different (Shamdasani 2003, 277, cited in Kenny 2015, 180).

Such an argument makes some historical sense. At the end of the nineteenth century and at the beginning of the twentieth, German-language scholarship was marked by an explicit and theorized division into natural sciences (*Naturwissenschaften*), which sought explanation via universal laws, and historical or cultural or spiritual sciences (*Kultur-* or *Geisteswissenschaften*), which sought understanding through the interpretation of distinctive social, historical, or personal wholes. Both Freud and Boas can be seen to have crossed this boundary, but in very different ways. Freud did so almost in spite of himself: a medical doctor thoroughly trained in the natural sciences, his unique contribution was to discover and interpret a distinctive kind of discourse in the particulars of dreams, slips of the tongue, and symptoms. Boas was coming from a very different background and had very different instincts. He was equally familiar with the natural sciences, having started out as a physicist, but his central interest was in the relationship between the world as science understands it and the world of subjective perception and apperception. This led him first to psychology, then to geography: a discipline, he argued in an early essay (1887), that straddled the divide between natural and cultural sciences. Boas always sought understanding from historical facts, and particularly avoided speculation built upon speculation, however "scientific"-sounding it might be. Both Freud and Boas, as we have seen, drew upon a distinct strand in the "psychology of peoples": in fact, in the preface to the book edition, Freud presents *Totem and Taboo* as a contribution to *Völkerpsychologie*, a term that is unfortunately translated "social psychology" in the Standard Edition of Freud's works (1913 [1955], 13). In other words, Freud was already set on a road that required a simple evolutionistic view of human history. He was not ready or able to hear Boas.

A recent article proposes the reverse. Robert Kenny (2015) gives good evidence that before 1909 Freud's interest in questions of myth and human evolution was secondary, and that they may have become a primary concern soon after the American voyage. Kenny's thesis is that Freud heard Boas loud and clear, recognized the direction in which anthropology was heading, and was, essentially, dismayed by it. Freud had assumed that anthropology, with its clear stratification of societies—and, in some cases, minds—into savage, barbaric, and civilized, or, in Wundt's case, totemistic, heroic, and humanistic stages, offered a straightforward parallel to his own discovery of "primitive" unconscious mental processes. Instead, Boas was saying that such parallels were bogus and that an enormous and complex historical world had to be explored, with each case analyzed, before legitimate generalities could be drawn. Boas championed the idea of unconscious mental processes, but his model required that each society, each historical period, be considered as a potentially unique case, analogous to the way a psychoanalyst considers each analysand. Such a view, denouncing premature theorization based on unanalyzed material, could, if one wished, be taken as a simple denial of the possibility of theory. That Freud took it this way is clear from the one mention he gives to "the most recent literature on the subject" in *Totem and Taboo*. It appears in a discussion of totemism, which, following Frazer and Wundt, Freud takes to be a universal stage of human social and mental development. Before beginning to review the literature, he explains why the literature he is reviewing contains no recent anthropological work:

> There is generally little difficulty in refuting the various views [of totemism] put forward: the authorities are as usual more effective in their criticisms of one another's work than in their own productions. The conclusion upon most of the points raised must be a *non liquet*. It is not surprising, therefore, that in the most recent literature on the subject (which is for the most part passed over in the present work) an unmistakable tendency emerges to reject any general solution of totemic problems as impracticable. (See, for instance, Goldenweiser, 1910.) (Freud 1913 [1955], 109; cited in Kenny 2015, 184)

The reference is to an article by Boas's student Alexander Goldenweiser that demonstrated the weaknesses of all the general theories of totemism and argued that attention should be shifted to the very different reasons for identifying clans with animals in each society. At least, this is the reference as given in the Standard Edition. In the German version (1913 [1924], 133), Goldenweiser is referred to via a brief summary of his article in a review of cultural anthropology by the Tylorian evolutionist R. R. Marett (1913, 160). Marett characterizes Goldenweiser as "insisting"

> that each "totemic complex" is the result of a separate set of historical causes, so that to explain them on the assumption of common origins is methodologically unsound.

And, Marett continues, there has been a subsequent "animated controversy" between Goldenweiser and the evolutionist Andrew Lang, who

> maintains that the hypothesis of more or less parallel development from a common starting-point is sound, in that it "works."

"No better criterion," writes Marett, "could be proposed."

For Freud, then, as for the remaining evolutionists, the objections of Boas and company were nihilistic and deserved to be countered—in Freud's case, by showing that the comparison between neurotic and primitive thinking "worked."

In November 1909 Freud wrote to Jung that "these things cry out for understanding, and as long as the specialists won't help us, we shall have to do it ourselves" (Kenny 2015, 180–81). Presumably the unhelpful specialists were the newest breed of anthropologist.

Boas's lesson, then, would have provoked Freud to double down on his reliance on Spencerian evolutionism and to valorize the apparent analogies between patients' experiences and primitive myths over what he might have learned from the ethnographies, grammars, and annotated texts of people who had been declared primitive. In this view, Boas's arguments affected Freud in the reverse of the way Boas would have hoped, provoking Freud to argue for the universality of his models by defending a general primitivity of thought and emotion through a rearguard defense of the anthropologically untenable classical evolutionists. This is what one might well call a reaction formation, and what was forgotten (read "repressed") was Boas, along with the open world of languages, societies, and histories that he championed.

NOTES

An earlier version of this article was presented in the panel "Ancestors," organized by Leila Monaghan, at the Annual Meeting of the American Anthropological Association, Denver, December 2015. I am grateful to the organizer for this opportunity to share my research, and to the Franz Boas Documentary Edition Project for supporting it. Access to documents was provided by the American Philosophical Society. Support was also received from the Social Sciences and Humanities Council of Canada.

1. An earlier version of this chapter also discussed Jung and his presence in Worcester. This proved too unwieldy for the present context.
2. The diary is held under restricted access at the Library of Congress; extensive sections have been translated and published in one venue or another.
3. One of the Sterns's children, Günther (1902–1992), would have a long literary and philosophical career, but under a pseudonym. Seeking a job as a journalist in Berlin, he was told that they already had too many Jewish-sounding bylines. Günther Stern then starting writing as Günther Anders ("Günther the Other"). In a nice twist, Anders would win the Sigmund Freud Prize for Scientific Prose in 1992.
4. See the documents labelled "Clark University: Academic Freedom Controversy" held at the American Philosophical Society in Philadelphia (APS documents number 31260, 31324, 31336).
5. In his letter of invitation from E. C. Sanford, then professor of psychology at Clark and soon to succeed Hall as president, Sanford takes care to note that "I have reason to know that your presence as lecturer and the conferring of the degree would be not less pleasing to Dr. Hall than to the rest of us" (Document 105240, Boas correspondence, APS).
6. The *Evening Standard* says the following about Freud: "Students of Dr. Freud's books on psychic analysis have doubtless fancied him a cold and cheerless person, but that prepossession vanishes when one confronts the man, bent and grey, but wearing the kindly face that age could never stiffen [he was only fifty-three!], more than selfishness [*sic*], and hears his own stories of his patients."
7. There is one particularly sinister note in the photo. The dapper young man with the moustache standing next to Ferenczi is Edwin Katzenel-

lenbogen (1882–1955), a Ukrainian Catholic of Jewish ancestry who had studied medicine in Germany and was at this point practicing psychiatry in the United States and teaching at Harvard. Katzenellenbogen was a strong proponent of eugenics and the sterilizing of epileptics, criminals, and other "defectives." In 1920 he returned to Germany, was seized by the Gestapo in 1943, and served the Reich for the rest of the war as the "inmate doctor" in Buchenwald. He was tried for war crimes but released for lack of evidence.

8. It was later revealed that Anna O was Bertha Pappenheim, who would go on to be a major feminist and one of the founders of modern social work.

9. It is not certain that Freud or Jung actually attended Boas's talk. Certainly it seems more than probable that Freud would have, given that Boas had given up his slot for him. Freud did subscribe to the *American Journal of Psychology*, in which Boas's lecture appeared (Kenny 2015, 190n94).

REFERENCES

Boas, Franz. 1887. "The Study of Geography." *Science* 9: 137–41.
———. 1906. "Some Philological Aspects of Anthropological Research." *Science* 23: 641–45.
———. 1910. "Psychological Problems in Anthropology." *American Journal of Psychology* 21: 371–84.
———. 1911. *The Mind of Primitive Man*. New York: Macmillan.
———. 1916. "The Origin of Totemism." *American Anthropologist* n.s. 18: 319–26.
———. 1938. *The Mind of Primitive Man*. Revised edition. New York: Macmillan.
Bock, Philip K. 1988. *Rethinking Psychological Anthropology: Continuity and Change in the Study of Human Action*. New York: W. H. Freeman.
Bunzl, Matti. 1996. "Franz Boas and the Humboldtian Tradition: From *Volksgeist* and *Nationalcharakter* to an Anthropological Concept of Culture." In *Volksgeist as Method and Ethic*, edited by George W. Stocking Jr., 17–78. Madison: University of Wisconsin Press.
Burnham, John C. 2012. "Anthropologist A. L. Kroeber's Career as a Psychoanalyst: New Evidence and Lessons from a Significant Case History." *American Imago* 69: 5–27.
Evans, Rand B., and William A. Koelsch. 1985. "Psychoanalysis Arrives in America: The 1909 Psychology Conference at Clark University." *American Psychologist* 40: 942–48.

Freud, Sigmund. 1900 (1953). *The Interpretation of Dreams*. Translated by James Strachey. Standard Edition of the Psychological Writings of Sigmund Freud, 4 and 5, 1–622. London: Hogarth Press.

———. 1910a. "The Origin and Development of Psychoanalysis." Translated by Harry W. Chase. *American Journal of Psychology* 21: 181–218.

———. 1910b. *Über Psychoanalyse. Fünf Vorlesungen*. Leipzig: Deuticke.

———. 1910 (1957). *Five Lectures on Psychoanalysis*. Translated by James Strachey. Standard ed. 11, 9–55. London: Hogarth.

———. 1911 (1958) *Formulations on the Two Principles of Mental Functioning*. Translated by M. N. Searle and James Strachey. Standard ed. 12, 218–26. London: Hogarth.

———. 1913 (1924). "Totem und Tabu." In *Gesammelte Schriften* 10, 3–194. Leipzig: Internationaler Psychoanalytischer Verlag.

———. 1913 (1955). *Totem and Taboo*. Translated by James Strachey. Standard ed. 13, 1–161. London: Hogarth.

———. 1915 (1957). *The Unconscious*. Translated by C. M. Baines and James Strachey. Standard ed. 14, 166–204. London: Hogarth.

———. 1925 (1959). *An Autobiographical Study*. Translated by James Strachey. Standard ed. 20, 3–76. London: Hogarth.

Freud, Sigmund, and Josef Breuer. 1895 (1955). *Studies on Hysteria*. Translated by James Strachey. Standard ed. 2. London: Hogarth.

Goldenweiser, Alexander. 1910. "Totemism, an Analytical Study." *Journal of American Folklore* 23: 178–298.

Jackson, J. Hughlings. 1884. "Evolution and Dissolution of the Nervous System." *Popular Science Monthly* 25: 171–80.

Janet, Pierre. 1889. *L'automatisme psychologique. Essai de psychologie expérimentale sur les formes inférieures de l'activité humaine*. Paris: Félix Alcan.

Jung, C. G. 1912 (1916). *Psychology of the Unconscious: A Study of the Transformations and Symbolisms of the Libido*. Translated by Beatrice M. Hinkle. New York: Dodd, Mead.

Kalmar, Ivan. 1987. "The *Völkerpsychologie* of Lazarus and Steinthal and the Modern Concept of Culture." *Journal of the History of Ideas* 48: 671–90.

Klautke, Egbert. 2013. *The Mind of the Nation: "Völkerpsychologie" in Germany, 1851–1955*. New York: Berghahn.

Kenny, Robert. 2015. "Freud, Jung and Boas: The Psychoanalytic Engagement with Anthropology Revisited." *Notes and Records of the Royal Society* 69: 173–90.

Kroeber, A.L. 1920. "*Totem and Taboo*: An Ethnologic Psychoanalysis." *American Anthropologist* n.s. 22: 48–55.

Laplanche, Jean, and Serge Leclaire. 1961 (1972). "The Unconscious: A Psychoanalytic Study." Translated by Jeffrey Mehlman. *Yale French Studies* 48: 118–75.

Leavitt, John. 2010. "Une voix royale? La possession dans la fondation des théories de l'inconscient." *Anthropologie et Sociétés* 34: 41–67.

———. 2011. *Linguistic Relativities: Language Diversity and Modern Thought*. Cambridge: Cambridge University Press.

Marett, R. R. 1913. "Cultural Anthropology." In *Encyclopedia Britannica Year Book for 1913*, 155–62. London: Encyclopedia Britannica.

Rosenzweig, Saul. 1992. *Freud, Jung, and Hall the King-Maker: The Historic Expedition to America (1909) with G. Stanley Hall as Host and William James as Guest*. Seattle: Hogrefe & Huber.

Shamdasani, Sonu. 2003. *Jung and the Making of Modern Psychology*. Cambridge: Cambridge University Press.

Simon, Robert I. 1967. "Great Paths Cross: Freud and James at Clark University, 1909." *American Journal of Psychiatry* 124: 831–34.

Stern, William. 1901. Review of Freud, *Die Traumdeutung*. *Zeitschrift für Psychologie und Physiologie der Sinnesorgane* 26: 130–33.

Stocking, George W., Jr. 1974. "The Anthropology of Franz Boas." In *The Shaping of Anthropology of Franz Boas, 1883-1911*. New York: Basic.

Trautmann-Waller, Céline, ed. 2004. *Quand Berlin pensait les peuples. Anthropologie, ethnologie et psychologie (1850–1890)*. Paris: CNRS.

STEPHEN O. MURRAY

5

Karl Popper's Enheartening of Derek Freeman's Attacks on Margaret Mead's *Coming of Age in Samoa*

When Derek Freeman's notorious book *Margaret Mead and Samoa* was published in 1983, I knew that much of what in it purported to be history of American anthropology was wrong—most spectacularly his contention that a Boasian paradigm had not been established before Mead's fieldwork and the popular book derived from it, *Coming of Age in Samoa* (1928), which he imagined to have been the foundation of American cultural anthropology, universally approved of and seminally influencing cultural anthropology.[1] Seeing that Freeman's book was dedicated to Sir Karl Popper (1902–1994) and invoked Popper's philosophy of science as Freeman's inspiration, I wondered if Sir Karl knew what was being done in his name. I titled my own first reflection on some of what was wrong with the method and historical conclusions of Freeman's writing about the culture of American anthropologists "The Poverty of Popperian History of Anthropology"—a title that was altered over my vociferous objection by Barbara Metzger, who had been copyediting *Current Anthropology* since its foundation by Sol Tax in 1960).[2]

Having read the Freeman:Popper correspondence (available on microfilm at the Popper Library in Celvese, Austria and at the Hoover Institution at Stanford University), I now know that Popper not only had access to a prepublication (1981) manuscript of Freeman's "refutation" of Mead (1928), but had urged Freeman on to publish it. Though he provided some tactical advice about toning down the prose (and caviling about one word in the proposed subtitle), Popper did not question any assertion in the manuscript or the notion that an ethnography could be "refuted." I now know that I was wrong to give Popper the benefit of the doubt about Freeman's assault on the late Margaret Mead's early work, leaving me to wonder if Popper had even read that book or knew anything about the history of American anthropology.[3]

The correspondence began with a fawning (or at least very flattering) letter from Freeman, dated 23 March 1973, in which Freeman wrote:

> I am reading with great enjoyment the papers contained in your recent volume *Objective Knowledge: An Evolutionary Approach*. I have long gained enlightenment and inspiration from your writings—for me, you are beyond all compare *the* philosopher of the twentieth century.
>
> Your recent work on objective knowledge is of particular interest to me as an anthropologist for it bears directly on anthropological problems of fundamental importance. Again, much of your recent work on the evolution of informational systems has illumined for me the relations between the evolving genetic and symbolic codes of human societies.
>
> One of your papers in *Objective Knowledge* which I had not seen previously is your Herbert Spencer Lecture of 1961. As it happens, I have myself recently completed a critical appraisal of the relation of Darwinian to Spencerian evolutionary concepts, giving special attention the varying extents to which Darwin and Spencer relied on Lamarckian assumptions [it would be published in 1974 in *Current Anthropology*].

After acknowledging receipt of the papers in April, on 24 July 1973 Popper wrote back that "The Evolutionary Theories of Charles Darwin and Herbert Spencer" "appears to me excellent as a very careful review of Marvin Harris. But as an autonomous piece of history it appears to me a little biased. It underrates Darwin's pro-Lamarckian utterances" (1973, 297n14). Freeman had attempted to do more than challenge Marvin Harris's history of evolutionary theory, and would continue to misrepresent Lamarckian strains in anthropological thinking (notably that of Franz Boas; see Murray 1990, 1991).

In a letter dated 8 August 1973 Freeman first mentioned he was smiting Mead and Boas in the introduction to a book on culture and human nature:

> I have delved deeply in the history of anthropological theory, and particularly the theories of Franz Boas and his followers, paying particular attention to its implicit ideological basis.
>
> Margaret Mead's book "Coming of Age in Samoa", which was first published in 1928 when it was greeted with rapture by Franz Boas and numerous other intellectuals and philosophers (including incidentally Bertrand Russell) ranks in fact as the Piltdown case of Social Anthropology. I can only hope that my book will provide a compelling demonstration of your view that criticism is indeed the method in which science tends to progress.

This is evidence that Freeman was thinking about attacking Mead's first book while she was still alive, though he did not submit his book manuscript for publication consideration until after she had died in 1978 (Popper papers, box 538, folder 3).

Popper sent Freeman some papers in 1976. In thanking him, Freeman (who was then in Borneo) broached the subject of meeting Popper in person soon in London, signing off the 6 August 1976 note with "With my deep appreciation of your epoch-making contributions to human understanding."

Freeman reiterated that hope in a note dated 24 May 1977 that accompanied a paper, "Towards an Anthropology both Scientific and Humanistic." Popper read it and made a number of negative annotations that he did not communicate to Freeman—for example, "No!" by Freeman's "contingent causality" and "Not so good" in the margin by "When it is realized that all values are a function of the capacity to make choices, the misconceptions to be found in cultures are seen to be cognitive choices made in the absence of adequate understanding."

What Popper did communicate to Freeman in a letter of 4 August 1977 is that "I consider it important to differentiate between scientific and ideological revolutions. My criticism of your paper is that it overrates what I should regard as ideologies (within Anthropology)."

Freeman did not reply to that. He arrived in the UK after Popper's Darwin Lecture. After meeting Popper for the first (and, I think, last) time in person, Freeman wrote that it was "generous of you to talk with me at such length on Friday afternoon last" and that "I shall try to follow your wise advise on the writing of my refutation of Margaret Mead—and to abjure, like death itself, the Kuhnian relativism" (26 November 1977).

More than a year later, on 1 December 1979, Freeman updated Popper on his project and sent a draft:

> I have also been continuing work on my refutation of the conclusions reached by the late Margaret Mead in her Coming of Age in Samoa, written after her stay in Samoa during 1925–26, which, as you will know, has been very widely read and very largely accepted by anthropologists and others. I regard this exercise as an exemplification within anthropology of the scientific methods in which you have so long instructed us .... I hope to be able to complete my book-length refutation of the conclusions of Dr. Mead during the coming year.

I found no indication anywhere in the Popper:Freeman correspondence that Popper had read *Coming of Age in Samoa* or knew anything of its relative status in either international or, specifically, American anthropology other than what Freeman wrote. Popper did not question any of Freeman's assertions about Mead's research of a popular (i.e., commercial rather than a technical or academic) book, or its uncritical acceptance—or more—by anthropologists. On 11 January 1980 (misdated 1979) he wrote:

> You had told me before about your criticism of Margaret Mead, but I must say I did not expect it to be quite as devastating as it turns out to be. As you indicate, she was somewhat unfortunate in hitting(?) on Samoa. The whole story is quite incredible. It is particularly incredible that so many anthropologists who wrote after accepted the whole thing without raising any difficulty.... Publish it as soon as possible.

In a letter dated 7 August 1981 Freeman informed Popper that in a week he would be sending off his book manuscript to Oxford University Press in New York and expressed considerable pride in its accomplishments:

I have produced a book that will have a radical effect on the thinking of both anthropologists and biologists, and find a permanent place in the history of the nascent science of anthropology. No where, I think, in all of the social sciences, is there a comparable instance of "the critical method of error elimination "having been used in such a detailed and decisive way.

I have called my book *On Coming of Age in Samoa: The Nemesis of an Anthropological Myth*. . . . In accordance with the advice that you gave to me in 1977, I have striven to keep the tone of the book detached and objective. As events finally fell out it was, in fact, a considerable advantage to have been able to write the final version several years after the death of Margaret Mead, and, after the publication of various eulogies as to the scientific significance of her Samoan researchs. As you will know she is principally known for her book *Coming of Age in Samoa* which, since its first publication in 1928 has become the most widely published and most widely read of all anthropological books.

Beyond putting gold on his own face, Freeman flattered Popper some more and anew: "Both in the Foreword to my book, as also in Chapter 19, I make explicit the great debt that I owe to your writings. I would, however, like to go beyond this, and, with your permission, to dedicate my book to you."

Popper exhibited no qualms about whether what Freeman had done was "Popperian" history of science (if, in fact, he considered anthropology a "science," which is uncertain) or any view on whether or how an ethnography could be falsified ("refuted" was Freeman's usual word choice rather than "falsification," the criterial feature of scientific theories for Popper [1963]). Popper said he greatly appreciated the gift of the dedication and demurred only about "Nemesis" in the subtitle, suggesting using "Downfall" or perhaps "Rise and Collapse" instead. Popper reiterated that "Nemesis is the revenge of the gods, that is all there is to it," so that Freeman was taking for himself the role of the gods.

After a note dated 21 September 1981 claiming that "I am happy to say my [then unpublished] book has been *very well* received by the Samoan people," in another note from Honolulu (20 October 1981) Freeman acceded to Popper's challenge and abandoned "nemesis," replacing it in the subtitle with "the demise of an anthropological myth."

In crowing that a reader commissioned by Yale University Press had described his book as likely to become "a landmark in the history of American science," and that "an eager interest has been evinced by Princeton and Harvard, as well as by Yale" in publishing the book, Freeman reported that the latest subtitle was "The Rise and Downfall of an Anthropological Myth." (Freeman did not mention what had happened during Oxford University Press's consideration of what he had submitted; however, he did say that he was inclined toward Harvard University Press, the eventual publisher.)

Popper remained uncritical of anything other than the subtitle: "Your book is excellent, and I liked the title very much. . . . I should like better if you would replace 'Downfall' by 'Fall,' simply because it is shorter and says the same; and the subtitle is a little long (*not too long*)" (10 December 1981).

In a 2 April 1982 letter Freeman reported "I had received very strong offers to publish from Yale and Princeton as well as Harvard," as well as asserting his belief that it would "influence the future course of anthropology."

On 15 April 1982 Freeman's uncritical fan cheered him on, writing that "it [the book in manuscript] is most impressive and it will be a great success. And, still more important, it will have a great influence. Your case is so strong that I do not expect that anybody will dare to defend M.M." In an undated note (possibly placed out of order in the Popper papers), Popper also wrote that "I am overjoyed at the success of your book, although my hope [is] that it will revolutionize standards for some time a little."

The case did not overwhelm those familiar with Samoa or with the history of Boasian anthropology. Freeman sent Popper various of his counterattacks, including one from the December 1983 issue of *Natural History* that included a reply to a Freeman letter by David Schneider. Since this is the only criticism of Freeman's book in Popper's files, I think it worth quoting Schneider's conclusion:

> The book is in fact more a personal attack on Margaret Mead than a serious work of scholarship. If Freeman protests too much his admi-

ration for Margaret Mead he also protests too much his devotion to the canons of science. One of these canons is that evidence be presented for statement of fact and the method of obtaining that evidence be fully explained. Freeman holds Mead's work of 1923 to scientific standards that he, in 1983, does not live up to in his own work.

On 16 January 1984 Popper sought to reassure Freeman: "I am sorry (1) that your books does not, as it should have at once a great influence on Anthropology; but it will in time (2) that you are understandably enough disappointed and irritated by its reception. I did not expect (1)."

Freeman refused to budge an iota on any of his claims about Mead's research, her popular book (mostly ignoring the ethnography of Samoa not aimed at the general public), the dependence of the Boasian paradigm on what Mead (1928) wrote, or anything else. No process of refining and correcting bold assertions based on cherry-picked quotations of a few words wrenched from their context was justified or legitimate in Freeman's messianic view.

On 18 June 1984 he wrote Popper that "the refutation contained in my book has successfully withstood all of the attempts made to rebut it.... I have, it is now evident, succeeded in making a not insubstantial contribution to the emergence of more scientific anthropology." I am among those who reject both claims. Perhaps more interestingly, in the same letter, Freeman wrote: "As I am sure you will agree, the writing of rejoinders is a crucially important stage in all those scientific controversies that finally lead to an advance in our understanding. It is also a very demanding stage." Reading the correspondence chronologically, I was eagerly awaiting Popper's response to the invitation to cheer on Freeman's self-representations as infallible (not a position that I think a "Popperian" should occupy). Popper did not, however, take the bait to approve of that. In a letter dated 23 December 1984 Sir Karl suggested that the problem must be that Freeman's opponents "can't read."

In the next Freeman:Popper letter, dated 12 December 1985, Freeman wrote: "I greatly appreciate your wise and enheartening comments on the irrational and highly emotional reactions of various American anthropologists to my refutation of Margaret Mead's preposterous conclusions of 1928" and "when all my rejoinders have appeared in the *American Anthropologist* I have no doubt that the cogency of my refutation will be recognized by all rational men and women" (box 538, folder 3).

In a letter dated 20 August 1987 Freeman wrote that "what is now clear is that my book is going to become a quite major turning-point in the history of anthropology," and thanked Popper for the interest he had taken in the book.

In a short letter of 12 November 1987 responding to a four-page draft entitled "On the Emergence in the Behavioural and Human Sciences of an Interactionist Paradigm" that Popper found overly deterministic, he flattered Freeman by "wonder[ing] when the American Association of Anthropologists [*sic*] will rescind their ridiculous anti-scientific view condemning your book, one of the outstanding events of this century."

In a letter of 24 February 1988 Freeman told Popper of what Freeman considered an "epoch-making" television documentary ("Margaret Mead and Samoa") in which an aged Samoan woman who was not one of Mead's informants said she reported having "lied and lied to Margaret Mead, if only in jest." Freeman again mentioned Bertrand Russell as one of those taken in by the "outright fictions" published by Mead "as though they were truth."

In a letter from Popper dated 16 March 1988, Popper thanked Freeman for his letter of 24 February 1988 and wrote that the story of joking/hoaxing Mead "is almost too good to be true." Indeed![4]

In a latter of 7 July 1988, Popper (uncritically) fed back Freeman's claims with an extra dash of melodramatic motive-attributing:

> Poor Margaret Mead! A little girl, catapulted by her teacher into a strange society, without any training, and with the definite task to find what her admired teacher knew that was there. If she failed in this task, total failure stared into her face: the loss of her teacher's friendship and interest. She had to prove herself. Will she succeed? No doubt she was deeply worried. She feared the worst, and made a great effort; and she succeeded beyond her wildest dreams. Her teacher was satisfied!! A load fell from her mind. This was all she had hoped to achieve. She never had dreamt of more. But it came: not only fame; but she changed the morals of millions. (box 538, folder 3)

This letter establishes Popper's acceptance of Freeman's very dubious claims of Mead as a volitionless puppet of Franz Boas, and makes clear that Freeman's project had Popper's imprimatur (albeit in private correspondence, not public acclamation of his admirer's work).[5]

A draft of a manuscript titled "Historical Analysis of the Samoan researches of Margaret Mead" (revealing that Mead was bisexual) led Popper to revise his earlier psychological conjectures. In a 12 May 1990 letter he wrote:

> I thought that MM was a naïve little girl when she went to Samoa to be duped. And I pitied her. It now looks very different: Clearly she was already an ideologist when she went, and far from naïve—and hardly a little girl.... She clearly had in an interest—to defend before herself her own perhaps a little "free" way of living as "natural" and "right."

The letter continued with advice to remove ad hominem attacks of Adam Kuper, then-editor of *Current Anthropology*, and to tone down some other shrill aspects of his polemic.

Popper moved from regarding Mead as a fool to regarding her as a knave, trying to justify her "perversions." Freeman would move in the opposite direction, from regarding her as a knave to regarding her as a fool (or, at least, one who had been naively fooled).

(Returning to chronological sequence.) It seems that Lowell Holmes (about whom Popper likely knew nothing except the aspersions Freeman made of him) was the occasion for more pop-psychology from Popper:

> My conjecture is that some children who have to learn to adapt themselves to parental or teacher's AUTHORITY learn to do so *too well*. They learn not only to believe the authorities, but they learn to believe much more: that intellectual duty—and, thus, intellectual honesty—consists in believing those who have power and influence (or, in a "democratic" society, those who "respect" the majority). (25 June 1988, box 538, folder 3)

In a letter from Freeman dated 28 July 1988 Freeman gushed that "your summation of the significance on 'poor Margaret Mead' was brilliantly insightful, and true in a powerfully poetic way."

On 14 December 1988 Popper wrote that the acceptance for publication by the *American Anthropologist* of Freeman's attack on Lowell Holmes (that would appear as Freeman 1989) "makes me no less harsh in my judgment about the both scandalous and laughable behavior of the *American Anthropologist* (and its members [?!]). I think they will be able to resist all admissions unto death. The next generation might think otherwise about this matter; or so I hope."

In a letter of 23 January 1990 Freeman told Popper that with "Fa'apua'a Fa'amû and Margaret Mead" in the December 1989 issue of the *American Anthropologist* "I can now fairly say *finis coronal opus*—it is the finishing touch that crowns the work" and that he would be teaching a seminar at Simon Fraser University (in Vancouver, BC) on "Sir Karl Popper, Refutation, and Margaret Mead," followed by a series of lectures at five campuses of the University of California. Freeman added that he was working on a book provisionally titled *A Myth Unmade* and that he hoped that "its influence on the future of anthropology will be decisive and lasting."

> This series of happenings, in which the intellectually elite of America, in particular, were totally misled by the idle jesting of Samoan girls must surely rank as one of the extreme instances of human folly in the twentieth century. And further, the obscurantism and unscientific opposition of my refutation together with the fulsome attempts to defend Mead's conclusions are now seen to be mere sophistry.

The last Popper-to-Freeman letter, dated 16 August 1991, expressed "hope [that] you can now bury the hatchet with satisfaction."[6]

CONCLUSION

I don't know if Popper was as convinced that every point Freeman made was God's Truth, as Freeman himself was. Though Popper clearly encouraged Freeman and praised his book, he does not seem to have read it with any care. That is, while there are many manuscripts, including early ones by Freeman not focused on Mead, with marginal comments in Popper's hand, I looked at each of the 475 pages of Popper's copy of the 1981 draft of *On Coming of Age in Samoa: The Nemesis of an Anthropological Myth* and could not find a single mark. There are two specific suggestions for a draft of "Holmes, Mead and Samoa" (Freeman 1989a) in a letter from Popper dated 2 March 1989. Moreover, Popper's 25 June 1988 letter makes it impossible to believe that Popper did not know what Freeman was doing.

Though Popper's conception of science was a series of conjectures and refutations, his eager disciple Derek Freeman was unwilling to accept any correction (refutation) to any of *his* conjectures or claims, and Popper showed no interest in finding out what rejoinders those (of us) refuting Freeman's histories of American anthropology or of Samoan mores of the mid-1920s advanced while, so far as I know, Freeman did not accept the slightest correction of any of his assertions about Boas and Boasians (either Margaret Mead or those who were trained by Boas in a Boasian paradigm that was well established before she went to Samoa). In contrast, Popper (1963) maintained that no theory, however well tested, can be conclusively established. Freeman never specified how his claims could, even in principle, be falsified. Many anthropologists (and others) have not considered what he did a sound basis for considering his proclamations "well-tested." If his "theory" was no more than that "human nature" has a biological component, that was something Mead had already clearly argued by 1949, though I don't think that even *Coming of Age in Samoa* was culture-determinist.

NOTES

1. With two exceptions (noted in the text), correspondence dated before 1985 are in box 247, folder 14, of the Sir Karl Raimund Popper papers; later ones are in box 538, folder 3 (misclassified in the Stanford microfilms, and identified by classification of the originals in Austria). I am grateful to the staff of the Hoover Institution Archives and to Nicole Sanger of the Popper Sammluing at Klagenfurt am Wörtheerse/Celvese, Austria, for assistance in accessing the correspondence; to Manfred Lube of the Popper Sammluin for granting permission for quotations from Karl Popper's letters to Freeman; and to Jennifer Freeman for granting permission for the quotations from her father's letters to Popper.
2. Obviously, the title was a hostile variant of Popper's title (1957) *The Poverty of Historicism*. Popper railed at historical determinism, which is not what is meant by "historicism" by those of us counterpoising it to "presentism." Indeed, what Popper meant by "historicism" is

very presentist. The bland title that was imposed on my article as "On Franz Boas and the Samoan Researches of Margaret Mead." Freeman's malpractice in smearing Mead, later extended to the alleged "hoaxing" of the young anthropologist, is definitively debunked (dare I say "refuted") by Shankman (2009, 2013).

3. The only other (sometimes) anthropologist I found in looking over the long list of his correspondents was Ernest Gellner (1925–1995) who was a professor of philosophy, logic, and scientific method at the London School of Economics until he moved to the anthropology department at Cambridge University in 1984 (i.e., was a philosopher colleague, Popper being on the LSE faculty from 1946 until his retirement in 1969). No anthropologist, not even Gellner, is indexed in Popper's 1976 autobiography.

4. In Shankman's summary of his 2013 article in *Current Anthropology*, he wrote: "Freeman claimed that Fa'apua'a was Mead's main informant, but this claim finds no support in Mead's field notes. More gravely, Freeman left out crucial passages from the interviews with Fa'apua'a that did not support his belief that Mead had been thoroughly hoaxed. When asked if Mead inquired about her sexual conduct or that of adolescent girls in Samoa, Fa'apua'a said 'No!' She also denied providing Mead with information on adolescent sex. Had the interviews with Fa'apua'a been available for other scholars to examine at the time of publication of *The Fateful Hoaxing of Margaret Mead*, his argument would not have seen the light of day. Based on the interviews themselves, the alleged hoaxing of Margaret Mead never occurred."

5. I now wonder why I did not write to Popper and ask him if he accepted Freeman's modus operandi as exemplifying how to do science or history. I was not generally shy of asking questions of my elders. It seems that no one else asked Popper if Freeman's work exemplified the methods or methodology prescribed either, alas.

6. On 20 December 1991 Freeman had sent Popper a very repetitious and typically outraged denunciation of *Current Anthropology* editor Adam Kuper (and my article published in CA), titled "A Memorandum on the Historical Scholarship and dated Editorial Practices of Professor Adam Kuper," seeking to stimulate a letter-writing campaign to Sydel Silverman, the president of the Wenner-Genn Foundation, which publishes *Current Anthropology*. From recipients of Freeman's document—which he said was going to all CA associates and others (but not to me)—Popper ignored the request for public support, as did other recipients of this screed, including Silverman.

REFERENCES

Freeman, Derek. 1974. "The Evolutionary Theories of Charles Darwin and Herbert Spencer." *Current Anthropology* 15: 211–37.
———. 1983. *Margaret Mead and Samoa: The Making and Unmaking of an Anthropological Myth.* Cambridge MA: Harvard University Press.
———. 1989a. "Holmes, Mead and Samoa." *American Anthropologist* 91: 758–62.
———. 1989b. "Fa'apua'a Fa'amū and Margaret Mead." *American Anthropologist* 91: 1017–22.
———. 1991. "On Franz Boas and the Samoan Researches of Margaret Mead." *Current Anthropology* 32: 322–30.
———. 1999. *The Fateful Hoaxing of Margaret Mead: A Historical Analysis of Her Samoan Research.* Boulder CO: Westview.
Mead Margaret. 1928. *Coming of Age in Samoa.* New York: Morrow.
———. 1949. *Male and Female: A Study of the Sexes in a Changing World.* New York: Morrow.
Murray, Stephen O. 1990. "The Poverty of Popperian History of Anthropology" [published as "Problematic Aspects of Freeman's Account of Boasian Culture."] *Current Anthropology* 31: 401–7.
———. 1991. "Boasians and Margaret Mead." *Current Anthropology* 32: 448–52.
Murray, Stephen O., and Regna Darnell. 2000. "Margaret Mead and Paradigm Shifts within Anthropology during the 1920s." *Journal of Youth and Adolescence* 29: 557–73.
Popper, Karl R. 1963. *Conjectures and Refutations: The Growth of Scientific Knowledge.* London: Routledge and Kegan Paul.
———. 1976. *Unended Quest: An Intellectual Autobiography.* LaSalle IL: Open Court.
Shankman, Paul. 2009. *The Trashing of Margaret Mead: Anatomy of an Anthropological Controversy.* Madison: University of Wisconsin Press.
———. 2013. "The 'Fateful Hoaxing' of Margaret Mead: A Cautionary Tale." *Current Anthropology* 54: 51–71.

HERBERT S. LEWIS

6

Anthropology's Camelot Myth—And What We Can Learn from It

As devotees of Arthurian legends and Broadway musicals know, "Camelot" refers to an imagined special place and a special time, summed up in the words of Lerner and Loewe: "Don't let it be forgot, that once there was a spot, for one brief shining moment that was known as Camelot." Apparently the presidency of John F. Kennedy, looked upon with nostalgia by some as "Camelot," inspired that lyric. Anthropology, too, has its Camelot myth, and this one is most assuredly not regarded with nostalgia; rather, it is remembered with embarrassment and anger. This myth concerns "Project Camelot," notorious in the mid-1960s; anthropologists of a certain age will remember the shame of it, as will those younger scholars who are familiar with the history of American anthropology. For those unfamiliar with the myth of Project Camelot, it is recalled as a plan by the United States Army "to use anthropologists' and sociologists' research to develop counterinsurgency tactics to quell uprisings (democratic or otherwise) in Latin America" (Price 2011). According to one influential and widely read account, "anthropologists played a formidable part" in this and other "paramilitary adventures" (Jorgenson and Wolf 1970; emphasis added). But do these claims conform to what actually happened?

In December 1964 the Director of the Special Operations Research Office (SORO) of American University in Washington DC released an announcement of a planned project for which they hoped to attract scholars "interested in the study of internal war potentials" (Horowitz 1967, 47).

Project Camelot is a study whose objective is to determine the feasibility of developing a general social systems model which would make it possible to predict and influence politically significant aspects of social change in the developing nations of the world. Somewhat more specifically, its objectives are:

> First, to devise procedures for assessing the potential for internal war within national societies;
> Second, to identify with increased degrees of confidence those actions which a government might take to relieve conditions which are assessed as giving rise to a potential for internal war; and
> Finally, to assess the feasibility of prescribing the characteristics of a system for obtaining and using the essential information needed for doing the above two things. (Letter sent to scholars, December 4, 1964. In Horowitz 1967:47)[1]

This was the high period of the Cold War, five years after the Cuban revolution and Fidel Castro's expressed intention to export revolution throughout Africa and Latin America. At the time Che Guevara was involved in military activities in Zaire (the Congo), and not long after that he would begin his ill-fated insurrectionary adventures in Bolivia. Although there has long been revisionist writing about that era, it should be remembered that the Soviet Union controlled Poland, East Germany, Czechoslovakia, Rumania, Hungary, Bulgaria, Lithuania, Latvia, and Estonia, while Mao Tse-tung and the Communist Party ruled China. North Korea, North Vietnam, Albania, and Yugoslavia were also under communist dictatorships.[2] There were active revolutionary movements in all three Portuguese colonies in Africa, as well as in Southeast Asia: Vietnam, Laos, Indonesia, Malaya, and, not long after that, the Philippines. Given these political realities the following statement from the same document seems at least as pitiful as it is disingenuous:

> By way of background: Project CAMELOT is an outgrowth of the interplay of many factors and forces. Among these is the assignment in recent years of much additional emphasis to the U.S. Army's role in the overall U.S. policy of encouraging steady growth and change in

the less developed countries of the world. The many programs of the U.S. Government directed toward this objective are often grouped under the sometimes misleading label of counterinsurgency (some pronounceable term standing for insurgency prophylaxis would be better). This places great importance on positive actions designed to reduce the sources of disaffection which often give rise to more conspicuous and violent activities disruptive in nature. The U.S Army has an important mission in the positive and constructive aspects of nation-building as well as responsibility to assist friendly countries in dealing with active insurgency problems. (quoted in Horowitz, 48)

That is how the directors of Project Camelot described their hopes. SORO, based at American University in Washington DC and funded by the research office of the army, had for some years been producing "country handbooks" (more than fifty) based on library research and "interviews with foreign nationals resident in the United States" (Beals 1969, 5). This work was carried out by a variety of graduate students and professors—from both the political right and the left (Price 2016, 252).[3] According to Beals, having accumulated these data and trying to codify and analyze them, it seemed to them like a great idea to "attempt a major breakthrough in the development of social science methodology and the achievement of predictability" (1969, 5). To this end, they brought together more than thirty highly regarded social scientists from leading universities.[4]

In view of the size and scope of the undertaking and the fact that there would be plenty of resources and oodles of money available for it—much more than social scientists were accustomed to—these scholars were quite interested, even enthusiastic. The total sum for four years was reportedly $6 million. Therefore, Beals writes, "a series of planning studies and conferences were undertaken" (1969, 5) but "the planning and design of the research program had not yet been completed or any decision reached about whether the project would move from the planning stage to the field" (1969, 6; cf. Dietchman 1976, 142). According to Seymour Dietchman, a long-time consultant for the intelligence and defense establishments, the program's designers hadn't even gotten around to "preliminary thinking and library research on theories of conflict, revolutionary warfare, and processes of change in diverse social systems." It is very interesting, and quite surprising, to read that they were planning to examine right-wing military coups such as those in Argentina (1943), Venezuela (1945), Peru (1963), Iran (1953), and Korea (1960). (1976, 145). But "the project never really got off the ground during the fall of 1964. The full project staff was never assembled or fully organized" (146).

It was no secret that the funding for this proposed international social science research project came from the Department of Defense's Army Research Office, nor was it intended to be. In fact, the organizers tried to enlist social scientists from other countries in this planned project, even some who were distinctly left-leaning. "Document Number 4" reproduced in Horowitz states that "CAMELOT is [an] unclassified, open project the results of which will be made available through normal scholarly channels. In addition it is anticipated that all the data will be made available to other scholars, in the United States and abroad, for their analysis" (1967, 62–63).

In the event this elaborate plan for a long-term multidisciplinary study of major social and political issues never came to pass, "a Chilean-born social scientist in the United States, *with only minor contacts with Project Camelot*, planned to visit Chile on personal matters and was offered a consultant's fee of $750 if he would informally explore the possible interest of Chilean social scientists in participating in the research should Chile be selected as a research location" (Beals 1969, 7; my italics). When news of Professor Hugo Nutini's extensive inquiries became public (most notably through a "vigorous attack" in the left-wing Chilean newspaper *El Siglo*), all hell broke loose. Beals writes that the ire of the Chilean Left was certainly enhanced by the fact that Chilean social scientists played a prominent role in the humiliating defeat of extreme left parties by the Christian Democratic Party. But the American ambassador was also furious, claiming that he had not been informed of the Nutini visit, and the episode brought out rivalries between the State Department and the Department of Defense. Not only would there be no Project Camelot, but American perfidy was loudly pronounced by politicians and academics internationally, and not only by those on the left. President Johnson "issued a directive requiring Department of State review of all foreign research sponsored or conducted by U.S. government agencies" and there were major attempts in congress to curb any more such overseas projects (7).

Above all Project Camelot had a powerful effect on American anthropology. It was of social and political value to anthropology and to academia as a cautionary tale, a warning against the collusion of science with government and military-sponsored research, especially in foreign lands. The revelations set off paroxysms of accusation and self-flagellation in the anthropological community; it was a marvelous subject for other social scientists and the press. In the words of Brown and Fernandez, "When news of the project slipped out in 1965, it created a major diplomatic scandal in Latin America and prompted anguished soul-searching in the North American academic world, the reverberations of which can still be heard today in anthropology" (1991, 111). As Murray Wax wrote, "Project Camelot is considered the paradigm of unethical research" (1979, 61).

At the 1965 AAA meetings Marshall Sahlins delivered a powerful and subsequently famous paper on the scandal, objecting to "any further engagement in strategic research by American anthropologists working under contract to defense, foreign policy, or intelligence agencies of the U.S. government. I happen to believe it is no good for the country or the peoples among whom we have lived. I am convinced it is no good for our discipline or our mortal selves" (1965, 79).[5] In 1966 the American Anthropological Association commissioned a respected and experienced elder, Ralph Beals, to conduct an "inquiry into the nature of social research, the influence of the political environment upon it, and the proper relationship between science and government." The "Beals Report," which went far beyond a concern with Project Camelot, was presented at a plenary session of the 1966 AAA meetings and, following its recommendations, the association established its Committee on Ethics in 1968, and adopted an extended statement of "Principles of Professional Responsibility" in 1971 (Lewis 2014, 37, 50). From the moment of its exposure, the Project Camelot fiasco has been a yoke around the neck of the discipline of anthropology—the field that took the lesson so much to heart. American anthropology was branded with a scarlet "C" for "Camelot," which "quickly became, and continues to be, a symbol of North American 'academic espionage' for Latin Americans" (Brown and Fernandez 1991, 111).

Here are recent examples of the stigmata. At the 2015 AAA annual meeting, a senior anthropologist, a veteran of the sixties, was taunting a fellow elder because of the latter's past participation in applied anthropology projects in the Andes. As the latter was defending the work his tormentor administered the coup de grace: "What about 'Camelot!?'" he demanded. The accuser had been a graduate student when the scandal first erupted, and he must have been familiar with this passage from a widely-read statement in *The New York Review of Books*:

> Then, suddenly, in the late Sixties a number of paramilitary adventures masquerading as scientific projects were launched, in which anthropologists played a formidable part. The best known of these enterprises was Project Camelot, sponsored by the US Army and the Department of Defense, and channeled through SORO. Despite its connection with leading social scientists at major American universities, it had only the dimmest connection with science; its counterinsurgency orientation severely undermined the credibility of North American social science in Latin America. The American Anthropological Association was quick to condemn the venture; resolutions passed in the aftermath of Camelot's collapse certified the righteousness of the Fellows. (Jorgensen and Wolf 1970)

David Price—the leading student of the relationship between anthropology, anthropologists, the CIA, and the military—claims, "In 1964, the U.S. Army's Project Camelot sought to use anthropologists and sociologists to study patterns of Third World social upheaval and revolution. Project Camelot planned to use anthropologists' and sociologists' research to develop counterinsurgency tactics to quell uprisings (democratic or otherwise) in Latin America" (2011, 23).

Similar claims of anthropologists' complicity in counterinsurgency activities under the direction of the military come from outside the discipline as well. The historian Andrew Zimmerman, writing of German colonial policy in East Africa, contends that "such farsighted plans to place anthropology directly in the service of counterinsurgency were taken up later in the century by, for example, anthropologists working with Project Camelot, or the U.S. Army Special Forces in their support of American invasions of Vietnam and elsewhere" (2006, 449).

This discourse of the complicity of anthropology with Camelot is remarkable because, except for the hapless Hugo Nutini, no anthropologists have been reported to have been involved in the stillborn project. Furthermore, Nutini was marginal to it, as is emphasized by Kalman Silvert (1967, 85n3), Seymour Deitchman (1976, 158–59), and Irving Horowitz, who wrote, "Whatever Mr. Nuttini [sic] was or was not, he certainly was not an employee or staff member of Project Camelot" (1967, 12). Price, however, writes that Nutini "regularly attended Camelot Monday meetings . . . as a consultant" (2016, 259).

In fact, the list of consultants to Project Camelot consists largely of sociologists, with a few psychologists and political scientists. The group consists of some of the best-known figures in 1960s social science, some of them known to be on the Left. These included the sociologists Jesse Bernard, James S. Coleman, Louis Coser (a founder of the journal *Dissent*), S. N. Eisenstadt, William Gamson, W. J. Goode, Samuel Klausner, William Kornhauser, Neil Smelser, and the economist Thomas Schelling.[6] It seems that this unclassified, un-secret project, conceived of in grand terms, was of interest to these major figures because it promised to give them the resources to undertake studies of social systems and social processes on a scale that was otherwise impossible. According to Kalman Silvert, "the enthusiasm of the social scientists involved is easily understood. The opportunity existed for a massive, richly supported, highly detailed study into the conditions for social change in general as well as into the more specific subject of revolution" (1967, 83). Jesse Bernard's essay in the Horowitz et al. volume presents the interests of several of the hopeful participants in "research which, like Project Camelot, is aimed at theoretical rather than at immediately practical goals" (1967, 128).[7]

Beals declared, "It should be emphasized that at no time was any part of Project Camelot classified or any deliberate attempt made to conceal its sponsorship. Contrary to what many assume, when the project came under question no research had been carried out or even authorized outside the United States" (1969, 6). Although David Price writes that "Johan Galtung was contacted in a futile effort to recruit him for Camelot's Chilean counterinsurgency program" (2011 23), Chile had not been decided upon as a site of interest for their general research, let alone for counterinsurgency. It would have been an unlikely choice, because there was little threat of leftist insurgency in democratic Chile of that decade. Galtung himself writes, "It should be emphasized that Nuttini [sic] was probably not really authorized to do this recruitment in Chile since Chile is said not to be on the original list of target nations for the project" (1967, 293n11).

Until the time that the project blew up there was no anthropologist other than Nutini involved. Theodore Vallance, who was director of SORO at the time of Project Camelot, wrote, "There were no anthropologists on the project staff (though there should and would have been except for the project's early demise" (1978, 411). The fact is that Project Camelot was basically anthropologist-free, bereft of ethnologists, and lacked the students of man and culture.[8]

The body of original literature on Project Camelot is not very large, but it bears out the argument I have been making. Ralph Beals (1969) presented the first synthetic account and Dietchman's 1976 book confirms Beals with greater detail. Using the same facts, Murray Wax produced an article critical of the critics, who, he claimed, "seem to prefer myth to fact. Authors cite such key sources as 'Horowitz 1967,' but do not seem to have troubled to digest its pages. The resultant discussion is inaccurate and even sloppy. Instead of clear ethical analysis, the reader is presented with fantasy and political polemic" (1979, 62).[9] The author argues that "in many ways Camelot was a political pawn in the interagency struggles within the U.S. (among the Defense Department, the State Department, and the CIA), just as it was in the struggles among rival political parties and factions in Chile, elsewhere in Latin America, and generally throughout the literate world" (1979, 78). He demonstrates how complex and confused the whole enterprise was and how far from a clever plot to undermine Chilean or any other government.[10]

Two other writers concerned about ethics and anthropology accept the same conclusions. James N. Hill writes, "Since that time, evidence has been presented which suggests that these allegations greatly exaggerated and oversimplified the actual situation with respect to Project Camelot. In fact it now seems, to some at least, that the allegations of clandestine anthropological research (which are still believed by many) represent myth rather than fact" (1987). Carolyn Fluehr-Lobban agrees that "it was not the high crimes of anthropologists involved in Project Camelot that precipitated the ... crisis, but the effects that a bollixed operation had on future research in Latin America" (2003, 8).[11]

In the light of these conclusions by serious scholars, why does Project Camelot still stand as that shameful episode in which anthropologists took part in clandestine research to quell revolutionary movements? The answer seems clear—and disturbing.

The scandal occurred at a time when the profession was in the midst of the turmoil of the 1960s, and many anthropologists—especially the younger generation and their elders of a radical/leftist persuasion—were prepared to believe anything negative about anthropology. Indeed, they were anxious to pin as many demerits as possible upon their field. (See, for example, the various charges levelled against anthropology in Dell Hymes [ed.], *Reinventing Anthropology*, as well as the historical discussion in Lewis 2009 [also 2014].) In that atmosphere Project Camelot was a godsend. As well as wonderful proof of anthropological sins, it was also an excellent case for those highly critical of the American position in the Cold War. Moreover, it was a warning and a powerful source of soul-searching and critique for social science. Anthropologists were, in fact, not guilty of complicity—but we imagined that we were. Ideas and slogans adopted in the anger—the fury—of the late 1960s should not stand for all time, however; in fact, they are due for serious reconsideration. It is time to set the record straight.

Sadly, what is more significant than this particular case is the disturbing fact that social scientists, as researchers after the "truth" (should there be such a thing), are just as emotional, sloppy, and lazy as common folk. There is a natural tendency to believe myths that match our predispositions rather than to investigate them. And, unfortunately, as Murray Wax points out, authors not infrequently "cite key sources ... but do not seem to have troubled to digest [their] pages." It is not uncommon for people to cite works that they believe support them without actually having read them.

A relevant and outstanding case is that of Kathleen Gough's famous short article "Anthropology and Imperialism": probably the single most widely cited reference when an author wants to support the claim that "anthropology is the child of Western imperialism" (1968). Although Gough does boldly proclaim that view of anthropology's birth in her third paragraph (12), she makes no attempt to document this statement, because that is not the point of her paper.[12] Her real concern is to call upon anthropologists to study the great economic and political problems of the modern world, including, and especially, imperialism and revolutions, from a Marxist and antiwestern point of view. And yet her paper is cited over and over again, as if it somehow gave evidence of anthropology's complicity with colonialism. It is beyond ironic that in a retrospective piece for a journal issue celebrating that paper, Kathleen Gough never refers to the very thing that gave her work immortality—indeed, its title (1993).[13] "Gough 1968" shares the honor of the most cited paper on the subject of anthropology and colonialism with "Asad 1973": "Anthropology and the Colonial Encounter." But it appears that Talal Asad's introduction to that work is not read carefully either. In it he writes, "It is a mistake to view social anthropology in the colonial era as primarily an aid to colonial administration, or as the simple reflection of colonial ideology" (1973, 18). Two decades later, referring to "some vulgar misconceptions on this subject," he wrote that "the role of anthropologists in maintaining structures of imperial domination has, despite slogans to the contrary, usually been trivial" (1991, 314)

In their conviction of the evils of anthropology, too many anthropologists and their interlocutors in fields such as sociology, literary and critical theory, cultural studies, and postcolonial studies seem willing to believe almost anything negative (Lewis 2014). Anthropology's Camelot myth stands as a double cautionary tale; in addition to the warning that social scientists took from it in the 1960s, it should now advise us against believing accusations of wickedness hurled in times of passion and partisanship.

A PARADOXICAL APPENDIX

The climax of Gough's oft-cited paper was a call for anthropologists to study revolutions:

> We need to know, for example, whether there is a common set of circumstances under which left-wing and nationalist revolutions have

occurred or have been attempted in recent years in Cuba, Algeria, Indo-China, Malaysia, the Philippines, Indonesia, Kenya, and Zanzibar. Are there any recognizable shifts in ideology or organization between these earlier revolts and the guerilla movements now taking shape in Guatemala, Venezuela, Colombia, Angola, Mozambique, Laos, Thailand, Cameroon, Yemen, or Southern Arabia? What are the types of peasantry and urban workers most likely to be involved in these revolutions; are there typologies of leadership and organization? Why have some failed and others succeeded?

She continues,

> I may be accused of asking for Project Camelot, but I am not. I am asking that we should do these studies in our way, as we would a cargo-cult or a kula-ring, without the built-in biases of tainted financing, without the assumption that counter-revolution, and not revolution, is the best answer, and with the ultimate economic and spiritual welfare of our informants, and of the international community, before us rather than the short-run military or industrial profits of the Western nations." (1968, 23)

But I have to agree again with Murray Wax: "In 1968 she outlined a series of research topics that appear remarkably like those which its social-scientific partisans ... wanted to achieve by Camelot.... Despite these disclaimers, I should judge that there was a certain community of scientific interest between Gough and the scientists who were recruited to Camelot" (69–70). I suggest that SORO could not have written their proposal any better than Gough did, and that the results of such studies would, in principle, be equally applicable for either revolution or counter-revolution.

NOTES

> I am grateful to the editors of *Anthropology Today* and *History of Anthropology Newsletter* for useful critical comments.

1. Ralph Beals adds "(c) identifying effective ways of averting as well as resolving conflicts" (1969, 4).
2. China had its own problems with counterinsurgency in Tibet.

3. Price offers an important cautionary note against the assumption that someone who was employed doing such work was a confirmed Cold Warrior engaged in nefarious counterinsurgency projects. Andre Gunder Frank, well-known for his critical Marx-inspired theoretical work, was one of those listed as employed "writing cultural descriptions for HRAF's Slavic Peoples Project." Price reports that Frank "gave little thought to what he was producing mostly because academically it was on the level of a high school textbook" (2016, 252). This work was one way that poor graduate students could get some support.
4. Solovey (2001) appends a list of the consultants.
5. Sahlins's paper was later published in Horowitz (1967) as "The Established Order: Do Not Fold, Spindle, or Mutilate." For those born in the computer age, this phrase originated in directions written on punch cards, a prehistoric system of data recording and processing.
6. Ironically, the man most responsible for breaking the story of Operation Camelot—the distinguished Norwegian sociologist and pioneer of peace and conflict studies, Johan Galtung—had been invited by Rex Hopper, the project's director, to participate in a planning seminar in Washington DC (Dietchman 1976, 158).
7. According to Theodore Vallance, "Army research civilians and some officers, and certainly the SORO officialdom, of which I was the head, were attracted to the idea of discovering how major social change takes place; we warmly—if naively—embraced the view that Camelot was to be a feasibility study rather than one designed to produce recommendations about 'counter-insurgency'" (1978, 411). See also Dietchman (1976) and Jacobs (1967).
8. It is not possible for me to guarantee that no anthropology graduate students, or even professionals, were ever hired to do background reference or bibliographical work, as with the "Handbooks." A reader of a draft of this paper reports having "done archival work revealing that prominent anthropologists were in fact recruited to work on the project in some function . . . even if in this case they declined."
9. He cites Boughey (1978) as well as Barnes (1977). Murray Wax, a man of the (democratic) Left, interested in Marxian approaches (Price 2004: 206–210) appropriately leads his article on Camelot with the famous quotation from Marx about men making their own history—but not just as they please (Wax 1978, 400).
10. Joy Rohde reports a different and interesting reaction to the sudden end of Project Camelot. The sociologist Dr. Robert Boguslaw, who had

joined the project as a senior scientist in the hope that it could help "democratize American foreign and military policy.... interpreted Project Camelot's abrupt cancellation, not as an indication that the project was intellectually or ethically flawed, but as a confirmation that the powerful figures who controlled the national security state would not allow a study with such radical democratic potential to move forward" (2009, 118).

11. Not long before Camelot, SORO had two projects in the field involving anthropologists. Both Task Colony in Peru and Task Simpatico in Colombia were carried out with the knowledge and support of those governments and were "designed to reduce the sources of disaffection" that might lead to violence. The Colony project "involved observation and analysis of Peruvian army efforts to assist the economic development and integration of the Indians in the trans-andean highlands into the Peruvian economy and society" (Dietchman 1976, 184–85). It is described by the researcher, Milton Jacobs, as a "study of migrations of Andean campesinos to the Amazonian jungle, where they were establishing farms and homes—a most uncynical and unsinister project" (1967, 364; see also Brown 1991, 111–12). (This was the era of active Túpac Amaru military uprising.) Beals writes that the Colony project "came under particularly heavy attack, perhaps because most of the participating group of Peruvian social scientists were known leftists" (1969, 8)—just the opposite of the Camelot case in Chile! For "Simpatico," a psychologist and an anthropologist were "trying to learn the villagers' attitudes towards the government, the army, and the turbulent events in their society" (Dietchman 1976, 186–87). 1964 was the beginning of the long-lasting conflict between FARC (FARC-EP) and the Colombian government and society. Both projects were concerned with "the study of the constructive role that the military in developing countries could play in improving social conditions" (1976, 185)—a doctrine called "civic action." Disingenuous or naïve—or both?

12. In fact Kathleen Gough devotes the fourth paragraph to modifying the declaration of the third by stressing that anthropologists "living closely with native peoples, ... tended to take their part and to try to protect them against the worst forms of imperialist exploitation" (13).

13. She did, however, confess that she had "tended to neglect" the imperialism of the Soviet Union and China "because I am a Marxist and was somewhat biased in my outlook" (1993, 280).

REFERENCES

Asad, Talal, ed. 1973. *Anthropology and the Colonial Encounter*. London: Ithaca Press.

Barnes, J. A. 1977. *The Ethics of Inquiry in Social Science*. Delhi: Oxford University Press.

Beals, Ralph. 1969. *Politics of Social Research: An Inquiry into the Ethics and Responsibilities of Social Scientists*. Chicago: Aldine.

Bernard, Jesse. 1967. "Conflict as Research and Research as Conflict." In *The Rise and Fall of Project Camelot: Studies in the Relationship between Social Science and Practical Politics*, edited by Irving Louis Horowitz, 128–52. Cambridge MA: MIT Press..

Boughey, Howard. 1978. *The Insights of Sociology: An Introduction*. Boston: Allyn & Bacon.

Brown, Michael J., and Eduardo Fernandez. 1991. *War of Shadows: The Struggle for Utopia in the Peruvian Amazon*. Berkeley: University of California Press.

Deitchman, Seymour J. 1976. *The Best-Laid Schemes: A Tale of Social Research and Bureaucracy*. Cambridge MA: MIT Press.

Fluehr-Lobban, Carolyn. 2003. "Ethics and Anthropology 1890–2000: A Review of Issues and Principles." In *Ethics and the Profession of Anthropology: Dialogue for Ethically Conscious Practice*. 2nd edition. Edited by Carolyn Fluehr-Lobban, 1–28. Walnut Creek CA: Altamira.

Galtung, Johan. 1967. "After Camelot." In *The Rise and Fall of Project Camelot: Studies in the Relationship between Social Science and Practical Politics*, edited by Irving Louis Horowitz, 281–312. Cambridge MA: MIT Press.

Gough, Kathleen. 1968. "Anthropology and Imperialism." *Monthly Review* 19 (11): 12–27.

———. 1993. "'Anthropology and Imperialism' Revisited." *Anthropologica* 35 (2): 279–89.

Hill, James N. 1987. "The Committee on Ethics: Past, Present, and Future." In *Handbook on Ethical Issues in Anthropology*, edited by Joan Cassell and Sue-Ellen Jacobs. Washington DC: American Anthropological Association.

Horowitz, Irving Louis, 1967. "The Rise and Fall of Project Camelot." In *The Rise and Fall of Project Camelot: Studies in the Relationship between Social Science and Practical Politics*, edited by Irving Louis Horowitz, 3–44. Cambridge MA: MIT Press.

Hymes, Dell, ed. 1974. *Reinventing Anthropology*. New York: Vintage.

Jacobs, Milton. 1967. "L'Affaire Camelot." *American Anthropologist* 69: 364–66.

Jorgensen, Joseph G., and Eric R. Wolf. 1970. "A Special Supplement: Anthropology on the Warpath in Thailand." *New York Review of Books*, November 19.

Lewis, Herbert S. 2009. "The Radical Transformation of Anthropology: History Seen through the Annual Meetings of the American Anthropological Association, 1955–2005." In *Histories of Anthropology Annual 5*, edited by Regna Darnell and Frederic W. Gleach, 200–28. Lincoln: University of Nebraska Press.

———. 2014. *In Defense of Anthropology: An Investigation of the Critique of Anthropology*. New Brunswick NJ: Transaction.

Price, David. 2000. "Anthropologists as Spies: Collaboration Occurred in the Past, and There's No Professional Bar to It Today." *Nation*, November 2, 2000.

———. 2004. *Threatening Anthropology: McCarthyism and the FBI's Surveillance of Activist Anthropologists*. Durham NC: Duke University Press.

———. 2011. *Weaponizing Anthropology: Social Science in Service of the Militarized State*. Petrolia CA: CounterPunch.

———. 2016. *Cold War Anthropology: The CIA, the Pentagon, and the Growth of Dual Use Anthropology*. Durham NC: Duke University Press.

Rohde, Joy. 2009. "Gray Matters: Social Scientists, Military Patronage, and Democracy in the Cold War." *Journal of American History* 96 (1): 99–122.

Silvert, Kalman H. 1967. "American Academic Ethics and Social Research Abroad: The Lesson of Project Camelot." In *The Rise and Fall of Project Camelot: Studies in the Relationship between Social Science and Practical Politics*, edited by Irving Louis Horowitz, 80–106. Cambridge MA: MIT Press.

Solovey, Mark. 2001. "Project Camelot and the 1960s Epistemological Revolution: Rethinking the Politics-Patronage-Social Science Nexus." *Social Studies of Science* 31 (2): 171–206.

Wax, Murray L. 1979. "The Reluctant Merlins of Camelot: Ethics and Politics of Overseas Research." In *Federal Regulations: Ethical Issues and Social Research*, edited by Murray L. Wax and Joan Cassell, 61–80. Boulder CO: Westview.

Zimmerman, Andrew. 2006. "'What Do You Really Want in German East Africa, Herr Professor?' Counterinsurgency and the Science Effect in Colonial Tanzania." *Comparative Studies in Society and History* 48: 419–61.

EVAN HABKIRK

7

A Model for Open Community Engagement

Six Nations, the GWCA, and the Production of Wartime Narratives

On 11 August 2014, 165 people from the Mohawks of the Bay of Quinte, the Mohawks of Wahta, Six Nations of the Grand River, and the neighboring communities of Brantford and Brant County filled the auditorium at the Woodland Cultural Centre outside of Brantford, Ontario, for the opening of the exhibit "Veterans, Warriors and Peacekeepers."[1] Curated by the Centre's Museum Director Paula Whitlow, the exhibit commemorated individuals from the three First Nations communities who served during World War I. The exhibit included little history about the war, focusing instead on the personal items, names, and, when possible, pictures of the over 450 Six Nations men and women who served.[2] Adding to this tribute, the opening of the exhibition included a twenty-minute presentation during which sixty-five of the veterans' descendants received reproductions of the flag of the 114th "Brock's Rangers" Battalion in honor of their ancestors' wartime service.[3] The original hand-embroidered flag was commissioned by the Six Nations Patriotic League in 1916, and presented to the battalion's D Company to mark the fact that it had been recruited from and trained at Six Nations of the Grand River Territory and that over half of the battalion was made up of Six Nations—and other First Nations—men from Ontario and Quebec.[4] For the attendees of this opening, it was clear that the Six Nations had not forgotten the people who had served, and what this service meant to them as a community.

This opening also marked one of the first events when the research of the Woodland Cultural Centre and the Great War Centenary Asso-

Fig. 3. The hand-embroidered battalion flag of the 114th Battalion, courtesy of the Woodland Cultural Centre.

ciation Brantford-Brant County-Six Nations (GWCA) was combined to create a joint public event. Formed in 2012, the GWCA board of directors, made up of librarians, academics, schoolteachers, museum professionals, and public historians, knew that Six Nations wartime narratives were different than those from Brantford and Brant County. Although the members of the GWCA brought to the organization over twenty accumulated years of local and Six Nations wartime scholarship, this research was based on non-Indigenous sources, including local histories, files from the Canadian Department of Indian Affairs, and newspaper accounts from *The Brantford Expositor*.

Wanting the project to reflect the Six Nations' perspective of their wartime participation, and to present this history to people both within and outside of the Six Nations, the GWCA sought an open community research model to facilitate community involvement. Although a public history project, the GWCA borrowed research models across various disciplines including anthropology, history, and public history to create a research model that brings academic research out of the universities and archives and to the general public. As such, not only would the Six Nations and the GWCA be creating their own wartime narratives, but the GWCA would be giving the Six Nations community final say in how their history was presented—demonstrating to the Six Nations community that the GWCA respected their knowledge and history, and that they wanted this relationship to continue for the entirety of the project and beyond. This interdisciplinary research model has led to the successful growth and following of the GWCA's public programming and—although it was tailored to the specific needs of the GWCA's mandate to create an interactive public memorial to the people and wartime participation of Brantford, Brant County, and Six Nations—it can be borrowed by other projects that require an open community consulting research model.

Although the GWCA actively sought a consulting relationship with the Six Nations before opening the call for a wide range of community partners, their first step in establishing community partnerships was the recruitment of Paula Whitlow to the GWCA's board of directors. Whitlow helped the GWCA establish their first community and Six Nations partnership. By partnering with the Woodland Cultural Centre, the GWCA was brought into working relationships with other Six Nations community organizations, such as the Six Nation Legacy Consortium, a group made up of historical and cultural groups mandated by the Six Nations Traditional Confederacy and Band Council governments to oversee ongoing historical Six Nations research; the Six Nations Public Library; and their local history group, and the Ohsweken Genealogy Society. These groups ensure that the work of the GWCA follows existing community narratives, and aids community researchers in becoming involved with GWCA projects; they also have final say in how their history is publicly presented. Through this approach, the GWCA has directly engaged the Six Nations community, whose members can contribute their original research, creating a digital memorial about their community's participation in First World War from their perspective, giving them a public platform to tell their history of the War and its place within the histories of Brantford and Brant County. This approach is necessary not only to challenge the dominant narratives about the Six Nations war effort, but also to ensure that a continuing and respectful relationship exists between the GWCA and the Six Nations community.

In November 2014, the GWCA launched its interactive and educational website. What viewers of the website do not see is the design and consulting work that went into its creation. Beginning in 2012, the GWCA met with the Six Nations Legacy Consortium and laid out their project and partnership plan. The procedure was simple: the GWCA, a registered charitable group, had already received funding from the Brant Community Foundation to pay for their website, and the GWCA research team and board of directors were in the process of writing historical articles for it. Before an article with Six Nations content went live, however, it would be handed over to the members of the Legacy Consortium for historical and narrative fact-checking. If any members of the consortium requested revisions, the GWCA would make them. This simple agreement ensured that the histories presented by the GWCA reflected the histories within the Six Nations community. In all, the Six Nations Legacy Consortium read, revised, and approved eleven articles for publication.[5] The information presented on the GWCA's website does more than simply highlight the role of the Six Nations in World War I; it has become a place for the promotion of cross-community understanding.

One article truly shows this process at work. The original draft of the manuscript for the article "Loyalty to the Crown" outlined the connections of Brantford and Brant County to the British Crown through their loyalist and imperial heritage, and the Six Nations alliance with the British that began with the British acceptance of the Two Row Wampum and was strengthened by the Silver Covenant Chain in 1667.[6] These relationships were celebrated during royal and vice-regal visits to the area, fourteen of which occurred between 1860 and 1919. For the communities of Brantford and Brant County, these occasions were celebrations, and were marked by outward expressions of loyalty as subjects under the British Crown. In contrast, the Six Nations viewed these visits as the return of their treaty and alliance partner to their homelands. For the Six Nations, these visits were a celebration, but, more important, a time to discuss aspects of their alliance that needed to be worked out. Since the GWCA website is a historical project whose mandate ends at 1919, the draft of "Loyalty to the Crown" ended with the Prince of Wales's visit to Brantford in 1919 and a story about the prince being presented at the end of his visit with a handmade silver pin fashioned by Catherine Silver, one of the oldest living women within the Six Nations Territory. When the article was returned to the GWCA from the consortium, a new final paragraph had been added about Queen Elizabeth's 2010 visit and her presentation of a set of eight inscribed silver bells to the Six Nations community on the Bay of Quinte, for their Royal Chapel. The addition of this paragraph highlights many aspects of Six Nations history neglected by GWCA in their draft of the article, including the fact that all Six Nations and Haudenosaunee communities in North America today are connected by a common historical past. The highlighting of the Six Nations–British alliance metaphor of silver, which needs to be continually cared for and polished, was understood and reciprocated by both the Six Nations and the British Crown, and in light of the fact that, to the Six Nations, the British/Six Nations alliance relationship continues to exist today. Without the consultation process, these important aspects of Six Nations history and worldview would have gone unrecognized by the GWCA.[7]

Early in the planning stages, the GWCA agreed that the website's educational articles should aid in their goal of cross-cultural understanding. After testing the articles' readability, the GWCA became aware that there were some aspects of Six Nations history, life, and culture not fully understood by those outside of their community . Through various committee and editing meetings, it was agreed that definition links would be added to clarify such concepts as the Six Nations annuity payments, Bread and Cheese Day, and treaties like the Two Row Wampum and the Silver Convenient Chain.[8] By adding these links to define terms common in Six Nations but unfamiliar to the non-Six Nations audience, the GWCA hopes that readers of the website will learn and understand the special place of Six Nations in the history of North America, and connect these historical experiences to contemporary issues faced by the Six Nations today.

The educational articles also serve as a way to show readers from the three Indigenous and non-Indigenous communities their shared and unique histories. To encourage readers to engage with these histories, the majority of the GWCA's articles highlight the similarities of wartime experiences, combining the common histories of Brantford, Brant County, and Six Nations; aside from "Loyalty to the Crown," other articles act to show the ways in which World War I united the three communities in a common sacrifice. "Three Communities Respond to War" illustrates the differences and similarities in how the communities responded to the war: with enthusiasm in Brantford, Brant County, and Six Nations, but also with caution by the traditional segments of the Six Nations community who wanted reassurances from the British Crown about their alliance.[9] Other articles, like "Agriculture" and "Six Nations Support of the War," show that while some wartime experiences were similar, they could also be vastly different.[10] Although the Six Nations were willing to aid in the greater agriculture effort and supported the war both monetarily and through other donations, these similarities to the non-Six Nations community were only superficial. A critical issue overlooked by most historians is that the Six Nations participated in these acts as a statement of their sovereign status as a separate national entity within Canada. By combining in a single article these two ideas of the significance of these events to both the Six Nations and non-Six Nations communities, readers get a dual understanding—that although these events appeared similar, there were differences based on the historical experience of each community.

However, articles like "Recruitment," "Battles," "Casualties in Perspective," and "The Halifax Disaster" demonstrate how the experiences of Six Nations, Brantford, and Brant County were all too similar. Not only was the number of the overall enlistment of Six Nations people on par with the rest of Canada per available population, but the Six Nations, Brantford, and Brant County all suffered together through their casualties.[11] This is best shown by the death of Cameron D. Brant and the 1917 Halifax Disaster. During the Halifax Explosion, Brantford and Brant County scrambled to raise money for the devastated city, only to find out midway through their fundraising that Six Nations soldier Adam Sandy had been killed by the blast.[12]

This was not the first time the three communities would be brought together. Every major battle became an occasion for community-wide grieving. One of the earliest deaths mourned was that of Cameron D.

Brant, a direct descendant of Joseph Brant who marked the first homegrown casualty for the three communities. In an act of solidarity, the City of Brantford wrote a condolence to the Six Nations Council, a transcript of which is available on the GWCA's website.[13]

In some cases, it was impossible to combine the three communities' wartime experiences. Instead, the GWCA created articles that highlight Six Nations-specific events of the war. Currently, two articles—"Cadets" and "Six Nations Conscription"—stand as examples of the different ways conflicting histories can be presented. For instance, in the "Cadet" article, the GWCA explains that the Mohawk Institute Cadet Corps, unlike its Branford counterpart, was a mandatory part of the residential school system in Canada. Although all cadet corps instilled the ideals of British patriotism to their youth charges, these lessons and drills were forced onto the Six Nations children at the Mohawk Institute.[14] The reasoning for separating the experiences of Six Nations in the Conscription Crisis of 1917 from the experiences of Brantford and Brant County was also due to vast differences. The City of Brantford and Brant County opposed conscription, fearing a loss of their industrial and agricultural workforces, while Six Nations opposed it on legal grounds, due to their alliance with the British Crown and their status as a separate nation.[15] These articles will soon be joined by two other articles about Six Nations postwar experiences with veterans' organizations and the soldier settlement program. All these articles bring to light the special status and historical experiences of Six Nations while also highlighting the inadequacies of the Canadian government's Department of Indian Affairs at the time.

During the GWCA's public launch of their website, representatives of various partner and community organizations were present, such as Wilfrid Laurier University; the local regiment, the 56th Field Artillery; the Six Nations Veterans Association; and Brant Museum and Archives. Equally important was the participation of the area's political representatives, including the members of the federal and provincial parliaments, chief of the Six Nations Band Council, the mayor of the City of Branford, and several city councillors, who praised together the multiple narratives told through the website.[16] What the GWCA did not know was the impact their website would have once it went live. From

April 2015 to July 2016, the website has had over 20,436 views. Viewers stay on the website for an average of five minutes and view three to four different pages; seventy percent are new and thirty percent are return visitors. Also interesting is the number of viewers coming from outside of Canada. Since April 2015, 12,900 viewers were from Canada, with 7500 viewers coming to the website from outside of Canada, mostly from the United States (2,600 viewers) and the United Kingdom (1,160 viewers). These numbers quantify for the GWCA the impact of their outreach, but also the number of viewers who are now informed about the Six Nations and other multinarratives of World War I.[17]

Further engaging the public and mobilizing knowledge, the GWCA has brought their information and website into the classroom. Led by GWCA board member and teacher Meghan Cameron, the GWCA education subcommittee—on which two members of the Six Nations subcommittee also sit—created three major Ontario curriculum-compliant lesson plans that can be adapted for different grade levels and into single period or multiday plans. As with website content, all Six Nations-specific lessons are vetted by Six Nations community members in order to ensure compliance with existing community narratives. The lessons explore whether or not Six Nation men could legally be conscripted, the history of Six Nations military and the 114th Battalion, and whether Six Nations were allies to the Crown or just ordinary Canadian soldiers. Using the GWCA website, students have digital access to primary documents like Six Nations treaties (including the Two Row Wampum and Silver Covenant Chain), transcripts of speeches from Six Nations leaders, artifacts such as the 114th Battalion colors, federal government documents, and transcripts from *The Brantford Expositor*. All these portray First Nations peoples as active agents in their history, connecting both Six Nations and non-Six Nations students to the larger history of Six Nations before, during, and after the war.

Currently these lessons are being tested in high schools in Brantford and Brant County, where Six Nations content is taught to a majority non-Six Nations audience. At the Brantford Collegiate Institute—a school with the second highest Six Nations enrollment in Brantford—these lessons have become important not only for non-Six Nations students, but also for Six Nations students, after seeing their community's history taught in their classrooms for the first time. With content reflecting the stories and perspectives they could engage with and relate to, these students became active participants in the teaching of these lessons, with teachers reporting the increased involvement of their usually disengaged Six Nations students. In the future, the GWCA hopes to create lesson plans with and for elementary school teachers. This will allow the content to be taught in Six Nations schools, since the Six Nations community at Grand River does not have a high school.

Community engagement and education, however, are the cornerstones of the GWCA's work. Wanting to bring the narratives of the war out of archival and personal collections, the GWCA has organized conferences, visits to classrooms and public service organizations, and an annual lecture series which has, on average, an attendance of thirty to forty people per lecture, mostly from the non-First Nations communities of Brantford and the County of Brant. Through this lecture series, the non-Six Nations public has been introduced to a variety of Six Nations topics, including how the Six Nations Confederacy Council—contrary to the opinion of the Canadian government—supported the war;[18] the effect of the local residential school, the Mohawk Institute, on Six Nations enlistment;[19] how the Six Nations home front supported the war;[20] and the prewar and wartime enlistment of Six Nations men in the army.[21] Sharing Six Nations narratives remains a constant imperative. Along with the annual lecture series, conferences held by the GWCA for museum professionals, teachers, and public educators always have one or more sessions highlighting the effects of the war on Six Nations people. Also requested by classroom teachers and service organizations, these lectures bring these histories, which would usually be confined in archives or within the Six Nations community, to a non-Six Nations public.

One of the more rewarding aspects of this project has been the gathering of personal narratives about individual artifacts that have been loaned to the GWCA by the public. The GWCA, noting concerns over the collecting of artifacts, and the increased market value of these artifacts due to the centenary of the war, has a strict non-collection policy. Although it is actively looking for artifacts, the GWCA is only interested in digitally copying them. This is done usually during digitization events held throughout the local community. If the owner of an artifact is insistent on donating their artifact, the GWCA will direct them to the most appropriate museum or archive. From these artifacts, the GWCA has been able to gather and share unique stories that highlight the complexity of the Six Nations wartime experience.

One of the first GWCA artifact stories was the Joseph Brant flagpole that held the colors of the 114th Battalion. The 114th Battalion was recruited out of the 37th Haldimand Rifles regiment, which, in the years before the war, was made up of mostly Six Nations men, with one company even being formed and stationed at the Six Nations Agricultural Fairgrounds. This pattern was repeated with the recruitment of the 114th Battalion. Not only was D Company of the battalion recruited from and stationed at Six Nations, Grand River, but over half of the battalion's recruits were First Nations men. For this reason, the Six Nations Patriotic League lobbied the Canadian Department of Militia to present D Company with a special battalion flag to celebrate the long-held Six Nations–British alliance. In the Woodland Cultural Centre's description of the flag, both Six Nations and the British were viewed as equals:

> The flag shows five clan symbols: the wolf, the eagle, the heron, the turtle and the bear. The turtle is situated at the base to symbolize the earth, Turtle Island. The bear clan is in homage to the first great warrior, Joseph Brant. His Mohawk name is Thayendanegea, meaning two sticks bound together, denoting strength, thus the image in the center which represents a war shield. The six arrows signify the Six Nations of the Iroquois Confederacy, Mohawk, Cayuga, Seneca, Tuscarora, Oneida, and the Onondaga Nation. The oak leaves and acorns symbolize life and sustenance from the Creator and the white pine the symbol of the Great Tree of Peace given to the Six Nations by the Peacemaker in the creation of the Great Law. The dragon and the lion are symbols for the Crown. The white hare is unidentified but is believed to symbolize the Ojibwe who were also members of the 114th Battalion.[22]

Six Nations scholar Rick Hill has also noted that the center crest in the flag, with the bear and the arrows, was the original seal of the Six

Nations Confederacy Council.[23] Less well-known, however, is that the Six Nations Patriotic League also funded the creation of a special flagpole for their flag.

When the GWCA began searching for the flagpole, they relied on the research of GWCA board member Geoffrey Moyer. Through this research, the GWCA discovered that a hand-carved mahogany bust of Joseph Brant had been commissioned by the Six Nations Patriotic League to accompany their hand-embroidered 114th Battalion flag, which, although it went with the battalion overseas, was never returned to Canada. With the aid of reporter Tristan Stewart Robinson in Glasgow, Scotland, the GWCA began their search for the flagpole where it was last sighted: during a propaganda tour of the 114th band, made up almost entirely Six Nations men, throughout Scotland. As they researched, Paula Whitlow at the Woodland Cultural Centre located a photograph of it. To the GWCA's surprise, the "flagpole" turned out to be a flagpole topper of the bust of Joseph Brant. Although this and another story about the 114th battalion remains on Robinson's website, no leads have come in yet about the location of the flagpole topper.[24]

Other stories come from the Six Nations community. The largest ongoing project of the GWCA involves collecting photographs of the over 5300 veterans from Brantford, Brant County, and Six Nations. As the Woodland Cultural Centre began putting together their exhibit, "Veterans, Warriors, and Peacekeepers," they also began compiling photographs of Six Nations World War One veterans.[25] In this process, Six Nations member Tesha Emarthle loaned the Woodland Cultural Centre a photograph collection and a 114th Battalion soldier's diary, belonging to her grandfather, Lloyd Curley. With Emarthle's permission, the diary and photographs were scanned, which enabled GWCA board member and reporter for *The Brantford Expositor* Vincent Ball to meet with Emarthle and write a story about Curley for the newspaper.[26] This diary was a rare find, as most artifacts like it were destroyed in the trenches. Moreover, Curley was killed in action with the 107th Battalion during the battle of Hill 70 on 14 August 1917; his diary and wallet were found by a British soldier in the aftermath of the battle and mailed to Curley's wife, Lulu. Through the Woodland Cultural Centre's partnership with the GWCA, this unique Six Nations story of the war was shared to the wide reading audience of *The Brantford Expositor*.

As the GWCA continues their work within the Brantford, Brant County, and Six Nations communities, artifacts are slowly coming out of people's basements and to the GWCA's attention. Non-Six Nations members even come to the GWCA with Six Nations historical information or scans of artifacts. When the GWCA receives these items, it sends them to the Woodland Cultural Centre, which passes them along to the appropriate Six Nations group for assessment. This approach has not only continued the respectful relationship between the Six Nations community and the GWCA, but has also aided in the return of objects to the community that were thought to have been lost forever.

Recently a photographic postcard came to the GWCA through researcher John Burger. While researching in the McMaster University archives, in Hamilton, Ontario, Burger came across a picture postcard of a man in full First Nations costume, holding a tomahawk. Written on the card was "Pte J Cook 64 Batt Canadian Indian Chief Shoreham Camp Dec 1916." Burger wrote to the GWCA to see if they had any information on J. Cook. After searching their records, they found that J. Cook was in fact John Cook, a Six Nations carpenter from Hartford, Ontario, who followed traditional Six Nations religious practices. After enlisting at the age of forty-three, Cook joined the band of the 114th Battalion. The band, during intermissions, would dress up in Wild-West-Show-styled clothing and perform for the audience. Burger was able to put the GWCA in contact with archivists at McMaster University, who allowed them to use the picture of Cook on their veterans' profile page, while securing Woodland Cultural Centre a picture of one of their veterans.[27]

Another artifact that came to the GWCA, in picture form, was a banjo signed by Six Nations veteran W. E. Davis. Photos of the banjo came to the GWCA from Alec Somerville, a retired police officer from Windsor, Ontario. Somerville, purchased the banjo in England as a restoration project and did not know about the signatures until he removed the banjo's skin. Somerville surmised that Davis, along with the other signatories, most likely signed the back of the banjo while the "E" anti-aircraft battery was on leave in Paris in 1917. Somerville, like Burger, asked the GWCA what information it had on Davis, since he was trying to identify all twenty-eight men who had signed the banjo. Unfortunately, the GWCA did not have a lot of information about Davis.[28] Somerville continued his research, and discovered through the Library and Archives Canada's digitization project of World War I service file, that Davis only spent one to two days in the 208th Battalion before being discharged for desertion.[29] Davis must have signed the banjo skin in either Toronto or Camp Borden, and the reference to the "E" anti-aircraft battery must have been added later. Since then, not only has the banjo been donated to the Canadian Military Museum in Ottawa, but the Six Nations community—who had very little information about Davis—now has Somerville's research and pictures of an artifact related to him.[30] These artifacts not only make a personal connection to World War I, but add to a growing community interaction, providing greater depth to the complex histories of the war at Six Nations Grand River. This has been especially true for Somerville, who, through this artifact, has been able to reconnect with his own past as a police officer in the neighboring non-First Nations town of Caledonia, Ontario, in 1954. After coming to Canada from Great Britain in 1953, Somerville served on the two-member Caledonia police force for six months before joining the Ontario Provincial Police, bringing him into contact with the people, history, and heritage of the area.

On 23 April 2015 the GWCA again teamed up with the Woodland Cultural Centre to commemorate the second battle of Ypres, where Brantford, Brant County, and Six Nations suffered their first wartime casualty. On 24 April 1915 Lieutenant Cameron D. Brant, great-great grandson of the famed Joseph Brant, was killed in action. The GWCA and Woodland Cultural Centre invited the public from all three communities to commemorate the effects of the battle on First Nations people, Canada, and the communities of Six Nations, New Credit, Brantford, and Brant County. The event was marked by two addresses. The first explained the battle, the soldiers' ordeal, and the effect of the massive casualties on First Nations communities and non-First Nations communities alike. The second presentation, given by New Credit librarian Darin Wybanga, highlighted the New Credit war effort and focused on the life and death of Cameron Brant. At the end of the evening,

Fig. 4. Somerville's banjo and the signature of W. E. Davis. Images courtesy of Alec Somerville.

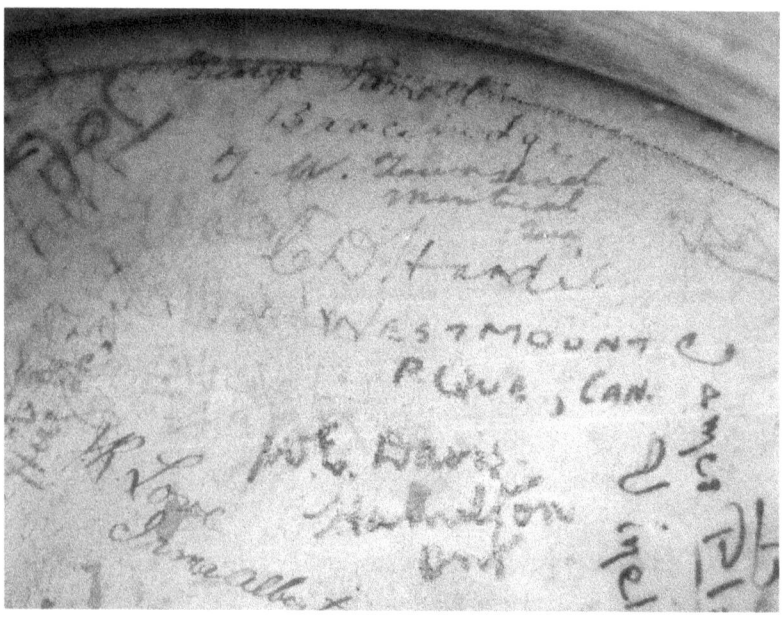

Fig. 5. Detail of Somerville's banjo and the signature of W. E. Davis. Images courtesy of Alec Somerville.

the names of all seventy casualties from the three communities were read while their pictures were projected on screen.[31] For ten minutes, while the names were read, the mixed audience of twenty-five people from Brantford, Brant County, and Six Nations remained absolutely silent, as they respected and reflected on their combined war dead and wounded, again aligning and remembering their combined and separate war efforts and sacrifices, just as their ancestors had done after Brant's death in 1915.[32]

This is the goal of the GWCA: public engagement and cross-cultural and cross-community understanding. The GWCA has created and continues to create programming, based on an open and continuing community consulting model, that will not only engage the public, but will create a permanent virtual memorial to the role Brantford, Brant County, and Six Nations played during World War I. By reaching out to the Six Nations community and giving them the final say in how their history is presented, the GWCA has ensured that community narratives from the people of Six Nations will not be stifled by the dominant Euro-Canadian communities that surround the Grand River Territory. As the GWCA continues to use this model and expand its presence in local communities during the centenary of the war, it hopes to foster new relationships with other community groups, collect more research materials, and share them on an extensive website and database that, taking World War I as an entry point, can be used to educate Six Nations and non-Six Nations communities alike about the unique position and history of the Six Nations of the Grand River Territory within North America.

NOTES

1. Woodland Cultural Centre, "Veterans, Warriors, and Peacekeepers Opening Full House," 2014. http://www.woodland-centre.on.ca/veterans-warriors-and-peacekeepers-opening-full-house.
2. Woodland Cultural Centre "Veterans, Warriors, and Peacekeepers Opening Full House," 2014. http://www.woodland-centre.on.ca/veterans-warriors-peacekeepers-exhibition-opening and http://www.woodland-centre.on.ca/veterans-warriors-and-peacekeepers-opening-full-house.

3. Woodland Cultural Centre, "Check Out youtube Video of 114th Flag Presentation Ceremony," 2014. http://www.woodland-centre.on.ca/check-out-youtube-video-114th-flag-presentation-ceremony and http://www.woodland-centre.on.ca/veterans-warriors-and-peacekeepers-opening-full-house.
4. Artifact identification tag, Flag of the 114th Battalion, Woodland Cultural Centre.
5. Eight articles are posted on the GWCA website, while two exploring Six Nations and veterans organizations and the Six Nations soldier settlement program will be released as the GWCA updates the website 2018–19.
6. The Two Row Wampum Belt was the first treaty made by the Five Nations (later Six Nations) with non-First Nations people. Beginning with the Dutch in 1613, this treaty outlined the conditions in which the two groups were to coexist with each other in North America. According to Tehanetorens Fadden, the two purple rows "symbolize two paths or two vessels, travelling down the same river together. One, a birch bark canoe, will be for the Indian People, their laws, their customs, and their ways. The other, a ship, will be for the white people and their laws, their customs, and their ways. We shall each travel the river together, side by side, but not in the same boat. Neither of us will make compulsory laws or interfere in the internal affairs of the other. Neither of us will try to steer the other's vessel." See Tahonetorens Fadden, *Wampum Belts of the Iroquois*, Summertown TN: Book Publishing Company, 1993, 74. The Silver Covenant Chain is an extension of the alliance created between the Six Nations and the British through the Two Row Wampum. Although the Two Row Wampum created the alliance, the Silver Covenant Chain strengthened it by giving it meaning and further protocols, represented both by chain links and by the fact that the chain is made from silver. According to the North American Indian Travelling College, "the first link [of the chain] represented peace between them [the Six Nations and the British]. The second link represented having a good mind, while the third [link] was a symbol of eternal friendship. It was said that should the chain become tarnished they [the Six Nations and the British] would sit together once again to polish the links, and renew the agreement." See Tsionni Fox and the North American Indian Travelling College, 1991, *Covenant Chain*, Cornwall, Ontario: North American Indian Travelling College.
7. GWCA, "Loyalty to the Crown," 2014. http://doingourbit.ca/loyalty-crown.

8. See GWCA, "Two Row Wampum" http://doingourbit.ca/two-row-wampum, "Silver Covenant Chain" http://doingourbit.ca/silver-covenant-chain, and "Bread and Cheese Day http://doingourbit.ca/bread-and-cheese-day in "Loyalty to the Crown" http://doingourbit.ca/loyalty-crown and "Annuity Money" http://doingourbit.ca/annuity-money in "Six Nations Conscription" http://doingourbit.ca/six-nations-conscription, 2014.
9. gwca, "Three Communities Respond to War," 2014. http://www.doingourbit.ca/three-communities-respond-war.
10. GWCA, "Six Nations Support of War" http://www.doingourbit.ca/six-nations-support-war and "Agriculture," 2014. http://www.doingourbit.ca/agriculture.
11. GWCA, "Enlistment Statistics by Province/Territory" in "Recruitment," 2014. http://doingourbit.ca/recruitment.
12. GWCA, "The Halifax Disaster," 2014. http://www.doingourbit.ca/halifax-disaster.
13. GWCA, "An Iconic Casualty," 2014. http://www.doingourbit.ca/casualties-perspective.
14. GWCA, "Cadets," 2014. http://www.doingourbit.ca/cadets.
15. GWCA, "Conscription Crisis, Brantford, Brant County" http://www.doingourbit.ca/conscription-crisis-brantford-brant and "Six Nations Conscription," 2014. http://www.doingourbit.ca/six nations-conscription.
16. Vincent Ball, "Do Your Bit by Visiting Great War Website." *Brantford Expositor*, November 19, 2014. A member of the Six Nations Confederacy Council could not be present, due to a death in the community.
17. Google Analytics provided to the GWCA through Digital Duck, Inc., August 2016.
18. Evan J. Habkirk, "Communities and Conflict: The City Brantford and Six Nations during the First World War" (lecture, the Great War Centenary Association Brantford–Brant County–Six Nations Speaker Series, Brantford ON, 2014).
19. Evan J. Habkirk, "Preparing for War?: The Cadet Movement in Brantford and Six Nations" (lecture, the Great War Centenary Association Brantford–Brant County–Six Nations Speaker Series, Brantford ON, 2014).
20. Allison Norman, "'In Defence of Empire': The Women of Six Nations and the Great War" (lecture, the Great War Centenary Association Brantford–Brant County–Six Nations Speaker Series, Brantford ON, 2015).

21. Evan J. Habkirk, "Six Nations Enlistment and the Creation of the 114th Battalion" (lecture, the Great War Centenary Association Brantford–Brant County–Six Nations Speaker Series, Brantford ON, 2016).
22. Artifact identification tag, Flag of the 114th Battalion, Woodland Cultural Centre.
23. Richard W. Hill Sr., *War Clubs and Wampum Belts: The Hodinohso:ni Experiences of the War of 1812* (Brantford ON: Woodland Cultural Centre, 2012), 82.
24. Tristan Stewart-Robinson, "The Independence Battalion" and "Six Nations Hunt for Lost World War I History," *Tomorrow Is Now*, 2013. http://tomorrow.is/yesterday/independence-battalion/#.v7yJ-zx9w-e and http://tomorrow.is/news/six-nations-hunt-lost-world-war-history/#.v7yk4zx9w-c.
25. Although the Woodland Cultural Centre's goal was to obtain pictures for all of the 450 men and women who served in World War I, by the time of the exhibit's opening, the Centre had just over 100.
26. Vincent Ball, "The World War I Diary of Lloyd Clifford Curley," *Brantford Expositor*, 2013. http://www.brantfordexpositor.ca/2013/11/10/the-ww1-diary-of-lloyd-clifford-curley.
27. GWCA, "John Cook," 2014. http://doingourbit.ca/profile/john-cook.
28. GWCA, "William Elmer Davis," 2014. http://doingourbit.ca/profile/william-davis-.
29. Service file of William Elmer Davis, Library and Archives Canada, http://central.bac-lac.gc.ca/.item/?op=pdf&app=cef&id=b2360-s055.
30. Peter Simpson, "Banjo is a Mystery from the First World War," *Ottawa Citizen*, 2013. http://ottawacitizen.com/entertainment/music/banjo-is-a-mystery-from-the-first-world-war.
31. Woodland Cultural Centre, "Doing Our Bit Commemoration, Thursday," 2015. http://www.woodland-centre.on.ca/doing-our-bit-commemoration-thursday.
32. GWCA, "Cameron Donald Brant," 2014. http://doingourbit.ca/profile/cameron-brant and "An Iconic Casualty" http://doingourbit.ca/casualties-perspective.

REFERENCES

Ball, Vincent. 2013. "The World War I Diary of Lloyd Clifford Curley." *The Brantford Expositor*. http://www.brantfordexpositor.ca/2013/11/10/the-ww1-diary-of-lloyd-clifford-curley.

———. 2014. "Do Your Bit by Visiting Great War Website." *The Brantford Expositor*.
Fadden, Tahonetorens. 1999. *Wampum Belts of the Iroquois*. Summertown TN: Book Publishing Company.
GWCA. 2014. "Agriculture." http://www.doingourbit.ca/agriculture.
———. 2014. "An Iconic Casualty" in "Casualties in Perspective." http://www.doingourbit.ca/casualties-perspective.
———. 2014. "Cadets." http://www.doingourbit.ca/cadets.
———. 2014. "Conscription Crisis, Brantford, Brant County." http://www.doingourbit.ca/conscription-crisis-brantford-brant.
———. 2014. "John Cook." http://doingourbit.ca/profile/john-cook.
———. 2014. "Loyalty to the Crown." http://doingourbit.ca/loyalty-crown.
———. 2014. "Six Nations Conscription." http://doingourbit.ca/six-nations-conscription.
———. 2014. "Six Nations Support of War." http://www.doingourbit.ca/six-nations-support-war.
———. 2014. "The Halifax Disaster." http://www.doingourbit.ca/halifax-disaster.
———. 2014. "Three Communities Respond to War." http://www.doingourbit.ca/three-communities-respond-war.
———. 2014. "William Elmer Davis" http://doingourbit.ca/profile/william-davis-.
Habkirk, Evan J. 2013. "Communities and Conflict: The City of Brantford and Six Nations during the First World War." Lecture presented at the Great War Centenary Association Brantford–Brant County–Six Nations Speaker Series, Brantford ON.
———. 2014. "Preparing for War?: The Cadet Movement in Brantford and Six Nations." Lecture presented at the Great War Centenary Association Brantford–Brant County–Six Nations Speaker Series, Brantford ON.
———. 2016. "Six Nations Enlistment and the Creation of the 114th Battalion." Lecture presented at the Great War Centenary Association Brantford—Brant County—Six Nations Speaker Series, Brantford ON.
Hill, Richard W., Sr. 2012. *War Clubs and Wampum Belts: The Hodinohso:ni Experiences of the War of 1812*. Brantford ON: Woodland Cultural Centre.
Library and Archives Canada, Service File of William Elmer Davis. http://central.bac-lac.gc.ca/.item/?op=pdf&app=cef&id=b2360-s055.
Norman, Allison. 2015. "'In Defence of Empire': The Women of Six Nations and the Great War." Lecture presented at the Great War Centenary Association Brantford–Brant County–Six Nations Speaker Series, Brantford ON.

Simpson, Peter. 2013. "Banjo is a Mystery from the First World War." *Ottawa Citizen*. http://ottawacitizen.com/entertainment/music/banjo-is-a-mystery-from-the-first-world-k-war.

Stewart-Robinson, Tristian. 2013. "The Independence Battalion." *Tomorrow is Now*. http://tomorrow.is/yesterday/independence-battalion/#.v7yJ-zx9w-e.

———. 2013. "Six Nations Hunt for Lost World War I History." *Tomorrow is Now*. http://tomorrow.is/news/six-nations-hunt-lost-world-war-history/#.v7yk4zx9w-c.

Woodland Cultural Centre. Artifact identification tag for the flag of the 114th Battalion.

———. 2014. "Check Out youtube Video of 114th Flag Presentation Ceremony." http://www.woodland-centre.on.ca/check-out-youtube-video-114th-flag-presentation-ceremony.

———. 2014. "Veterans, Warriors, and Peacekeepers: Exhibit Opening." http://www.woodland-centre.on.ca/veterans-warriors-peacekeepers-exhibition-opening.

———. 2014. "Veterans, Warriors, and Peacekeepers Opening Full House." http://www.woodland-centre.on.ca/veterans-warriors-and-peacekeepers-opening-full-house.

———. 2015. "Doing Our Bit Commemoration, Thursday." http://www.woodland-centre.on.ca/doing-our-bit-commemoration-thursday.

ANTHONY F. C. WALLACE
With an editorial note by Regna Darnell

8

Guns and Ivy
An Anthropologist's Memoir

The death of Anthony F. C. Wallace earlier this year left considerable work incomplete. With the permission of the executor of his papers, the American Philosophical Society, HoAA is pleased to present one such piece. It was written as the introduction to a planned book-length monograph. Tony shared it with me, including two additions to show the intended scope of the full work. I raised the possibility of separate publication for the introduction, but his health precluded editorial revisions and the matter lapsed. After some consideration, I have decided not to incorporate the two excerpts into the introductory text. I have made minimal changes to the text, simply correcting obvious typographical and formatting errors. Tony's lucid prose stands on its own, but readers should realize that he would certainly have integrated more fully the material that follows.

The genre of memoir inadequately captures the tenor of the project. Wallace begins with his reflections on war among the Tuscarora and other Hodenosaunee peoples with whom he spent much of his professional life. In *Tuscarora: A History* (2012) he told the story of how he came to see the Tuscarora community on its own terms and to understand the violence implicit in the imposition of social science categories, however well-meaning, upon those realities. Only in the context of its contrast to Tuscarora modes of understanding did Wallace turn to his own experience of war. The longer manuscript (of which the proposed table of contents appears here, following the text), documents the war as he experienced it and frames in retrospective terms how it became "the Second World War," a considerable generalization from any single person's experience. The text moves back and forth between "his" war and the Tuscarora tradition of war, as he came to understand it through orally transmitted collective memory of the experiences of warriors and their communities.

The first excerpt deals with Wallace's personal experience of World War Two. The second deals with the discipline of anthropology in the era of my generation's war, the undeclared one in Vietnam. During my graduate school years, Wallace was responding to then-contemporary crises that, however unique they might seem to those experiencing them, would later come to make sense in a cross-cultural perspective. In those years the discipline of anthropology was reimagining itself, with repercussions that continue to resound today. As he was in the war, Wallace was a witness. He served as president of the American Anthropological Association in 1970–71 and attempted to steer a balanced course through the turbulence of those years. His exemplars of Project Camelot, the AAA Code of Ethics, and the anthropological reception of Patrick Tierney's critique of the discipline in the Amazon reflect the polarized climate. The overall frame exploring the meaning of war for an anthropological understanding of human nature and sociality returns to the core piece on "war and the boundaries of kinship."
—**Regna Darnell**

WAR AND THE BOUNDARIES OF KINSHIP

On our planet there is probably no village that does not have a story of war to tell. But some villages have had a peaceful time in recent years. I live in a village at the mouth of the Niagara River, where it flows into Lake Ontario, a few miles below the Falls. The residents of Youngstown, New York, have recently been celebrating two hundred years of peace with Canada. The people in the Canadian town across the river, Niagara-on-the-Lake, have been celebrating two hundred years of peace with the United States. The last war between us was the War of 1812. There is a children's playground in Youngstown, and in it a small garden of flowers, called "The Peace Garden," planted by local children who brought plants of their own (or their mothers') choosing. Tuscarora Indian children from the reservation nearby brought sunflowers, native to the country. The Peace Garden was dedicated several years ago by officials from both sides of the river, who said a few words of international well-wishes and resolved to continue the peace.

But the dark days of the war are remembered as well. The British capture of the American Fort Niagara and its garrison at the mouth of the river about a mile north of Youngstown was commemorated in a predawn re-enactment. But perhaps the most emotional, and paradoxical, commemorative occasion was the unveiling of the Tuscarora Heroes Monument. The ceremony was held on December 19, 2013, at the center of the town of Lewiston, a few miles up the river from Youngstown, on the two hundredth anniversary of the burning of Lewiston after the fall of Fort Niagara. I attended the event with a couple of Indian friends. It was a cold evening, but at least a thousand people showed up, both whites and Tuscaroras from the reserve just above the town, the Indians wearing corn-husk ribbons in honor of their ancestors, whose rescue of white refugees from Lewiston was the scene portrayed in the sculpture.

The re-enactment began after dark, at about 6:30. The street was lit by the flames from propane tanks mounted in oil drums, representing the burning of the town. A squad of reenactors dressed as U.S. soldiers in uniforms of the time retreated up the street, firing muskets. Then came a squad of British soldiers, firing their guns. Then a crowd of women and children in white pajamas, screaming and yelling (chosen for their loudness), followed by a gaggle of British Indians, whooping and waving tomahawks, and, at last, the Tuscarora heroes coming to the rescue with their guns and tomahawks, covering the retreat of their white neighbors up Ridge Road.

After this re-enactment, Tuscarora chief Sacarissa and various town, county, state, and U.S. officials, made brief remarks, and then the plastic wrap was pulled off the bronze statues (crafted by a renowned local sculptor, Sarah Geissler). The crowd swarmed about the work, which was a finely detailed representation of a fleeing white woman, baby under her arm, reaching out to grasp the hand of a Tuscarora warrior, while another warrior faces off the threatening crowd of Canadian Indians pursuing her.

It is claimed that this re-enactment was the largest public event in the United States that commemorated the War of 1812. It expresses universal values: both a deploring of the pain and chaos of war, and a celebration of the charitable side of human nature. It echoes the statement of a Tuscarora Indian in 1709 on the importance of coming to the aid of neighbors in distress:

> They are very kind, and charitable to one another, but more especially to those of their own Nation; for if any one of them has suffer'd any Loss, by Fire or otherwise ... it is all their Duties to help him, as he would do to any of them, had the like Misfortune befallen them.... The same Assistance they give to any Man, that wants to build a Cabin, or make a Canoe. They say, it is our Duty thus to do; for there are several Works that one Man cannot effect, therefore we must give him our Help, otherwise our Society will fall, and we shall be depriv'd of those urgent Necessities which Life requires." (Lawson 1709 [1966], 178–79)

Not emphasized in the public doings was the fact that all of the Tuscarora women and children also became refugees, along with the white folks, and their village was burned to the ground. The women and children moved on to the east, among the Oneidas, and their warriors entered the war as a unit in the U.S. army, fighting along the lower St. Laurence. The people did not return to the reserve above Lewiston until well after the end of the war, in 1814. Thus the year 2013 is a double anniversary of Tuscarora wars. In 1713 the Tuscarora Fort Neoheroke in North Carolina was destroyed by an army of whites and their Indian allies, with hundreds of casualties and prisoners taken into slavery. This catastrophe ended the Tuscarora War (1711–13) and set in motion the Tuscarora migration north into New York. These events were commemorated at East Carolina University by a three-day conference, featuring historical talks and a visit to the site and the monumental wall under construction there in commemoration of the battle. I attended the conference and gave a talk on the survival of the Tuscarora Nation.

These two anniversaries of war stimulated widespread interest among Tuscarora residents in their nation's history. Neil Patterson Sr. and his family provided the Lewiston Historical Association with advice and information. Neil Patterson Jr. planned and led a trek north along the old migration route to the present reservation. And a "History Group" led by chiefs, clan mothers, and teachers from the Tuscarora School collected documents and oral history, and organized the travel of nearly two hundred Tuscaroras to attend the "Tuscarora 300" event in North Carolina. These activities were supported by a grant from the American Philosophical Society and led by Tim Powell, to help advance the program—already underway at the Tuscarora Elementary School—to revitalize the Tuscaroras' knowledge of their history, culture, and language.

Part of the effort of the History Group was to "unpack" the story of the Tuscarora Heroes. There remains little today in the way of living memory passed on by word of mouth from the contemporary participants and observers of the event in 1813. In 1883 a Tuscarora Indian chief, Elias Johnson, published a history of the Tuscarora Nation that included an account of the encounter, based on oral testimony, that is the main source of information now available to local historians. This narrative reveals little about the War of 1812 beyond the Niagara Frontier. It came as a surprise to many Tuscaroras and local whites to learn the larger realities of the War of 1812: the surprise preemptive attack in 1811 by U.S. troops led by Governor Henry Harrison on Tippecanoe, the Shawnee Prophet's village in Ohio; the invasion of Canada by the U.S. Army in 1812, leading to the events the following year on the Niagara Frontier and the burning of Lewiston; the revival and defeat of the northern confederacy led by Tecumseh; Andrew Jackson's onslaught against the Creeks in Georgia, some of whom were followers of the Shawnee Prophet, Tecumseh's brother. The Tuscarora intervention, involving an exchange of fire with other Iroquois warriors from Canada, and the death of a Canadian Mohawk, led to a breach of the Six Nations Confederacy between the Canadian and American councils that has still to be fully repaired. And beyond the fighting on American soil, the War of 1812 must be seen as part of the world war between Great Britain and Napoleon's France, over the countries of Europe and their empires in North and South America, Africa, and Asia, and, in an even larger sense, the colonizing of the Indigenous (in accord with Canadian usage) peoples on all the continents by the Christian nations of Europe. All of these levels of reality had to be rediscovered by the Tuscarora History Group from the literature and primary sources and revealed as the background information for the commemoration of the rescue of white refugees from Lewiston by the Tuscarora Heroes. The skirmish at Lewiston was a microcosm of this vast panorama of battle.

In the midst of all this activity devoted to rediscovering the history of Tuscarora wars and migrations, I was prompted to think of writing a book about my experiences in my own war, World War II, and in its aftermath. My own experiences were those of tens of millions of other common soldiers who survived their wars and returned as veterans to countries cleaning up from the last war and preparing for the next one. And, as it was for the Tuscaroras, it turned out to be a task of historical research for me to discover what had been going on in and around my own limited zone of combat. For many years I had been bothered by a gap in my memory of six or seven hours that blotted out the circumstances of a battle in France in 1944 and by a vague amnesia for much of the rest of the campaign of the Fourteenth Armored Division in Alsace. I retained only fragmentary memories, like a succession of brief video clips, and was barely aware of the strategy and progress of the campaigns in which the Fourteenth Armored Division was involved. But I became increasingly aware, as events unfolded in the Cold War, in Korea and Vietnam, and, most recently in Iraq and Afghanistan, of the pervasive effect of war on the lives of individuals and institutions as nations repeatedly prepare for the next one.

One of the places where the cycle of war has continued for hundreds of years is the border between France and Germany. I remember becoming viscerally aware of the antiquity of this struggle during the campaign in Alsace. We came across an old stone wall, partly covered with vegetation. The locals told us that these were the remains of the *Heidenmauer* (or "Heathen Wall"), built to keep out the pagan German tribes. It must have been constructed in late Roman times, after Gaul had been Christianized. A few weeks later, the battle at Hatten was fought among the bunkers and pillboxes of the old Maginot Line, built by France after World War I in preparation for the next war with Germany. Eventually we broke through the Siegfried Line in Germany, similarly built by Germany during preparations for the next war with

France. No matter who lived on either side of the river, the series of wars continued. I remember lying on the grass and looking up at the contrails of bombers in the blue sky, and thinking that we were traveling over ground where armies had been marching for thousands of years. This line of thought leads to the classic model of war as a dance of death between nations.

I was talking about these ideas with my research partner, Deborah Holler, and I told her of an incident in a town in Germany when I "liberated" a pair of boots for a barefoot man just released from a slave-labor camp so that he could begin his pilgrimage, a walk back to his home in the Ukraine. She suggested that perhaps I should write an account of my own wartime experiences. Personal memories, narrative vignettes, might serve as a way of introducing larger issues. Stories from one observer's life in a world of wars might help to reveal the penetration of war, from childhood to old age, throughout the fabric of society, and also some of the human strivings toward lasting peace. I could illustrate these matters with examples from the two nations in which I have been embedded, Tuscarora and the United States, and in whose wars I have some personal interest. And it would illuminate some chapters in the history of my discipline, anthropology.

And the anthropologist in me cannot help but go back to the Iroquois, the Haudenosaunee, the People of the Longhouse, for a theme that runs through the tortuous maze of events that make up every war. This theme is the obligations, and boundaries, of kinship.

The action of the Tuscarora Heroes presented not only the Tuscarora Nation but also the entire confederacy with a dilemma of political kinship. The public ideology was expressed in the condolence ceremony, the central ceremonial event of the league, which was performed after the death of a chief. It depicted the normal state of human relationships, as based on kinship in its various forms, in networks of consanguinity and affinity, from the nuclear family to the clan to the nation, and to interaction between nations. Central bonds within the kinship network are mother and child, father and child, uncle and nephew, brother and sister (elder and younger), and husband and wife. Such relationships, over several generations, unite all the members of the characteristic Iroquois dwelling, the longhouse. The longhouse, and the kin relationships within it, provide the metaphor—and, I would suggest, the active template—for the ideal system of relationships among nations. In the language of the Great Law of the Confederacy, and in the language of recorded treaties, the sides address one another as father and son, as elder and younger brother. War between nations by these bonds of kinship is unthinkable. War only occurs between nations who are beyond each other's boundaries of kinship—in effect, between members of the league and alien nations.

Within the nation and within the confederacy, injuries inflicted by an identified or suspected fellow member were responded to by the victim's kin in private negotiations with, or in revenge against, the perpetrator's immediate family. There were no police or courts to intervene. War was launched against another nation only when the perpetrator could be identified as a member of a nation not belonging to the confederacy. In such a case, the perpetrator's kin could not be sought out. The entire offending nation was deemed guilty and a threat, and any and all of its members—warriors, women and children, the aged and infirm alike—were subject to attack by the aggrieved. Such "mourning wars" were feuds that could go on for generations as each side sought to even the score. Thus the agonizing issue between the American Tuscaroras and the Canadian Mohawks was whether confederate solidarity would prevail over national alienation.

Do considerations of the boundaries of international kinship apply to "my" war, World War II? The answer is certainly "yes." It was Nazi ideology, as expressed in Hitler's *Mein Kampf* and Alfred Rosenberg's *Mythos der 20st Jahrhundert* that encouraged and justified Germany's assault on Poland, the Soviet Union, and the western powers. The issue of kinship, of ethnic Germans and, indeed, Aryans worldwide, as an endangered people, folk, and race, was central to Germany's rationalization for launching World War II in Europe.

The principal victims of the Nazi Holocaust were Jews. Their survivors after the war renewed an ancient demand, after an earlier diaspora, to reconstitute the state of Israel on its own territory. The Jewish people too are a kinship group, but whether in the sense of a descent group, a religion, or a nation is not always clear to users of the term. I was talking over the matter with a rabbi, after the war, on a ship taking us to Star Island, off the coast of New Hampshire, for a conference on "Science and Religion." He told me, in an emphatic tone of voice, "The Jews are not a religion, they are not a descent group or race, they are a Nation."

Once violence is underway, at the other end of the population scale, the importance of the bond of kinship in the fog of war is displayed dramatically in the camaraderie of small groups. The boundary of kinship shrinks from nation to "the band of brothers." I am reminded of the lines from Matthew Arnold's "Dover Beach":

And we are here as on a darkling plain,
Swept by confused alarms of struggle and flight,
Where ignorant armies clash by night.

The team becomes a family, fighting to save one another, lost in a world of strangers bent on their annihilation.

I use the word "family" (and the word "kinship") in the larger sense. The boundaries of KINSHIP are defined in my usage here not merely by genealogy (marriage and descent), but also by proximity (neighborhood), by collaboration, by sharing language and values. It is the work of political, economic, religious institutions to define these boundaries. KINSHIP is the mantra whose invocation mobilizes nations to go to war.

EXCERPT 1: WARTIME EXPERIENCE

I served in World War II in a signal company, a support unit that provided radio and wire communications to the battalions "up front," and that on occasion came under fire itself. Here I became aware of battle as a confusing mess of ignorance and error. And in the years after the war, during an academic career, I came to see the aftermath of war in the civilian world—cleaning up after the last one and preparing for the next—as in some ways more destructive than battle itself, penetrating the lives of individuals and warping the priorities of nations.

The Battle of Hatten

The battle at Hatten, in northern Alsace, was fought between a small American force led by the Fourteenth Armored Division and a larger

German army of several armored ("panzer") divisions. Our radio halftrack was parked on the edge of this battle, and I knew little of what was going on. Discovering the magnitude and significance of the battle at Hatten has been an example of the kind of historical research that the Tuscarora History Group had to undertake.

In December 1944 concern about the developing danger of a German breakthrough in northern Alsace, a second Bulge, had already prompted Eisenhower to order that a defense line be formed out of the remaining elements of the Seventh Army, most of whose reserves had moved north to defend Bastogne. A thin little group was hastily cobbled together to defend a line in northern Alsace: from the foothills of the Vosge mountains, around Bitche, all the way west to the Rhine, about seventy miles. This defense line was composed of three units, called task forces, and our DAO had been assigned to lead Task Force Hudelson, which was made up of one infantry battalion and one cavalry squadron from the Fourteenth Armored, at first with minimal tank support. We had been on the way to join them when we got lost [ED: this event is discussed in preceding section].

Elements of five German divisions attacked a few days later on New Year's Eve. In the ensuing battle in the towns of Hatten and Rittershoffen, from January 10th to the 21st, the Fourteenth Armored, now with its reserve tank and infantry battalions brought up from the south, fought off the German Thirty-Ninth Panzer Corps. We were hunkered down, operating the radio, during the eleven days of fighting. The little town of Hatten was flattened: of 305 houses standing at the outset, all were destroyed but five. Combined death on both sides amounted to about 2500. The division had 150 tanks knocked out in combat and at one point was running low on ..30-caliber machine gun ammunition, and the DAO was responsible for renewing the supply. I was assigned to go along with a truck driver with orders to pick up ammunition. There was nothing we could find nearby, and we had to go all the way to the docks at Marseilles to pick up a load (about two and a half tons) of .30-caliber machine-gun ammunition. It took two days to travel the seven-hundred-or-so-mile round-trip. A couple of days later the word came from Hatten that the ammunition was defective, old and corroded, and that it jammed the guns.

We did not know it then, of course, that the attack on northern Alsace was the beginning of what the Germans referred to as *Operation Nordwind*. (Our lost half-track may have been the first to encounter Northwind.) It was launched by two separate armies. The northern force was commanded by Hitler himself, the southern by Heinrich Himmler. Both were ceremoniously referred to as *Reichsführer*. Himmler was the commander of the ss, who manned a large part of the tank divisions and administered the concentration camps (Dachau among them). The plan, apparently, was for Hitler's force to break through the flimsy American defenses in northern Alsace, sweep down to capture Haguenau and Strasbourg, and then swing north to annihilate Patton's Third Army defending Bastogne. In a belligerent speech to his division commanders three days before the attack in the north, Hitler emphasized the importance of Operation Northwind:

> Thus this second attack has an entirely clear objective—the destruction of the enemy forces. No questions of prestige are involved. It is not a question of gaining space. The exclusive aim is to destroy and eliminate the enemy forces wherever we find them. It is not even the task of this operation to liberate all Alsace. That would be wonderful.... But that is not what matters. As I said before, what matters is the destruction of the man power of the enemy. (1944 [1951], 164–65)

Having contained the German advance at Hatten, the Fourteenth Armored and other units in northern Alsace were ordered on January 21st to withdraw and move south to help defend a line along the Moder River, next to the Forty-Fifth Infantry, the Seventy-Ninth Infantry, and the 101st Airborne.

Our withdrawal began in a less than orderly way. Rumor had it that the Germans had broken through to the north. It was a cold day with freezing rain on top of snow. Tanks, trucks, and other vehicles were sliding off the road. I was riding with the code clerk in some sort of staff vehicle while the rest of the crew were following. My driver was a tall, skinny Irishman from Boston who loved to drink beer but who became intoxicated, as someone said, by even the smell of beer. He was probably nervous, was certainly not a good driver on snow and ice, and he failed to make a sharp turn in the road. We burst through a hedgerow, zoomed across a snowy field, crashed through another hedgerow, and miraculously were back on the road. The captain later found us another code clerk. We all eventually got together somewhere east of Haguenau, where elements of the 101st Airborne had halted the German advance. I remember driving by Haguenau and wondering at a black layer of smoke that covered the city like a cap, held in place, I suppose, by an atmospheric inversion layer.

By mid-January the German forces had reoccupied most of the territory we had over-run a couple of months before. But Hatten remained an icon of the successful defense of northern Alsace. The Fourteenth Armored issued a little pamphlet comparing the importance of saving Hatten to the Soviet victory at Stalingrad. Lt. General Devers, commander of the Sixth Army Group, called the Battle of Hatten-Rittershofen "one of the greatest defensive battles of the war." The Fourteenth Armored received two Presidential Unit Citations. German commanders declared that the Fourteenth Armored defense of Hatten was "heroic" and "one of the hardest and most costly battles that had ever raged on the western front." It was said to have been the largest tank battle on the Western Front during the war in Europe.

The cost in casualties of Operation Nordwind was, for the Germans, by some estimates, about 23,000 men, for the U.S. about 29,000. It cost the German army on the Western Front all of its reserves and ended its capacity to continue the assault in the Ardennes.

What made Hatten a place of strategic importance to both the Americans and the Germans was its geographical location. Hatten and nearby Rittershoffen were only small country villages. Their two thousand or so inhabitants were mostly farm families who tilled the rich black earth and raised livestock in the surrounding fields. These fields made good tank country, a mostly treeless plain, frozen solid in winter. The villages themselves could be easily bypassed by tanks. But the plain around Hatten was only a few miles wide, lying between two natural obstacles to the passage of a mechanized army: the wooded foothills of the Vosges mountains to the northeast and the Forest of Haguenau to the southwest. This narrow corridor had been used by invading German armies in 1870 and 1914. Across it now stretched the aging bunkers of the Maginot Line, built by France in 1920 and abandoned in 1940.

In December 1944 the U.S. Seventh Army chose to form its defenses along the Maginot Line across the plain at Hatten.

Task Force Hudelson, led by units of the Fourteenth Armored, including some tanks, field artillery, a battalion of tank destroyers, and infantry, were at Hatten on January 1, 1945. They were in a position to stop the panzer divisions, not because they were any match for the German armor, but because they could obstruct the German supply trains, particularly trucks carrying gasoline. Tanks consume a lot of gasoline and, after the prolonged battle in the Ardennes, German forces were running low on fuel. Thus the German panzers could not simply bypass Hatten on their way south to Haguenau and Strasbourg. They had to eliminate the tanks, tank destroyers, and field artillery of the Fourteenth Armored based in Hatten first, to secure safe passage of the main force of Operation Nordwind. As the bloody battle went on, the Seventh Army dispatched its last reserve division, the remainder of the Fourteenth Armored, to join the task force at Hatten. In the end, after stalling the main thrust of the Sixth German Army Group, personally commanded by Hitler, for eleven days, the forces at Hatten were ordered on January 20 to withdraw south to Haguenau to assist the 101st Airborne and other infantry divisions along the Moder River in the defense of Haguenau, through which the German army had to pass to reach the Rhine at Strasbourg.

Nordwind ground to a halt at Haguenau.

EXCERPT 2: PROJECT CAMELOT

As the Cold War evolved, defense agencies increasingly undertook to support social science research by several disciplines. Linguistics departments received funds for the study of foreign languages in parts of the world where the U.S. had strategic interests. The anthropology department at Penn had a program of research in sub-Saharan Africa but was not now recruiting faculty for ethnographic research in North Africa. Nevertheless a student from our department went to Ethiopia for his dissertation. On his return, he brought me back a striking, colorful painting on vellum of Christ carrying a sword, no doubt an image (or perhaps an omen) of Armageddon as anticipated by Coptic Christians. Other odd coincidences of geography and ethnographic interest come to mind. In one of my seminars, a student casually told of being on a dig in Iran (then ruled by the shah, with close interchanges between the University of Tehran and our university museum), where they would look down over the edge of an escarpment and watch Iraqi tanks maneuvering along the border. Another student, doing research on Fiji—who was unable to turn in her dissertation because, she said, it had been eaten by rats—went on to start a business in Hong Kong, married the chief of British security there, and followed him to the Caribbean when he was appointed governor of the Cayman Islands. She applied to do a dissertation on social organization among the native population of the Caymans, with me as her supervisor, but was turned down by the department.

The recruitment of anthropology departments by defense agencies became increasingly centralized under the rubric of "counterinsurgency." Populist movements of indigenous peoples protesting the rule of conservative elites were rising in countries whose rulers welcomed an American military presence and provided strategic resources and conveniences of transportation. Demands for economic reform, educational opportunities, and land redistribution were seen by established governments as leftist, if not Marxist, in tone and by the U.S. as Cold War maneuvers. Even "liberation theology" in Latin America was eventually deemed to be too closely aligned with Communist ideology for the Roman Catholic Church to encourage. "Counterinsurgency" became the watchword for U.S.-supported political and military efforts to suppress these movements, some of which I would deem to have been genuine revitalization movements, whatever political ideology inspired them. The Soviet bloc had similar problems and energetically suppressed resistance to Communist rule in eastern Europe and Asia. The Cold War was becoming a hot war in the third world, where civil wars and even inter-nation wars were being fought by proxies for the two great powers.

Anthropologists already knew a good deal about the communities in which the proxy wars of insurgency and counterinsurgency were being fought. Anthropologists had the languages, the fieldwork skills, and often the trust of native peoples. Thus it was obviously important for the U.S. defense establishment to recruit anthropologists to help in the counterinsurgency program. This was no longer, as had been the case in Korea, a series of battles between well-trained armies wearing uniforms and equipped with tanks and aircraft. It had become a war in the shadows carried on by the assassination of the enemy's leaders and even minor officials and by the arrests of students, union activists, and intellectuals, many of whom simply "disappeared."

The spearhead of the defense establishment's move into the anthropologists' domain was the celebrated "Project Camelot." Along with dozens of department heads and senior cultural anthropologists, I was invited to attend a conference in Washington DC, at which Camelot was introduced to the academic community. Institutions were invited to apply for grants to carry out research in sensitive insurgency areas in Latin America, including Mexico, Guatemala, and the Andean nations, where Penn had long-established programs of archeological and anthropological research. Camelot would provide information on insurgent populations. In effect, the anthropologist would be employed, as usual, to enter the community as a friend, to carry out legitimate ethnographic research, but, incidentally, to pass on to local authorities information about political activism, perhaps even the names of insurgents, who could then be observed, apprehended, perhaps tortured, and killed.

I was so outraged that I walked out of the meeting. Many anthropologists were also opposed to any such effort to co-opt the whole profession into service in an undeclared war. Some of my colleagues remained, however, and brought back the cheery news of riches to come in the form of lots of money from the Defense Department for grants and fellowships. At a business meeting during the annual conference of the American Anthropological Association, the redoubtable Margaret Mead pounded her walking stick on the floor and declared, "We would accept money from the devil himself if it got our students into the field." Her remark was hissed by some on the floor.

The Code of Ethics

The American Anthropological Association had been moved to take positions on clandestine research as long ago as the 1920s. Franz Boas, the dean of American anthropology, had opposed the entry of the United States in World War I, and after the war publicly condemned the

War Department for employing four anthropologists to work undercover as spies in Mexico. Academic criticism of his stand against clandestine research even during wartime led to his resignation from the National Research Council and reprimands from the American Anthropological Association (AAA) and the Bureau of American Ethnology. The issue presented itself again during World War II and its immediate aftermath. In 1948 the council of the AAA adopted a resolution opposing secret research that might "harm informants or groups" and condemning consent to the censorship or suppression of the publication of findings. With the revelation of intelligence-gathering under the guise of research in Vietnam and Laos, in 1967 the AAA issued a resolution condemning any "constraint, deception, and secrecy in science." An even more forceful resolution was adopted in 1971, and renewed in 1998, declaring that "anthropologists' paramount responsibility is to those they study" and outlawing "clandestine and secret research."

But the problem did not go away. In 2000 Patrick Tierney published a sensational piece of journalism, *Darkness in El Dorado*, that accused anthropologists Napoleon Chagnon and James Neel, both respected scientists, of deliberately spreading a measles virus among the Yanomamo Indians of the upper Amazon. Measles epidemics had long been known to have decimated American Indian populations that carried no genetic resistance to the disease. Actually, Chagnon and Neel had merely collected blood samples to determine the level of antibodies against the virus, a procedure that a colleague of mine in the Department of Anthropology at Penn, Nobel laureate Baruch Blumberg had carried out a worldwide search for any human population that had not been reached by the 1919 flu epidemic, as judged by antibody presence or absence. Allegedly the Yanomamo project was funded by the U.S. Atomic Energy Commission to provide information about epidemics that might follow the destruction of medical facilities in a nuclear attack. Tierney had supposedly discovered this scheme in interviews with an unimpeachable source, the workers for the order of St. Francis de Sales, which had established a mission among the Yanomamo. The book was favorably reviewed in the *New York Times*, there was public outrage, the AAA—already sensitized to the issue of clandestine research—denounced the project, and Chagnon took early retirement. But a later investigation demonstrated that the charges were groundless and that the evidence had been fabricated, and the scientists' innocence was vindicated.

I had met Chagnon some years before, in connection with the 1967 AAA conference on war and the subsequent volume of papers, to which both of us had contributed. At that time Chagnon reported on his exemplary research on Yanomamo warfare. He returned to the field for the next thirty years, making classroom videos of Yanomamo life and publishing some of the most respected texts and monographs on indigenous Indian cultures in South America. The Yanomamo were, originally, a tribe of at least ten thousand people, village residents of the upper Amazon, along the borders of Brazil and Venezuela. The area had attracted thousands of illegal white invaders prospecting for gold and driving off the Yanomamo, indifferent to the weak efforts of the government to protect them. Who really stood to gain from a genocidal measles epidemic among the Indians of the upper Amazon? Who stood most to gain from discrediting Yankee anthropologists who spoke up for the rights of the Indians? As recently as 2012 the Yanomamo were reported to be still under armed attack in the Huximu massacre, in which a helicopter gunship virtually wiped out a Yanomamo village.

As the wars in Iraq and Afghanistan dragged on, the army developed a program labeled "Human Terrain System" (HTS), which provided for embedding anthropologists and other social scientists in combat units. In response, in 2007 and again in 2009, the AAA reaffirmed the code of ethics adopted in 1971 opposing participation in counterinsurgency intelligence gathering.

These various statements of a code of ethics, and even the mistaken and withdrawn condemnation of Chagnon and Neel, add up to a general position that anthropology, along with other sciences and fields of scholarship, constitutes a special community. Like law, medicine, and the clergy, the anthropologist is committed to "do no harm" to his or her clients, and should not be forced to disclose information received in the course of research, which should be regarded as privileged communications.

Proposed Table of Contents

Introduction: War and the Boundaries of Kinship
The 14th Armored Division
Preparing for War
The Division Ammunition Office
Combat Command A at Barr
The Battle Hattern
Hersbruck
Dachau and Berschtesgaden
The Ashman at Dachau
Niemoeller
Bettleheim
The Eagle's Nest
Cleaning up the Battlefield
Preparing for the Next War
Indian Claims
Redeemer Nations
Afterword: What Has Anthropology Learned about War?

REFERENCES

Arnold, Matthew. 1869. *Dover Beach: Poems*. London: Macmillan.
Hitler, Adolf. 1944 [1951]. "Hitler's Speech to his Generals, 28 December 1944." In *Hitler Directs His War: The Secret Records of His Daily Military Conferences*, edited by Felix Gilbert, 157–74. New York: Oxford University Press.
Lawson, John. 1709 [1966]. *A New Voyage to Carolina*. Facsimile reprint of the 1709 London edition. Ann Arbor MI: University Microfilms.
Tierney, Patrick. 2000. *Darkness in El Dorado: How Scientists and Journalists Devastated the Amazon*. New York: W. W. Norton.
Wallace, Anthony F. C. 2012. *Tuscarora: A History*. Albany: SUNY Press.

CONTRIBUTORS

REGNA DARNELL, Department of Anthropology, University of Western Ontario. email: rdarnell@uwo.ca.
CHRISTIAN FEEST, independent scholar. email: christian.feest@t-online.de.
FREDERIC W. GLEACH, Department of Anthropology, Cornell University. email: f.gleach@cornell.edu.
EVAN HABKIRK, University of Western Ontario. email: ehabkirk@uwo.ca.
JOHN LEAVITT, Département d'anthropologie, Université de Montréal. email: john.leavitt@umontreal.ca.
HERBERT S. LEWIS, Department of Anthropology, University of Wisconsin, Madison (emeritus). email: hslewis@wisc.edu.
STEPHEN O. MURRAY, El Instituto Obregón. email: som1950@hotmail.com.
CATHERINE A. NICHOLS, Department of Anthropology, Loyola University, Chicago. email: cnichols@luc.edu.
DRITON NUSHAJ, Department of Anthropology, University of Western Ontario. email: dnushaj@uwo.ca.
NANCY J. PAREZO, Deprtment of Anthropology and American Indian Studies, University of Arizona. email: parezo@email.arizona.edu.
ANTHONY F. C. WALLACE (1923–2015), Department of Anthropology, University of Pennsylvania.

Lightning Source UK Ltd.
Milton Keynes UK
UKHW042153201218
334349UK00001B/137/P